M'Culloch v. Maryland

LANDMARK LAW CASES

AMERICAN SOCIETY

Peter Charles Hoffer
N. E. H. Hull
Series Editors

MARK R. KILLENBECK

M'Culloch v. Maryland

Securing a Nation

UNIVERSITY PRESS OF KANSAS

Published by the University Press of Kansas (Lawrence, Kansas 66045), which was
organized by the Kansas Board of Regents and is operated and funded by Emporia
State University, Fort Hays State University, Kansas State University, Pittsburg State
University, the University of Kansas, and Wichita State University

Library of Congress Cataloging-in-Publication Data

Killenbeck, Mark Robert.
McCulloch v. Maryland : securing a nation / Mark R. Killenbeck.
p. cm. — (Landmark law cases & American society)
Includes bibliographical references and index.
ISBN 0-7006-1472-9 (cloth : alk. paper) — ISBN 0-7006-1473-7 (pbk. :
alk. paper)   1. McCulloch, James W.—Trials, litigation, etc..   2. Bank
of the United States (Baltimore, Md.)—Trials, litigation, etc.
3. Maryland—Trials, litigation, etc.   4. Banks and banking, Central—Law
and legislation—United States—History   5. Exclusive and concurrent
legislative powers—United States—History   6. State rights—History
I. Title.   II. Series.
KF228.M318K55 2006
346.73'0821223—dc22   2006010983

British Library Cataloguing-in-Publication Data is available.

Printed in the United States of America

10 9 8 7 6 5 4 3 2 1

The paper used in this publication meets the minimum requirements of the
American National Standard for Permanence of Paper for Printed Library Materials
z39.48-1992.

For Hans Brisch, Friend and Mentor

CONTENTS

The lives of landmark cases are never short. They have their origins in long-standing quarrels and continue to grow years, sometimes centuries, after they are formally decided. For no case is this truer than *M'Culloch v. Maryland* (1819). Sown in the debates over the powers of Congress in 1787, grafted onto national fiscal policy by Alexander Hamilton in the 1790s, and fully mature in the years after the War of 1812, the institution of a national bank split the nation into parties, sections, and classes. Arguably more important than its better-known companion *Marbury v. Madison* (1803), *M'Culloch* marked the high-water mark of the Marshall Court's nationalism. Its holding — that Article I of the federal Constitution could be read in an expansive way, and that states might not undermine acts of Congress — not only gave teeth to the supremacy clause but also laid a sure constitutional foundation for a strong Union. It did not slay the dragon of states' rights, but it caused a furor among states' rights advocates.

This much is well known to students of our law history. Mark Killenbeck's lively and swift-moving account of the events and ideas before, during, and after 1819 case goes far beyond this conventional reading of the case. Coming as it did in the Panic of 1819, the decision supported the highly unpopular Second Bank of the United States. Sensibly, Killenbeck fits the case into the often troubled history of early national banks and traces the fate of the Second Bank after the decision. Maryland was not the only state to try to tax the Bank out of existence, and Killenbeck recovers this highly interesting litigation. The battle over the Bank would engulf the other branches of government — President Andrew Jackson announcing his intention to kill the bank and powerful members of the Senate like Henry Clay and Daniel Webster rushing to its defense.

Killenbeck also examines the debate that followed the case between Marshall and Judge Spencer Roane of Virginia, among others. Many impassioned critics of the bank assaulted the Court. Writing privately, both James Madison and Thomas Jefferson criticized the decision's implicit acceptance of "loose construction of the Constitution." Killenbeck gives fair hearing to these critics and to Marshall, sometimes discounted as a legal scholar, who proved himself an able opponent in these newspaper wars.

Killenbeck demonstrates how, like a stone thrown into a pond, the opinion spread itself over related issues, the most important of which was slavery. The great debate over the admission of Missouri as a slave state threw its shadow over *M'Culloch*. This shadow would lengthen as the Bank, national unity, and the role of the high court were all swept into the maelstrom of antebellum political conflict. But the decision survived, just as the Union survived, and has become one of the foundations of federal law.

Definitude is an elusive concept, particularly in constitutional history and theory. If any account of *M'Culloch* comes close to that goal, however, it is this one. We even learn what happened to the clerk of the Maryland branch of the Second Bank after the decision.

ACKNOWLEDGMENTS

This project had its origins in my work on the Rehnquist Court's federalism decisions, and many of the thoughts expressed here were initially developed in a number of articles on that subject. Two of these dealt expressly with *M'Culloch v. Maryland* and the history of the Bank of the United States: "Pursuing the Great Experiment: Reserved Powers in a Post-ratification, Compound Republic," 1999 *Supreme Court Review* 81; and "Madison, *M'Culloch*, and Matters of Judicial Cognizance: Some Thoughts on the Nature of Judicial Review," 55 *Arkansas Law Review* 901 (2002). Work on this book in turn led me to write two chapters that explored aspects of the case and the Bank: "*M'Culloch v. Maryland*," in Melvin I. Urofsky, ed., *The Public Response to Controversial Supreme Court Decisions* (Washington, D.C.: Congressional Quarterly Press, 2005); and "The Bank Was Saved, and the People Were Ruined: James William McCulloh and the Second Bank of the United States," in Melvin I. Urofsky, ed., *100 Americans Who Made Constitutional History* (Washington, D.C.: Congressional Quarterly Press, 2004). And it spawned an article on how I teach *M'Culloch*, "It's More Than a Constitution," 49 *St. Louis University Law Journal* 749 (2005).

There is a forest-and-trees, chicken-and-egg quality to this body of work. Nevertheless, to the extent that any of the material from the articles and chapters is repeated in some form in this book, it appears with the permission of the original publishers.

One of the problems involved in dealing with this case is a simple matter of spelling: What exactly is the name of the case and, for that matter, of the individual whose actions gave rise to it? In this book I have adopted the spelling used in the official reports of the Supreme Court, *M'Culloch v. Maryland*. There are nevertheless a substantial number of individuals and publishers who forsake the apostrophe and embrace the variant *McCulloch v. Maryland*. I opt for the approach taken by most participants in these events. And, as I explain in both chapter 5 and the epilogue, I also opt for the spelling that James William M'Culloh himself employed for his own name, a further possible source of confusion for which I apologize (sort of).

A number of individuals played important roles in bringing this project to completion. Various members of the staff of the Law Library at the University of Arkansas School of Law helped me secure copies of scarce original source material, in particular Ms. Lorraine Lorne. The staff at the Maryland Historical Society Library in turn helped me identify and secure copies of important materials in the library's collections.

One of the greatest debts I owe is to Michael Briggs, the editor in chief of the University Press of Kansas, and Peter Hoffer, the coeditor of the Landmark Law Cases and American Society series with whom I worked. The gestation period for this manuscript was uncommonly long, and I suspect that there were points at which both Michael and Peter suspected that the book would not come to term. Their patience and support sustained me, and this volume is immeasurably better because of them.

Finally, a note about Hans Brisch, to whom this volume is dedicated. Hans set me on the path that led to this project when he hired me to work with him at the University of Nebraska. Over the course of thirty-plus years his example reminded me constantly of the importance and power of friendship and education. Hans passed away on February 22, 2006, taken from us far too early on the very day when, 187 years earlier, *M'Culloch* came before the Court. The coincidence is telling and haunting, and like all who knew him I miss him more than I can possibly say.

Prologue

February 22, 1819. George Washington's birthday. We live in a time in which Washington's birthday is largely ignored, recognized simply as one aspect of what is styled as Presidents' Day, an occasion that is significant — if at all — mostly for the fact that it is a federal holiday and an excuse for department store sales. But in 1819 Washington had been dead a scant twenty years, and a grateful nation still found it appropriate, indeed necessary, to revere the individual described on the occasion of his death as "first in war, first in peace, and first in the hearts of his fellow citizens."

And so the nation paused to honor him in a variety of ways. In the capital city that bore his name the festivities concluded with a "spirited Ball" at Cranford's Hotel. "The farther we travel from his era," Washington's *National Intelligencer* observed the next day, "the more profound will be the respect entertained for his memory." And in New York City, where the nation's first president took his initial oath of office, the city's elite gathered for a similar event, "a very respectable ball and supper in honor of Washington's birthday," during which a typical toast was offered: "The memory of George Washington — A man unequaled in the history of men — The flight of a thousand years will but increase the diamond brilliancy of his fame."

None of this was especially remarkable. During the early years of the nation, patriotic events and celebrations were an important part of the social fabric. They provided the occasion for a collective reaffirmation of the importance of the great American experiment in democratic government. They also offered a degree of relief from the burdens imposed by day-to-day life in what was still a fledgling, largely undeveloped nation.

This particular February 22 was nevertheless unique. For on February 22, 1819, the nation's past, present, and future came together in the unfolding stories of an individual, Andrew Jackson, and an institution, the Second Bank of the United States.

In the early months of 1819, Andrew Jackson was either a hero or a villain, depending on how one viewed his conduct as commander of the forces that had recently subdued the Seminole Indians. That tribe had made a habit of raiding settlements in Georgia and then retreating to the sanctuary of their villages in Spanish Florida. Jackson's role in the prosecution of what became known as the First Seminole War had cemented his reputation with the general public. But that popular response was at odds with his actual record in those events, which was decidedly mixed. He had indeed subdued a tribe President James Monroe characterized as having "long violated our rights, & insulted our national character." But Jackson had also risked an international crisis with both England and Spain. He approved the execution of two British subjects accused of complicity in the Seminoles' actions, in one instance overruling the court-martial recommendation that the accused be flogged and confined for one year at hard labor. And while he fulfilled an unspoken goal of the administration by invading and seizing Spanish Florida, he did so without formal authorization and in a manner that could not help but embarrass the Spanish.

Jackson's conduct was debated at length in the House of Representatives in January and February 1819, and a series of measures contemplating his censure were soundly rejected. Whatever the misgivings many might have held about his actions — and they were both profound and in large measure justified — the "people's House" refused to turn its back on him. Indeed, Representative George Poindexter of Mississippi captured perfectly the popular mood when he declared that "whatever may be the opinion of others, for one I should not hesitate to say, in the language of the sage of Monticello, 'Honor and gratitude to him who has fulfilled the measure of his country's glory!'"

Jackson felt vindicated. Leaving Washington in the wake of the congressional debate, ostensibly to visit his godson at West Point (he never made it there), Jackson moved up and down the East Coast and was hailed every step of the way. There was one brief setback, occasioned by a report filed in the Senate on February 24 characterizing Jackson's conduct in Florida as "a departure from that mild and humane system . . . honorable to the national character." But, sensing the public mood, the Senate tabled the report. Jackson's devastation on first hearing of the document gave way to a renewed, even strengthened sense of personal and political triumph. His journeys thus became a continuous sequence of adulatory gatherings that would take him back to his home at the Hermitage in Tennessee and, eventually, to the White House.

One such event was the ball and supper held in Washington's honor in New York. Jackson had arrived in the city a few days earlier to great acclaim. As one local newspaper noted, "Whenever the General went into the streets it was difficult to find a passage through them, so great was the desire of the people to see him." This enthusiasm carried over into the evening of February 22. When Jackson entered the room, he "was saluted by a discharge of artillery from a miniature fort raised on the orchestra." And what was ostensibly a celebration of Washington's life and accomplishments became an evening during which the focus in important respects shifted to "the saviour of the south."

Ironically, that same morning a dialogue began a few hundred miles to the southwest that would settle, at least for the time being, the fate of an institution with which Jackson would become inextricably linked, the Second Bank of the United States. For on February 22, 1819, the Supreme Court of the United States met in its chambers in Washington to hear the first of nine days of oral arguments in a case that was styled *M'Culloch v. Maryland*. Two questions were before the Court: Did Congress have the power to create the Bank? And if it did, could the State of Maryland use its sovereign power to tax to impose a levy on notes issued by that institution?

The legislation creating the Second Bank had been passed in 1816. It was arguably a Bank of the United States in name only. Although the United States held one-fifth of the stock and the president appointed five of its twenty-five directors, the Bank was actually a private corporation. But the relationship between the federal government and the Bank was such that it was appropriately named. And in both form and function it was the virtual mirror image of the First Bank of the United States, the brainchild of Alexander Hamilton that came into being in 1791 when President George Washington signed the measure authorizing it on February 25, 1791, just three days after his fifty-ninth birthday.

The creation of the First Bank had been marked by a protracted and intense debate about whether Congress had the power to authorize such an institution. Among those opposed to the measure were James Madison and Thomas Jefferson, who argued eloquently and at length that the Constitution did not expressly grant such a power and that such authority could and should not be inferred. Hamilton disagreed and provided the president with an extensive written opinion to that effect, a document and argument that carried the day. The First Bank was largely successful, but it labored under a twenty-year charter that was allowed to expire in 1811 in the wake of yet another debate about its constitutionality. The absence of a central bank was deeply felt during the War of 1812, and the Second Bank was eventually created and given its own twenty-year charter after a protracted series of events within which constitutional concerns seemed largely to have vanished.

The Second Bank nevertheless proved controversial. Various unfortunate decisions on its part were widely believed to have contributed substantially to a severe economic downturn that became known as the Panic of 1819. The wider question of the nature and scope of federal authority had in turn been a persistent source of concern throughout the early years of the nation. The Federalist regimes of Washington and John Adams, which stood for a strong central government, had been succeeded by the Republican administrations of Presidents Jefferson, Madison, and Monroe. The so-called Revolution of 1800 should accordingly have signaled a transition to an era within which federal authority was limited and the sovereign prerogatives of the states respected and preserved.

But events did not unfold in that manner. For example, as president, Thomas Jefferson would approve a number of initiatives that consolidated and expanded federal authority in ways that were at odds with the positions he embraced in the contentious 1790s. Madison in turn gave his stamp of approval to the creation of the Second Bank, observing that the constitutional questions seemed settled by the prior long-standing acceptance of the First Bank. State rights proponents disagreed. In particular, Jefferson and his Virginia allies criticized measures they believed inconsistent with the letter and spirit of a Constitution that "was intended to lace" the federal government "up straitly within the enumerated powers, and those without which, as means, these powers could not be carried into effect."

By February 1819 the Second Bank had become a dominant symbol of that continuing conflict, an institution savaged by its critics as a

4 { *Prologue* }

"scheme of dishonor" and an "evil established by law." Maryland was accordingly simply one of the many states that enacted measures designed to limit if not eliminate the Bank's operations within their borders. Its attempt to impose a tax on the notes issued by the Bank was then simply one important reflection of a current of opposition within which the Bank was in many respects a symptom rather than the disease itself.

Public interest in the case was accordingly high, a fact of which the Court itself was well aware when, on Saturday, March 6, 1819 — just three days after oral arguments concluded — Chief Justice John Marshall announced the opinion and judgment of a unanimous Court.

Congress did indeed have the authority to create the Bank. The fact that such an institution was not expressly mentioned in the text did not matter. The powers of the national government were both express and implied, and the test to be invoked an arguably simple one: "Let the end be legitimate, let it be within the scope of the constitution, and all means which are appropriate, which are plainly adapted to that end, which are not prohibited, but consist with the letter and spirit of the constitution, are constitutional." Maryland in turn could not interfere with the Bank's activities by exercising its authority to tax. Since "the power to tax involves the power to destroy," a state's exercise of that sovereign prerogative must necessarily yield in the face of the considered judgment of the nation that a national bank was both necessary and proper. "Such a tax," Marshall concluded, "must be unconstitutional."

The decision delighted the Bank's supporters and enraged its opponents. And while there is no indication in Andrew Jackson's papers that he was at that point aware of or concerned about the *M'Culloch* litigation, it soon became quite clear that he did not approve of either the Court's decision or the institution it preserved.

Jackson's views on banking in general, and the Second Bank in particular, were clear. He believed that banks were an unalloyed evil, corrupt institutions that themselves facilitated profligacy and corruption by others. And Jackson made certain that everyone knew this. In a memorial directed at the Tennessee legislature in July 1820, he argued against the establishment of a state bank, asserting that "the imprudent speculator may be enabled to extricate himself from his pecuniary embarrassments but the burthen must ultimately fall upon the honest farmer and industrious tradesman." Banks were also illegal, no matter what the Supreme Court said. As Jackson reminded William Berkeley Lewis in a letter that same July, "you know my op[in]ion as to the Banks, that is, that the Constitution of our state, as well as the Constitution of the United States prohibited the Establishment of Banks in any state."

Nine years later, President Jackson seized the opportunity to transform these sentiments into national policy. In his first annual message in December 1829, he laid down the challenge, observing — the clear holding in *M'Culloch* notwithstanding — that "Both the constitutionality and the expediency of the law creating this bank are well-questioned by a large portion of our fellow-citizens." In July 1832 he explained his thinking and excoriated the Bank, vetoing an attempt to renew its charter. "The Congress, the Executive, and the Court must each for itself be guided by its own opinion of the Constitution," he observed, and it was his belief that the Bank was neither a necessary nor a proper exercise of the powers granted to the national government. And in September 1833, he sealed the Bank's fate, ordering the removal of the federal deposits from its branches and by that act ensuring that the Bank would cease to exist when its charter expired on March 4, 1836.

Arguably, then, John Marshall and his colleagues simply granted the Bank a stay of execution when they decided *M'Culloch*. And they did so at precisely the same moment that Andrew Jackson was emerging triumphant from an episode that, had it gone the other way, would almost certainly have denied him both the presidency and the platform that would allow him to transform his anti-bank beliefs into public policy reality.

Jackson's views on these matters thus enjoyed a short but important life. By 1837 the Bank itself had ceased to exist. Jackson in turn used his appointment powers as president to place a number of individuals on the Supreme Court whose judicial philosophies were at odds with those of Marshall and his colleagues. Indeed, for a brief period it appeared that *M'Culloch* would go the way of the Second Bank, as Jackson and his successors pursued a strategy designed to bring the question of the Bank's constitutionality before a reconstituted Court that would almost certainly have reversed the Marshall Court holding.

Today, however, *M'Culloch* dominates the constitutional landscape. Various commentators routinely characterize it as one of the most important cases, if not the most important case, in the history of the Supreme Court. One study has described it as the most influential opinion ever issued by the Court, a judgment reached by a process that calculated a historical value index for each of its major decisions. Justice Felix Frankfurter in turn characterized one phrase in the Marshall opinion — "we must never forget, that it is a *constitution* we are expounding" — as "the single most important utterance in the literature of constitutional law — most important because most comprehensive and compelling" given "the conception of the nation which Marshall derived from the Constitution."

There are some who disagree, arguing that the *M'Culloch* decision is both unfortunate and overrated. One member of the current Supreme Court, Justice Clarence Thomas, has in turn made it quite clear that he disagrees with many of the central points made in *M'Culloch*, albeit, at least not to date, not with its ultimate conclusions. But these remain minority views. The consensus is that the principles for which *M'Culloch* stands lie at the heart of the American constitutional order, that this is one case that no one interested in the Constitution or the history of this nation can afford to ignore.

There are two principal reasons for this. As a threshold matter, *M'Culloch* confirmed that the Supreme Court would play an important role in the political process, even as it placed important limits on the nature and scope of the Court's authority. As such it was one of a string of Marshall Court decisions within which the Court placed itself at the heart of a significant national political dispute. At the same time, the Court seemed to be saying that it would exercise this role with restraint, deferring to the judgments of Congress except in those hopefully rare cases where that body clearly exceeded its constitutional authority. *M'Culloch* is, then, an essential decision for parsing the parameters of what we call judicial review, the power of the Court to declare the actions of a coordinate federal branch, or of the states, unconstitutional.

M'Culloch was also at the time and remains today an incredibly important holding on federal-state relations. It made it clear that the powers of the federal government — be they express or implied — while limited, are supreme. As such it became an essential foundation for much of what followed, in particular the extraordinary expansion of federal authority that arose in the wake of the Great Depression as President Franklin D. Roosevelt's New Deal initiatives made the national government an active participant in many areas that had heretofore been seen as the province of the states. The Supreme Court played a key role in this process, initially striking down many of these measures but then changing course, relying on the authority of *M'Culloch* as it held that the federal government did indeed have what seemed to be a virtually limitless authority to act for the public good.

Recently a more conservative Court has called some of these precedents into question. It has, in the name of state sovereignty, declared several federal statutes unconstitutional and in doing so has rekindled the debate about federalism, about the proper allocation of authority between the nation and the states. This is, as Justice Sandra Day O'Connor once declared, "perhaps our oldest question of constitutional law." And it is one that cannot be fully appreciated, much less answered in any meaningful sense, without understanding and accounting for the events that precipitated the *M'Culloch* litigation and the nature and scope of what the Marshall Court held in that case.

CHAPTER I

The Constitution and the First Bank

When the First Federal Congress convened in New York on March 4, 1789, the new nation faced many problems, some of the most important of which were financial. The American Revolution had been an extraordinarily expensive undertaking, and the Continental Congress had been especially ineffective in funding the war. The first national government, convened pursuant to the Articles of Confederation, had in turn fared no better financing the peace. The new federal Congress would accordingly have to act quickly and decisively in the face of what seemed to be a series of intractable economic difficulties. There was no common currency, and there were no centralized means for either financing the government or controlling economic activity. The newly formed government carried a crushing load of debt, and its credit, that is, its ability to borrow to pay its expenses, was virtually nonexistent. The financial and commercial systems in the new nation were in turn chaotic, reflecting the realities imposed by an unworkable approach to government within which each state had retained considerable authority to go its own way in such matters. In addition, the states had incurred considerable debt, much of which they were unwilling to honor.

President George Washington recognized the significance of the problems and the need to place the nation's financial affairs in the hands of someone who had the experience and status to chart a course that could garner both congressional approval and public support. His first choice was Robert Morris, a Philadelphia financier and merchant who had played a critical role in the funding of the Revolution. Morris's support for the new nation was clear. He had, for example, used his own funds and credit at various points to pay Washington's troops and expenses. But Morris was facing financial problems of his own and declined. He did, however, have a suggestion, observing, "My dear general, you will be no loser by my declining . . . for I can recommend to you a far cleverer fellow than I am for your minister of finance in the person of your former aide-de-camp, Colonel Hamilton."

Washington did indeed know and respect Alexander Hamilton, the illegitimate son of a Scot who had settled in the West Indies after a series of financial failures in the mother country that he was doomed to repeat in his new home. Born in 1755, Hamilton spent the first seventeen years of his life trying to survive with his mother and brother after his father abandoned them. After her death in 1768 he lived under the care of first a guardian and then local patrons. His intelligence and industry set him apart, and his mentors provided the means for him to leave the West Indies, in theory to study medicine and, at least from their perspective, to return to the islands and practice. Hamilton eventually ended up in New York, where he matriculated at Kings College, the precursor to Columbia University. But like many men of his generation, he found his studies interrupted and his plans changed by the political turmoils of the day and the outbreak of the Revolution.

Hamilton enlisted in a local regiment and rose to the position of captain of an artillery company. This brought him to Washington's attention, and in the wake of Washington's defeat by the British in New York in late 1776 Hamilton joined his staff as his aide with the rank of lieutenant colonel. This was a position, Washington observed, where he needed someone to "think for me, as well as execute orders." Hamilton did so, for the most part admirably. In particular, he was with Washington at Valley Forge, where — as did John Marshall — he witnessed firsthand the problems caused by a weak central government and willful states. In a letter to George Clinton, governor of New York, Hamilton complained of "men [who] have been fonder of the emoluments and conveniences, of being employed at home, and local attachment, falsely operating, has made them more provident for the particular interests of the states to which they belonged, than for the common interests of the confederacy." Ironically, Hamilton became a victim of his own ambitions in 1781, engaging in a terse and disrespectful exchange with Washington that led to his resignation. He then returned to New York, where he practiced law and eventually again entered the world of politics and policy as one of the three anonymous authors of *The Federalist Papers*.

When Washington responded to Morris, he reportedly observed, "I always knew Colonel Hamilton to be a man of superior talents, but never supposed he had any knowledge of finance." But Morris assured him that Hamilton had the requisite knowledge, a judgment that grew out of a detailed exchange between Morris and Hamilton on the values of and need for a national bank.

In September 1780 Hamilton wrote James Duane, a prominent New York Federalist, and outlined his impressions of "the principal defects in the present system." One of these, which he addressed at some length, was the need to provide "a stable foundation for [the government's] schemes of finance." In April 1781, in turn, he wrote Morris, expressing the "greatest satisfaction of your nomination (to) the department of finance" and taking "the liberty to submit to you some ideas, relative to the object of your department." The discussion that followed was lengthy and thoughtful. It included a detailed proposal for a national bank, which Hamilton regarded as "an expedient essential to our safety and success," for there was "no other that can give to government that extensive and systematic credit which the defect of our revenues makes indispensably necessary to its operations."

Morris was impressed. He also believed that it was essential that a national bank be created, an institution he envisioned as the "principal Pillar of American Credit." In May of that year he drew up his own Plan for Establishing a National Bank, with Observations. That proposal led the Continental Congress to charter and create the Bank of North America, an action that would eventually be cited as support for the notion that a national congress could in fact create corporations. Shortly after developing and presenting his own plan, Morris responded to Hamilton's letter, indicating that he had "read it with the attention which it justly deserves" and that Hamilton himself would "very soon see the Plan of a Bank published and Subscriptions opened for its establishment, having already met with the Approbation of Congress." He stressed both that "I esteem myself much your Debtor for this piece" and that he believed that "the Publick are also Indebted to you."

Washington signed the bill creating the Treasury Department on September 2, 1789. Nine days later he nominated Hamilton to head that department, an appointment that was confirmed the same day. The problems the new secretary faced were massive and complex, but arguably reducible to three immediate needs: repairing the public credit, cultivating and protecting appropriate streams of revenue for the new government, and creating a central authority to assist in the management of both the government's financial affairs and the conduct of the economy.

Hamilton first turned his attention to the question of debt. At the time he assumed his position, the federal government owed some $54 million and the states an additional $25 million. Hamilton presented his proposed solutions to Congress in January 1790 in his *Report on the Public Credit*, in which he argued for the issue of new series of securities that would pay off the federal debt and assume that of the states. The proposal was controversial, with regard to both its scope and its details. In particular, Hamilton's support for federal assumption of state debts was deeply troubling for a number of individuals. The measure was nevertheless approved after six months of intense debate, and Hamilton had taken care of one piece of the puzzle.

He then addressed the revenue problems, focusing on the reality that as matters then stood, import duties provided more than 90 percent of the national government's income. The problem here was not that the money was not available, but rather that the ability to secure and spend it needed to be protected. Revolutionary-era Americans had developed a justified antipathy toward British customs measures and had elevated smuggling to a patriotic art form. This hostility and these habits persisted under the new government and posed a threat to its revenue stream. Hamilton responded by creating the Customs Service and the Coast Guard. He also created the Sinking Fund, an account that would receive surplus revenues from import and tonnage duties and use those moneys, which would themselves draw interest, to ensure that there would always be sufficient funds to pay the principal and interest owed on the new securities. These innovations, combined with the credit measures, began to place the new government on sound financial footing, such that by late 1790 the government was actually generating a sizable surplus.

Hamilton then turned his attention to the management of the government's finances and oversight of the economy. His approach to these matters emerged in December 1790 in yet another detailed and thoughtful document, *The Second Report of the Further Provision Necessary for Establishing Public Credit*. This title reflected the fact that it was written largely in response to a resolution of the House of Representatives asking Hamilton to provide "such further provision as may, in his opinion, be necessary for establishing the public credit." But it became known simply as the *Report on a National Bank*, for in it Hamilton recommended that Congress authorize a bank modeled after the Bank of England. Although styled as the Bank of the United States, it would actually be a private corporation, albeit one with close government involvement. Hamilton believed that such an approach was "the best guide of policy for a bank from the point of view of management of it and investment in it and the only security for a careful and prudent administration." As Hamilton asked in words that proved unfortunately prophetic, "What nation was ever blessed with a constant succession of upright and wise Administrators?"

The Bank would sell stock, and its debts would never exceed the amount of that capital stock. It would be the depository for the federal government's funds and could assist in the collection of federal revenue. It would lend money to private entities and the government. And its banknotes would be legal tender, "payable on demand, in gold and silver," and "receivable in all payments to the United States." This last provision was especially important, for it would make it at least possible that there would finally be a secure and uniform medium of exchange, replacing a system within which foreign coins and local banknotes were the dominant modes of payment.

Hamilton began the *Report* with the observation "that a National Bank is an institution of primary importance to the prosperous administration of the finances, and would be of the greatest utility in the operations connected with the support of the public credit." He stressed that "his attention has been drawn to devising the plan of such an institution, upon a scale which will entitle it to the confidence, and be likely to render it equal to the exigencies of the public," emphasizing that the merits of his proposal "entitle[d] it to the confidence . . . of the public."

Hamilton's own confidence in these matters was arguably not misplaced. It certainly comported with his expansive reading of the Constitution and with his conviction that it was the duty of the new government "to do good to mankind," at least as Hamilton defined that good. The public response to the institution once it was created eventually demonstrated that Hamilton had accurately read the minds of the body politic. But the proposal to establish a Bank nevertheless became one of the most controversial of the many issues that arose in the early years of the Republic, and much of the debate that followed focused on a threshold question: Did Congress have the power to create such an institution?

Hamilton's *Report* did not express any concern about the constitutional issues that soon engulfed his proposals. His extensive discussion and justifications were directed at objections to banks and banking per se, not to the constitutionality of the Bank itself, an issue to which he never alluded. This is hardly surprising given Hamilton's expansive reading of the Constitution, which he presumably believed was entitled to respect given his dominant role in describing the commercial dimensions of that document in *The Federalist*. But it seems at least curious that an advocate as accomplished and insightful as Hamilton did not mention what arguably became the most important consideration in the debates.

The matter was first taken up by the Senate. The *Report* was referred to a special committee on December 23, 1790, and a bill adopting Hamilton's recommendations was reported to the full Senate on January 3, 1791. It was discussed initially on January 10 and ultimately approved on January 20. Because the Senate met in secret until 1794, accounts of its debates are necessarily sketchy. There is nevertheless little evidence that anything approaching a majority in the Senate thought that this otherwise quite controversial measure was unconstitutional. For example, in his diary entries for the period, Senator William Maclay refers to the bank debates several times but never mentions questions about the constitutionality of the measure. Indeed, his entry on the day the bill was introduced stated simply, "This day the Bank bill reported, It is totally in Vain to oppose this bill. the only Useful part I can Act is to try to make it of some Benefit to the public, which reaps none from the existing Banks." And he noted — his own intense opposition to the proposal notwithstanding — that "The debates" themselves "were conducted rather in a desultory Manner."

Maclay did dwell on one aspect of the debate that became increasingly important over time. He believed that the bank was "an Aristocratic engine . . . operating alike a Tax in favor of the Rich against the poor" and, as such, "opposed to republicanism." That theme recurred in the public comments of other senators found in their papers or the press. Pierce Butler of South Carolina argued that the Bank proposal reflected "an Aristocratick influence subversive of the spirit of our free, equal government." Richard Henry Lee of Virginia, in turn, maintained that "banking is the kind of Traffic that tempts by interest to abuse." These essentially populist, anti-bank sentiments were coupled with reservations about the fact that the proposal created a national bank. Senator James Gunn of Georgia believed that "the great object of the Bank Bill is to consolidate the monied Interest of America and strengthen, in an astonishing degree, the Executive Department of the General Government."

The constitutionality of the measure did generate some comment. Butler, for example, was troubled by one aspect of the proposal, observing that the "exclusive privilege" — that is, the fact that during the life of the Bank no similar institution could be created — "is considered as a violation of the Constitution." James Monroe asserted, albeit hesitantly, that the proposal "exceed[ed] the powers of Congress; it appears to me that they have no authority to grant an exclusive charter to any one company. Tis not given in the enumeration of the powers in the constitution, nor does it appear to me to flow from any that are enumerated, but in this I may be wrong." And while Maclay noted in December that "the power of incorporating may be inquired into," he seemed to concede the point by stating, "but the old Congress enjoyed it," an allusion to the fact that the Confederation Congress had chartered the Bank of North America. To the extent that they were even raised, then, the constitutional objections seem to have been limited in both number and scope.

The tenor of the debate changed once the bill made its way to the House. One individual who vigorously supported the measure, Representative Fisher Ames of Massachusetts, predicted that the Bank would experience "a hard battle to maintain before its passage." That turned out to be the case. And while the debates were wide-ranging, and included many of the anti-bank and anti–national government themes just noted, the constitutional questions became the most important considerations.

This should not have been a surprise, as the focus of the debate was on a series of issues that had been at the forefront in the ratification process. How should the Constitution be read? Did it grant to the new federal government only those powers expressly mentioned? Or were there also implied powers, authorizations to act that were not enumerated but nevertheless followed logically from those that were? And what were the implications of all this for the supposedly sovereign states?

One of Hamilton's coauthors addressed these issues in *Federalist 45:*

> The powers delegated by the proposed Constitution to the federal government are few and defined. Those which are to remain in the State governments are numerous and indefinite. The former will be exercised principally on external objects, as war, peace, negotiation, and foreign commerce; with which the last the power of taxation will, for the most part, be connected. The powers reserved to the several states will extend to all objects which, in the ordinary course of affairs concern the lives, liberties, and properties of the people, and the internal order, improvement, and prosperity of the State.

The speaker was James Madison. And his views of these matters were significant, as he is appropriately recognized as the "Father of the Constitution" given his extraordinary role in the creation and ratification of that document.

Born in 1751, Madison was a member of the Virginia aristocracy who studied at the College of New Jersey — better known today as Princeton University — and displayed a striking aptitude both for his studies and for original thought. Plagued by poor health, he undertook a political rather than military role during the Revolution, serving in a variety of capacities in the Virginia state government. Then, in December 1779, his colleagues on the Virginia Council of States elected him to the Continental Congress, setting him on a path toward national leadership that eventually made him the fourth president of the United States.

Madison spent four years in Philadelphia developing a deep awareness of both the nature and the origins of the problems the Confederation faced. He then returned to Virginia, serving in the state assembly even as he continued to ponder the difficulties posed by the Articles of Confederation, an approach to national government that in large measure relied on the good graces of thirteen constantly bickering and decidedly sovereign states. In September 1786 he was a member of the Virginia delegation that attended a meeting in Annapolis, Maryland, which was convened at the insistence of Virginia to discuss whether federal authority over a particular national concern, commerce and trade, should be substantially strengthened. In May 1787, in turn, he returned to Philadelphia as one of Virginia's representatives in the Constitutional Convention, during which he became one of its undisputed leaders.

Madison also participated actively albeit anonymously in the ratification process in New York as one of the three individuals who, as Publius, wrote *The Federalist Papers*. He then played an important role in implementing the text as a member of the House of Representatives, serving from his election to the First Federal Congress in 1789 (narrowly defeating yet another future president, James Monroe) until he retired from the House in 1797. That "retirement" proved to be anything but, as Madison remained deeply interested and actively involved in national affairs.

Madison's argument in *Federalist 45* was technically correct: the Constitution was by design a document that divided powers between the nation and states, arguably allocating only a small number of essential areas of national interest to the new federal government. Of course, as Article VI of the Constitution — the supremacy clause — made clear, while enumerated and limited, the powers of the federal government were also both "complete" and "supreme." This was a radical change from the Articles of Confederation, and it was debated at length and contested with vigor by those individuals who feared that the newly formed national government would become all-powerful at the expense of the supposedly sovereign states. The supporters of the Constitution denied repeatedly that this would happen. In an important speech addressing concerns raised in the Pennsylvania Convention about the scope of the powers granted, one of the most important figures of the founding era, James Wilson, observed:

They have asserted that these powers are unlimited and undefined. These words are as easily pronounced as limited and defined. . . . [I]t is not pretended that the line is drawn with mathematical precision; the inaccuracy of language must, to a certain degree, prevent the accomplishment of such a desire. Whoever views the matter in a true light will see that the powers are as minutely enumerated and defined as was possible, and will also discover that the general clause [Article I, Section 8] . . . is nothing more than what was necessary to render effectual the particular powers that are granted.

In some instances, assurances of this sort were sufficient and ratification followed. In others, acceptance was accompanied by calls for amendments, one of the most frequently requested being for language that reaffirmed the importance and sovereignty of the states. In response, in June 1789 now Representative James Madison fulfilled a campaign promise by proposing a series of amendments that would eventually become what we now call the Bill of Rights. During his discussion of these measures, he noted, "I find, from looking into the amendments proposed by the State conventions, that several are particularly anxious that it should be declared in the constitution, that the powers not therein delegated should be reserved to the several States. Perhaps words which may define this more precisely than the whole of the instrument now does, may be considered as superfluous. I admit they may be deemed unnecessary; but there can be no harm in making such a declaration."

The declaration in question became the Tenth Amendment. But that provision did not replicate the formulation contained in the Articles of Confederation, which spoke of those powers retained by the states that were not "expressly delegated." Rather, it provided simply that "the powers not delegated to the United States by the Constitution, nor prohibited by it to the States, are reserved to the States respectively, or to the people." That very precise language became an important element in the argument about whether Congress indeed had the power to create a national bank.

Formal debate in the House began on February 1, when the bill was "read the second time, and ordered to be engrossed for a third reading." At this point William Smith of South Carolina expressed his belief that the bill had a series of technical defects and moved that it be recommitted so that amendments could be considered. James Jackson of Georgia then indicated that he "was opposed to the principles of the bill altogether" and "urged the unconstitutionality of the plan," characterizing it as "a monopoly" that "contravenes the spirit of the Constitution." John Laurence of New York disagreed, arguing that "the Government of the United States is vested by the Constitution with the power of borrowing money; and in pursuance of this idea, they have a right to create a capital, by which they may, with greater facility, carry the power of borrowing on any emergency into effect." The motion to recommit was defeated, with 23 in favor and 34 against. But Representative James Madison of Virginia stressed that "there was the greatest propriety in discussing the constitutional question in the Committee of the whole," and that process began the next day, with Madison himself taking the lead.

When debate continued, Madison devoted the first part of his lengthy address to "a general review of the advantages and disadvantages of a bank." He found six potential positive results but qualified them with the observation that "the most important of the advantages would be better obtained by several banks properly distributed, than by a single one." He also described four possible disadvantages, most notably that the plan before them "did not make so good a bargain for the public as was due to its [own] interests." He then came to the heart of the matter, observing that "in making these remarks on the merits of the bill, he had reserved to himself . . . the right to deny the authority of Congress to pass it." Stressing that "he had entertained this opinion from the date of the constitution," he noted that his initial reservations arose from a matter on which he presumed to speak with considerable authority, for "he well recollected that a power to grant charters of incorporation had been proposed in the general convention and rejected."

Madison was referring to the fact that during the Convention he had moved that a motion by Benjamin Franklin to amend the "post roads" clause also include "a power to provide for cutting canals where deemed necessary." Responding to Franklin, Madison "suggested an enlargement of the motion into a power 'to grant charters of incorporation where the interest of the U.S. might require & the legislative provisions of individual States may be incompetent'. His primary object was however to secure an easy communication between the States which the free intercourse now to be opened, seemed to call for — The political obstacles being removed, a removal of the natural ones as far as possible ought to follow."

Franklin's motion was so modified but ultimately failed, gaining the support of only three states: Pennsylvania, Georgia, and (ironically, as subsequent events established) Virginia. The accounts of this debate are sketchy, but one factor in the negative decision was apparently the very issue Hamilton now broached, the specter of "establishment of a Bank." Rufus King of Massachusetts observed that "the states will be prejudiced and divided into parties by it — In Philada. & New York, It will be referred to the establishment of a Bank, which has been a subject of contention in those Cities." James Wilson publicly disagreed: "As to Banks he did not think with Mr. King that the power in that point of view would excite the prejudices & parties apprehended." Privately, however, he conceded that the bank question had been an especially divisive issue.

In 1791 the question for Madison was simple: "Is the power of establishing an *incorporated bank* among the powers vested by the constitution in the legislature of the United States?" An examination of the document, reinforced by his knowledge of the origins and fate of the Franklin motion, provided the first, obvious step in Madison's constitutional analysis: there was no express provision in Article I granting Congress the power to create corporations, much less to incorporate a bank. In particular he stressed "the peculiar manner in which the federal government is limited. It is not a general grant, out of which the particular powers are excepted — it is a grant of particular powers only, leaving the general mass in other hands. So it had been understood by its friends and foes, and so was it to be interpreted." And he emphasized that "an interpretation that destroys the very characteristic of the government cannot be just."

Madison then examined in detail the clauses that might support an inference that Congress had the power. He argued that the measure before Congress gave no indication that the Bank would either tax or borrow money, at least as those terms could properly be understood. This left the necessary and proper clause, which he declared "must, according to the natural and obvious force of the terms and the context, be limited to means *necessary* to the *end*, and *incident* to the *nature*, of the specified powers." Madison maintained that the establishment of a Bank would not be "direct and incidental" but instead simply "conducive to the successful conducting of the finances." This went too far. "If implications, thus remote and thus multiplied, can be linked together, a chain may be formed that will reach every object of legislation, every object within the whole compass of political economy." Both the terms of the Constitution and the realities attendant to its ratification counseled against this course, which implicated the promise "that the powers not given were retained" and violated the "fundamental principle that the terms necessary and proper gave no additional powers to those enumerated." Moreover, Madison believed that the Bank was at best merely "convenient" or "conducive," rather than "essential."

The Bank debate occupied the better part of the House's attention for several days. Much of it focused on the question of implied powers. Fisher Ames in particular tried to move that discussion from the abstract to the particular: "But why should we lose time to examine the theory when it is within our power to resort to experience? After being tried by that test the world has agreed in pronouncing the institution [of banks] excellent." More tellingly, "If Congress cannot make laws conformable to the powers plainly implied, though not expressed in the frame of government, it is rather late in the day to adopt it as a principle of conduct." In effect, Ames stated, this meant that "a great part of our two years' labor is lost, and worse than lost to the public, for we have scarcely made a law in which we have not exercised our discretion with regard to the true intent of the Constitution." Michael Stone of Maryland disagreed. "The end of all Government is the public good," he argued, "and if the means were left to legislation, all written compacts were nugatory." He then maintained "that the sober discretion of the Legislature, which in the opinions of gentlemen ought to be paramount, was the very thing intended to be curbed and restrained by our Constitution."

Debate ended on February 8. Madison took the floor to both reexamine the constitutional questions and argue that specific defects in the bill required that it be revised and amended if it were to become law. The states, he stressed, were in a position to do many, if not all, of the things claimed for the Bank, and "the exercise of this power on the part of the United States, involves, to all intents and purposes, every power which an individual state may exercise." Assurances provided by the Bank's supporters were in turn illusory. "The constructions of the constitution . . . which have been maintained on this occasion," Madison declared, "go to the subversion of every power whatever in the several States." Elbridge Gerry "rose to reply . . . but the House discovering an impatience to have the main question put, after a few remarks, he waived any further observations." A vote was taken and the bill passed by a comfortable margin, with 39 in favor and only 20 opposed.

A sectional bias was evident, with every vote against the measure coming from individuals who represented southern states and only five individuals from that region supporting it. As William Branch Giles of Virginia noted, "I have observed with regret a radical difference of opinion between gentlemen from the Eastern and Southern states, upon the great governmental questions, and have been led to conclude that the operation of that cause alone might cast ominous conjectures on the promised success of this much valued government." The observation was telling, both as to the Bank and for conflicts yet to come about the respective powers and prerogatives of the federal and state governments. Southern and western states in particular exhibited a pronounced animosity toward banks and banking. They also harbored continuing reservations about the authority of the federal government and the implications for the states of a doctrine of implied power.

The Bank debate may also have been influenced by another issue that was alive at the time, the eventual location of a permanent capital city. This had proved to be an especially contentious issue for the new government. In 1790 it became part of the process that unfolded as Congress considered Hamilton's proposal that the national government assume the state debts. Jefferson in retirement maintained that the eventual passage of that measure was the result of what is now styled as the Compromise of 1790, an agreement that secured critical support for assumption in return for a measure that initially placed the capital in Philadelphia and then, after ten years, on the northern bank of the Potomac River in a tract to be carved out of Maryland.

But as the Bank debate unfolded that compromise seemed at risk. Senator William Maclay noted in his diary that "the Potomac interest seem to regard [the Bank] as a machine which, in the hands of the Philadelphians, might retard the removal of Congress." Hugh Williamson of North Carolina was somewhat more circumspect, observing in a letter to the governor of that state that "the Virginians are afraid of the Bank lest it should hurt the Potowmack Scheme." Indeed, in a letter of February 17, 1791, Fisher Ames both belittled Madison and purported to reveal the true basis for his opposition. He began by stating, "We have been occupied a long time with the debate on the bank bill. Mr. Madison has made a potent attack upon the bill, as unconstitutional. The decision of the House . . . is strong proof of the little impression that was made. Many . . . laughed at the objection deduced from the Constitution." He then emphasized the ramifications of the reality that the Bank, if approved, would have its headquarters in Philadelphia, presumably for the full twenty-year life of its initial charter: "The great point of difficulty was, the effect of the bank law to make future removal of the government from this city to the Potomac less probable. This place will become the great center of revenue and banking operations of the nation. So many interests will be centered here, that it is feared, ten years hence, Congress will be found fast anchored and immovable."

Ames may well have been correct, at least to the extent that he maintained that the two issues — the Bank and what became the District of Columbia — could not be separated. During the course of the Bank debate, an attempt had been made to limit the initial charter to a term of ten years, a limitation that roughly coincided with the date proposed for establishing the permanent capital. President Washington had in turn made the capital's location a live issue by formally requesting on January 24, 1791, that Congress amend the Residence Act to reflect his preferred location. A bill to that effect was introduced in the Senate and read for the first time on February 17. But the next day — over the opposition of all ten senators from the southern states of Georgia, Maryland, North Carolina, South Carolina, and Virginia — a second reading was postponed for one week.

The new date for consideration thus became Friday, February 25, which was also the final day of the ten-day period provided by the Constitution during which Washington could approve or reject the Bank bill. Representative Alexander White of Virginia commented on this development at the time, observing that "the second reading of the Bill was postponed till next Friday. . . . There are various conjectures with regard to their motives. I shall not repeat any of these, but only state the Fact. I will mention another Fact. The President must within that period approve or disapprove the Bill for establishing a Bank."

There are, then, compelling reasons to believe that the debate on and disposition of the Bank bill was influenced as much by personal and regional concerns as it was by considered judgment about the constitutional propriety of the measure. There is nevertheless little doubt that all parties at least appeared to and almost certainly did treat the constitutional questions quite seriously. This seems to have been especially true of Washington, who requested formal opinions on the Bank's constitutionality from his attorney general, Edmund Randolph, and from his secretary of state, Thomas Jefferson.

Randolph provided his written opinion on February 12, 1791. Like Madison, he began with the "obvious," that "the power of creating corporations is not *expressly* given to Congress." He then explained at some length why a power by implication must be rejected, tying his analysis both to an examination of those powers actually conferred and to the "real difference between the rule of interpretation, applied to a law & a constitution." A constitution, he maintained, is "simply a summary of matter" and "is therefore to be construed with a discreet liberality," while laws are the "detail," to be examined "with a closer adherence to the literal meaning." He nevertheless found it necessary to read the enumerated powers according to "common sense and common language" and rejected an expansive reading of those powers as one likely to "stretch the arm of Congress into the whole circle of state legislation." "The phrase, 'and proper,'" he concluded, could not be read that way, for "if it has any meaning, [it] does not enlarge the powers of Congress, but restricts them."

Jefferson weighed in three days later. Consistent with his views on the question of state sovereignty, he began with a discussion of the reserved powers question, noting, "I consider the foundation of the Constitution as laid on this ground that 'all powers not delegated to the U.S. by the Constitution, not prohibited by it to the states, are reserved to the states or to the people'. . . . To take a single step beyond the boundaries thus specifically drawn around the powers of Congress, is to take possession of a boundless field of power, no longer susceptible of any definition." He then examined each of the various powers that had been expressly conferred on the national government that might support such an action and found them wanting. The proposed bank would neither lay taxes nor borrow money. It could not in turn be seen as an appropriate means of regulating commerce, as the activities it undertook "would be void, as extending as much to the internal commerce of every state, as to it's external." That was inappropriate, "For the power given to Congress, by the Constitution, does not extend to the internal regulation of the commerce of a state (that is to say of the commerce between citizen and citizen) which remains exclusively with it's own legislature; but to it's external commerce only, that is to say, it's commerce with another state, or with foreign nations or with the Indian tribes."

Jefferson's attack on the invocation of the "necessary and proper clause" was especially sharp, turning on his sense that there was a profound difference between "the means which are 'necessary' " and "those which are merely 'convenient' for effecting the enumerated powers." He argued:

> If such a latitude of construction be allowed to this phrase, as to give any non-enumerated power, it will go to every one, for there is no one which ingenuity may not torture into a *convenience, in some way or other*, to *some one* of so long a list of enumerated powers. It would swallow up all of the delegated powers, and reduce the whole to one phrase as before observed. Therefore it was that the constitution restrained them to the *necessary* means, that is to say, to those means without which the grant of the power would be nugatory.

Drawing on his pronounced belief that the proposed measure invaded areas reserved to the states, Jefferson maintained that endorsing the proposal meant that "Congress should be authorised to break down the most antient and fundamental laws of the several states." It was accordingly essential to limit drastically any exercise of implied federal powers: "Nothing but a necessity invincible by any other means, can justify such a prostration of laws which constitute the pillars of our whole system of jurisprudence."

Jefferson's views were important. He was also from Virginia and was also a member of its landed elite. Born in 1743, he attended the College of William and Mary and entered the practice of law. His political life began in local government and eventually took him to the Continental Congress, where he achieved national prominence as the principal author of the Declaration of Independence. He returned to Virginia, serving first in the legislature and then as governor from 1779 to 1791. He then went to France, initially as a trade commissioner and then as Benjamin Franklin's successor as the Confederation's minister to that nation.

Jefferson was not accordingly a delegate to the Constitutional Convention, although he participated vicariously in that process via an extensive correspondence with Madison. He was nevertheless highly regarded, an active participant in the political process who also became the primary spokesman for a restrained view of the new government's authority. Part of this reflected his deep concern about individual rights and his fears that the Constitution posed dangers in that regard. Jefferson believed that "the further the departure from direct and constant control by the citizens, the less has the government the ingredients of republicanism." In 1787 he argued that the draft Constitution posed this threat and in particular that a Bill of Rights was necessary. He also maintained that the sovereignty and authority of the states should be preserved, declaring that the Constitution should "make us one nation as to foreign concerns, and keep us distinct in Domestic ones," an approach that would represent a "proper division of powers between the general and particular governments."

Washington then turned to Hamilton, indicating that he had received the Bank bill and that "the constitutionality of it is objected to." Washington noted that Randolph and Jefferson had offered their opinions and that both had argued against the measure. He declared, "I now require, in like manner, yours on the validity & propriety of the" proposal so that "I may be fully possessed of the Arguments *for* and *against* the measure before I express any opinion of my own."

Hamilton was in a difficult position. The president had received the bill on Monday, February 14. The Constitution required that he act within ten days, Sundays excluded. Hamilton accordingly needed to have his response to Washington quickly because the deadline for action was Friday the twenty-fifth. Hamilton wrote apologetically to Washington on the twenty-first, indicating that "he has been ever since sedulously engaged in it, but finds it impossible to complete before Tuesday or Wednesday *morning* early," and that he was "anxious to give the point a *thorough examination.*" He then completed his defense of the measure in a final burst of activity that began on Washington's birthday, February 22, and had him laboring through the night, eventually delivering his lengthy written opinion the morning of the twenty-third.

Hamilton examined each of the arguments against the constitutionality of a Bank and responded to each of them in considerable detail. He maintained at the outset "that principles of construction like those espoused by the Secretary of State and the Attorney General would be fatal to the just & indispensable authority of the United States." The linchpin in his argument was his expansive reading of the nature of sovereign powers, an interpretive gloss that not coincidentally echoed in important respects the arguments raised by Madison and others when they debated what became the Tenth Amendment:

> Now it appears to the Secretary of the Treasury that this *general principle* is *inherent* in the very *definition* of *Government* and *essential* to every step of the progress to be made by that of the United States; namely — that every power vested in a Government is in its nature *sovereign*, and includes by *force* of the *term*, a right to employ all the *means* requisite, and fairly *applicable* to the attainment of the *ends* of such power; and which are not precluded by restrictions & exceptions specified in the constitution; or not immoral, or not contrary to the essential ends of political society.

To believe otherwise, he maintained, was to think the unthinkable, for "the United States would [then] furnish the singular spectacle of a *political society* without *sovereignty* or of a people *governed* without *government.*"

Hamilton then took up the question of implied powers, treating this as an obvious and settled matter. "It is not denied that there are *implied* as well as *express* powers and that the former are as effectually delegated as the latter." He argued that the Bank had "a natural relation to . . . the acknowledged objects [and] lawful ends of the government." And he maintained that Jefferson's limited take on how the term "necessary" should be defined was inappropriate, since both "the grammatical" and "the popular sense" of the term supported the construction that a given act needed simply to be that "which the interests of the government or person require, or will be promoted, by the doing of this or that thing." The determinative constitutional criterion thus became "the *end* to which the measure relates as a *mean*. If the end be clearly comprehended within any of the specified powers, & if the measure have an obvious relation to that end, and is not forbidden by any particular provision of the constitution — it may safely be deemed to come within the compass of the national government."

Washington's decision was not an easy one. Four people whose views he trusted had weighed in. Madison had argued at length during the debates in the House that the Constitution did not authorize the creation of such an institution and repeated these arguments in discussions with Washington while the president mulled over the matter. Randolph and Jefferson in turn had taken the same position in writing. Hamilton alone believed otherwise, bolstered by the fact that the Senate and House had ultimately passed the measure by comfortable margins.

Washington's struggles were detailed by Madison in his Detached Memoranda, a series of observations written after he stepped down from the presidency. His comments are lengthy, but they capture nicely both the letter and the spirit of the problems presented by the Bank bill:

> The constitutionality of the National Bank, was a question on which his mind was greatly perplexed. His belief in the utility of the establishment & his disposition to favor a liberal construction of the national powers, formed a bias on one side. On the other, he had witnessed what passed in the Convention which framed the Constitution, and he knew the tenor of the reasoning and explanations under which it had been ratified by the State Conventions. His perplexity was increased by the opposite arguments and opinions of his official advisers Mr Jefferson & Mr Hamilton. He held several free conversations with me on the Subject, in which he listened favorably as I thought to my views of it, but certainly without committing himself in any manner whatever. Not long before the expiration of the ten days allowed for his decision, he desired me to reduce into form, the objections to the Bill, that he might be prepared, in case he should return it without his signature. This I did. . . .
>
> From this circumstance, with the manner in which the paper had been requested & received, I had inferred that he would not sign the Bill: but it was an inference nowise implying that he had precluded himself from consistently signing it.

Madison's draft veto was never used. Washington signed the bill on Friday, February 25, 1791. There were no signing statements then, a current practice through which presidents express a variety of opinions, constitutional and otherwise, on the measures they approve. Washington's papers in turn provide no real indication of either his own feelings or which arguments he found persuasive. It may be that his views on the nature and scope of the president's veto power played a role in his decision to sign the measure. Washington exercised that power with restraint, noting in a 1793 letter (perhaps with a bit of disingenuous modesty) that "I never had such confidence in my own faculty of judging as to be over tenacious of the opinions I may have imbibed in doubtful cases." It is also entirely possible that any inclination he might have had to heed the arguments against the measure were set aside, ironically, in the face of Jefferson's own admonition that "if the *pro* and *con* hang so even as to balance his judgment, a just respect for the wisdom of the Legislature, would naturally decide the balance in favor of their opinion."

And, as we have already seen, it may be that because Washington was a Virginian, and someone who had taken a decided stance on the issue, that the question of the capital's eventual location played a role in his thinking. For some, the connection was obvious. In a letter of March 30, 1791, John Rutledge Jr. — who had just resigned from a seat on the Supreme Court to return to his home state of South Carolina — observed that Washington had "stood on the bank of a precipice from which had he fallen he would have brought down with him much of that glorious reputation he has so deservedly established but fortunately for his country and very fortunately for himself what was dreaded did not take place."

Washington's struggle to balance constitutional concerns and regional interests was telling. Ultimately, the practical needs of the nation triumphed over parochial concerns, and the First Bank of the United States came into being with a twenty-year charter and in a form that reflected virtually every aspect of Hamilton's original proposal. A second bill making some minor technical adjustments was passed and signed into law a few days later. But that reality did not diminish the significance of Hamilton's accomplishment, and he had every reason to be pleased. He had conceived and brought into existence an institution that would provide desperately needed help in settling the financial affairs of the nation. And as part of this process he had countered what he believed to be an incorrect and potentially dangerous attempt to impose tight constraints on the nature and scope of federal authority. These were extraordinary accomplishments, secured in the face of formidable opposition. As Hamilton noted in a May 26, 1792, letter to Edward Carrington, "A mighty stand was made on the affair of the Bank. There was much *commitment* in that case. I prevailed."

CHAPTER 2

The Life and Death of the First Bank

Public response to the Bank was quite favorable. A Boston newspaper was perhaps a bit too effusive when it declared that its creation "established public confidence and credit, reconciled the jarring interests of discontented states, and cemented the people in the bonds of harmony, peace, and love." But the thrust of the commentary was correct. By and large the body politic recognized both the need for and the advantages of having a Bank of the United States, and it actively expressed that support when the Bank's stock was first offered for sale at its headquarters in Philadelphia on July 4, 1791. As one observer noted, "The publick promptly went berserk." Investors believed that the stock would pay substantial dividends, and the initial Philadelphia offering sold out in one hour. And so, Jefferson complained, "The bank filled and overflowed in the moment it was opened."

The excesses that accompanied the initial sales of the Bank's stock were regrettable but predictable. The Bank was both a private corporation and dedicated to profit, and a certain amount of this sort of activity reflected the inevitable nature of the beast. A more telling issue was the continuing hostility expressed by Jefferson and his allies, who refused to accept their defeat. This was perhaps best captured by Fisher Ames, who observed in January 1792, "I do not believe that the hatred of the Jacobites toward the house of Hanover was ever more deadly than that which is borne by many partisans of state power towards the government of the United States. . . . The hour of victory is dangerous. The federalists have triumphed; they have laid their own passions asleep; they have roused those of their adversaries."

The Bank did not always help matters. For example, in its first months of operation it issued a substantial number of bank notes and credits, fueling a sharp increase in the prices of government and bank securities. Hamilton was concerned about this, noting that "the rapid and extraordinary rise . . . was in fact artificial and violent such as no discreet calculation of probabilities could have supposed." Recognizing this, the Bank eventually changed directions and restricted credit, causing securities prices to plunge. The ensuing financial dislocations became known as the Panic of 1792, in essence the first market crash in the nation's history.

Episodes of this sort were the exception rather than the rule. Overall the Bank pursued a measured course of action that made it a valued and valuable institution. As time passed, it paid modest dividends, and the market price of its stock remained relatively constant. It made a number of important loans to the government and was a secure depository for government funds. Its record was such that much of the controversy that surrounded its creation faded, and it certainly benefited from the fact that the reins of government stayed in Federalist hands for the first nine years of its existence. But the positive record of the Bank itself was not matched by a parallel reduction in the political strife that characterized the debates surrounding its creation. The rifts exposed there did not disappear. Rather, they intensified over the course of the 1790s, with the opposing sides each becoming more distrustful and contemptuous of each other.

The full extent of the hostility is perhaps best seen in Jefferson's reaction to the attempts on the part of the Bank's supporters to establish a branch office in Virginia. The very notion of branch offices was controversial. Hamilton had, for example, opposed their creation, fearing that they would fuel local hostility to the Bank, especially by financial interests that would feel threatened by the presence of the Bank in their communities. But the Bank's board did not agree and pursued the creation of a number of branches. When it seemed possible that one of these would be opened in Virginia, Jefferson complained bitterly to Madison in a letter within which he initially reverted to the position he had taken in 1791, observing, "The [state] assembly should reason thus. The power of erecting banks and corporations was not given to the general government it remains then with the state itself." He then made a startling transition, in a statement that revealed the full extent of his hostility. Characterizing Congress as a "foreign legislature," he declared:

For any person to recognize [their acts] in a case belonging to the state itself, is an act of *treason* against the state, and whosoever shall do any act under colour of the authority of a foreign legislature whether by signing notes, issuing or passing them, acting as a director, cashier or in any other office relating to it shall be adjudged guilty of high treason & suffer death accordingly, by the judgment of the state courts. This is the only opposition worthy of our state, and the only kind which can be effectual.

The Bank's directors retreated from their initial decision, and the opportunity did not arise to test the extent to which Jefferson's allies shared his sentiments that support for the Bank constituted treason. But the episode illustrated a course of political and social conflict that fueled the gradual creation of what we now know as the two-party system. The founding generation assumed that while there might be disagreements about details and means, all actors within the political system would together pursue the common good. Madison in particular condemned "the violence of faction" in *Federalist 10*, characterizing it as "a majority or minority of the whole, who are united and actuated by some common impulse of passion, or of interest, adverse to the rights of other citizens, or to the permanent and aggregate interests of the community."

Hamilton agreed, albeit noting in *Federalist 26* that "the spirit of party, in different degrees, must be expected in all political bodies." But the successes Hamilton enjoyed brought matters to a head, and organized opposition to his programs emerged, championed by a group that styled itself as the Democratic-Republicans, a name that subsequently simply became the Republicans. That label was designed to cast doubt on the bona fides of the group now formally known as the Federalists, a party Jefferson and his allies associated with inclinations toward monarchy. The conflicts were bitter and continuous, playing themselves out throughout Washington's administration (from which Jefferson resigned in December 1793) and in the pages of an increasingly partisan press.

In many instances the Bank was simply the catalyst for political disputes whose implications ultimately reached more widely. In May 1793, for example, John Taylor of Carolene County, Virginia, one of the most important advocates of the Republican position, wrote Madison, urging a more proactive stance against the Bank. "Upon reflection it seemed to me, that at the next session of Congress, and at its very commencement, a direct, firm and resolute attack should be made upon the bank law. The newspapers are improper channels through which to make a considerable impression on the public mind, because they are a species of ephemera, and because the printers are not orthodox in general as to politics." He indicated that one aspect of this movement might be the publication of a pamphlet he had written. And he argued that the Bank should be treated much as Cato the Elder viewed the threat to Rome posed by Carthage, urging Madison to make "a Carthago est deleta business of the bank Law."

Taylor's pamphlet appeared in 1794. Titled *An Enquiry into the Principles and Tendency of Certain Public Measures*, it expressed his belief that the current administration — by which he principally meant Hamilton — was pursuing "a design for erecting aristocracy and monarchy" within which "a *money impulse*, and not the *public good*, is operating on Congress; and that taxes are imposed upon motives, other than the general welfare." And the Bank was "the master key of that system, which governs the administration," the foundation for a system of "tyrants and slaves — an aristocracy enormously rich, and a peasantry wretchedly poor, approximate in its morals."

One facet of the conflict Taylor sought occurred in January 1794, when the Senate debated at some length a proposed constitutional amendment that, as introduced, had two components. The first would have barred members of Congress from "holding any office in any institution of the nature of a Bank, under the authority of the United States." That provision reflected the fact that a substantial number of senators and representatives had been elected to the board of the Bank in 1791, fueling justifiable apprehensions about conflicts of interest.

The second clause was more telling, for it declared that "no power to grant any charter of incorporation, or any commercial or other monopoly, shall be hereby implied." The amendment would have been added as a new clause in Article I, Section 9, within which are set out the "prohibited powers," that is, those things that Congress could not do. It would accordingly have cast serious doubt on the constitutionality of the Bank. It would not necessarily have doomed it, assuming that a constitutional defense could be mounted via the argument that the Bank was authorized by one of the enumerated powers. But as Madison and others had demonstrated during the 1791 debates, that was at best a risky proposition.

The Senate began discussion of the amendment on Tuesday, January 14, 1794. Debate continued through Thursday, January 16. The measure was changed to make clear its target, substituting the phrase "Bank of the United States" for the initial language speaking of "an institution in the nature of a bank . . . under the authority of the United States." The clause denying any implied power to create a bank was then deleted "on motion," with no vote recorded. The measure was then put to a vote and failed, with twelve senators voting in favor and thirteen against.

The Senate still met largely in secret in 1794, and neither the official *Journal of the Senate* nor the unofficial *Annals of Congress* provides any details of the actual debate. But it is clear from the length of the debate that the Senate treated this as a serious matter and that there were a substantial number of senators, albeit not a majority, who were hostile to the Bank. Indeed, consideration of the constitutional amendment was followed on the sixteenth by debate on a bill introduced by Pierce Butler of South Carolina that declared it "inexpedient that the government of the United States should continue to hold any stock in the Bank of the United States, or have any political connection with the said Bank, or any other connection with it, otherwise than in common with other banks within the United States." It is likely that the issues posed by this measure had already been discussed at length, for it too was rejected that same day, by an identical vote.

The Bank continued to be a subject of concern through the end of the decade. But as significant as it was, it was overtaken in importance by a series of controversies within which the fault line continued to reflect the fundamental difference in perspectives embodied by the Federalist and Republican parties.

Matters came to a head in 1798 when the administration secured the passage of what became known as the Alien and Sedition Acts. John Adams, who had served as Washington's vice president, had succeeded him in office, defeating Jefferson in the election of 1796. Adams was one of the towering figures of the times. He had been trained as a lawyer, had played a key role in the fight for independence, and was a political philosopher who had thought deeply about the nature of government and the nature of man. He was also deeply unhappy as vice president, observing in a letter to his wife, Abigail, "My country has in its wisdom contrived for me the most insignificant office that ever the invention of man contrived or his imagination conceived."

During the 1780s Jefferson had become close to Adams, who spent most of those years in Europe negotiating the treaty that ended the Revolution and pursuing commercial agreements with France, Holland, and England. But when he returned from France, Jefferson encountered a John Adams who, in his estimation, was determined to undermine the victories of the Revolution by pursuing an aristocratic rather than republican form of government. The offenses were numerous, but their hallmark was Adams's proposal that Congress designate the chief executive "His Highness of the President of the United States of America, and Protector of the Rights of the Same." This imitation of royalty deeply offended Jefferson, who called it "the most superlatively ridiculous thing I ever heard of."

The 1796 election was close, but in the end Adams prevailed, securing seventy-one electoral votes to Jefferson's sixty-eight. But in a twist of fate dictated by the manner in which the Constitution structured the process at that time, Jefferson became Adams's vice president, as the person who had secured the second-highest number of electoral votes.

Jefferson was initially cautiously optimistic. In a letter to Madison he observed, "If mr. Adams can be induced to administer the government on it's true principles, and to relinquish his bias to an English constitution, it is to be considered whether it would not be on the whole for the public good to come to a good understanding with him as to his future elections. He is perhaps the only sure barrier against Hamilton getting in." But whatever hopes he might have entertained were shattered with the passage of the Act for the Punishment of Certain Crimes, otherwise known as the Sedition Act of 1798.

This measure made it a crime to write, speak, or publish anything that was "false, scandalous, and malicious . . . against the government of the United States, or either house of the congress . . . or the president of the United States, with the intent to defame . . . or bring them . . . into contempt or disrepute; or to excite against them . . . the hatred of the good people of the United States." Charges were brought against a number of individuals, all opponents of the administration. Convictions were secured, and fines and prison sentences imposed. In some instances, notably those of Thomas Cooper and James Callender, it came to light that Jefferson had both supported and assisted them. This caused a break in the relations between Jefferson and Adams, who believed that Jefferson's involvement with "a host of Republican libellers" was "not only a blot on his moral character but proof he was a captive of party."

The Sedition Act was widely condemned as an assault on free speech, in spite of Federalist avowals that it simply codified the common-law doctrine of seditious libel. Indeed, in one important respect the act actually improved the situation for government critics because it allowed them to plead the truth of their statements in defense. A pair of companion measures in turn gave the president substantial authority over aliens, including the authority to expel any alien deemed "dangerous to the peace and safety of the United States" or about which there were "reasonable grounds to suspect" that he was "concerned in any treasonable or secret machinations against the government."

Taken together, the Alien and Sedition Acts became the catalyst for a broad campaign against the Federalist regime, symbols of Republican beliefs that the government was in the hands of individuals with no respect for individual rights and a penchant for increasing federal power at the expense of the states. Jefferson and Madison became covert leaders in the reaction against these measures, drafting resolutions against them that were promulgated by the legislatures of two states controlled by the Republicans, Virginia and Kentucky.

Jefferson's Kentucky Resolutions were particularly pointed. He described the Constitution as creating a "compact" that established "a general government [for] special purposes, delegated to that government certain de[fi]nite powers, reserving, each state to itself, the residuary [m]ass of right to their own self-government." And — in language directed at the measures at hand, but with clear implications for the Bank — he stated that "whenso[ev]er the General government assumes undelegated powers, [its] acts are unauthoritative, void, & of no force." He also wrote that the measures should be deemed "altogether void & of no force," phrasing that conjured up the specter of nullification, that is, the authority of a given state to declare a federal measure unconstitutional. And he declared "that these & successive acts of the same character, unless arrested at the threshold, necessarily drive these states into revolution & blood," a notion that found subsequent form in the doctrine of secession and the Civil War.

Madison was more measured but nevertheless made clear his concerns and his belief that the states had both the authority and the obligation to respond to such measures. Thus, in a passage that captured eloquently much of the political turmoil that permeated the drafting, ratification, and implementation of the Constitution, he stated:

> That this Assembly doth explicitly and peremptorily declare, that it views the powers of the federal government, as resulting from the compact to which the states are parties; as limited by the plain sense and intention of the instrument constituting that compact; as no farther valid than they are authorised by the grants enumerated in that compact, and that in case of a deliberate, palpable and dangerous exercise of other powers not granted by that compact, the states who are parties thereto have the right, and are in duty bound, to interpose for arresting the pro[gress] of the evil, and for maintaining within their respective limits, the authorities, rights and liberties appertaining to them.

Madison's sense that the states had the "duty" to "interpose" seemed to suggest a political response to such matters, as opposed to Jefferson's more radical pronouncement that the federal statutes should be perforce deemed null and void. At the same time, Madison made it quite clear that measures like the Alien and Sedition Acts subvert "the general principles of free government" and "ought to produce universal alarm."

The Virginia Resolutions passed in the form in which Madison submitted them; Jefferson's Kentucky Resolutions passed in modified form, albeit one that preserved much of his message of state autonomy. Both resolutions were then sent to the governor of each state and widely published. Seven states issued responses, all of which were negative, provoked in large part by the pairing of the two sets of measures and the fears engendered by Jefferson's rhetoric. In particular, these states expressed a belief that the Supreme Court of the United States, and not the individual states, should determine whether a given federal law was constitutional. In some instances, notably that of Massachusetts, they applauded the Alien and Sedition Acts, declaring them "not only constitutional, but expedient and necessary."

Madison responded in *The Report of 1800*, a lengthy defense of both the Virginia Resolutions and the principles for which he believed the Republican Party stood. In the report he stressed:

The Constitution of the United States was formed by the sanction of the states, given by each in its sovereign capacity. It adds to the stability and dignity, as well as to the authority of the constitution, that it rests on this legitimate and solid foundation. The states then being the parties to the constitutional compact, and in their sovereign capacity, it follows of necessity, that there can be no tribunal above their authority, to decide in the last resort, whether the compact made by them be violated; and consequently that as the parties to it, they must themselves decide in the last resort, such questions as may be of sufficient magnitude to require their interposition.

Madison observed, however, that such "interposition" be limited to " 'the case of a *deliberate, palpable* and *dangerous* breach of the constitution, by the exercise of *powers not granted* to it.' "

He also doubted that the Court could serve as an effective check, noting "that there may be instances of usurped power, which the forms of the constitution would never draw within the controul of the judicial department." That argument highlighted the reality that there are limits to federal court jurisdiction, especially when the conflict in question poses a political as opposed to a legal issue. More tellingly, he argued that the resolutions contemplated only "those great and extraordinary cases, in which all forms of the constitution may prove ineffectual against infractions dangerous to the essential rights of the parties to it."

Taken together, the Kentucky and Virginia Resolutions and Madison's report came to stand for what became known as "the Spirit of '98," a series of doctrines that expressed core Republican assumptions about the residual sovereignty of the states and the limits that should be imposed on the nature and scope of federal authority. And it was against this backdrop that Jefferson challenged Adams in the momentous election of 1800. The contest was bitter, protracted, and closely contested. And when the electoral votes were counted, the results were inconclusive. Adams had secured sixty-five votes in the Electoral College, one more than his running mate, Thomas Pinckney. Jefferson in turn had seventy-three, as did his vice presidential aspirant,

Aaron Burr. This left the decision in the hands of the House of Representatives, within which each state had one vote.

Ironically, Alexander Hamilton played a key role in a process from which Jefferson emerged victorious. The new Congress had not yet been seated, which meant that the House was still under the control of the lame-duck Federalists. More tellingly, Burr now loomed as a threat, given a constitutional system that awarded the presidency to the individual with the highest number of electoral votes. In December Burr indicated in a letter to Jefferson he "would never think of diverting a single vote" from him. But there were now rumors that the Federalists might support Burr in preference to Jefferson, and Burr was no longer disclaiming any interest in accepting the ultimate political prize.

It was at this point that Hamilton intervened. On hearing that there would be a tie vote in the Electoral College he sent a letter to Oliver Wolcott, arguing as follows:

> There is no doubt but that, upon every virtuous and prudent calculation, Jefferson is to be preferred. He is by far not so dangerous a man; and he has pretensions to character.
>
> As to Burr, there is nothing in his favour. His private character is not defended by his most partial friends. He is bankrupt beyond redemption, except by the plunder of his country. His public principles have no other spring or aim than his own aggrandizement. . . . If he can, he will certainly disturb our institutions to secure to himself *permanent power* and with it *wealth*. He is truly the *Catiline* of America.

The concluding allusion — to an individual who had a reputation for personal dissipation and who allegedly plotted against the Roman Republic in 63 B.C. — was a powerful one for the educated individuals who were making the decision, steeped as they were in the classics. Hamilton's sentiments in these matters were in turn a mixture of statesmanship and pique. He and Burr were not yet full enemies, a relationship that had not yet evolved into the conflict that led to Hamilton's death at Burr's hands in 1804. But Hamilton had no regard for Burr. As he stressed in a letter to Gouverner Morris, "If there be a man in the world I ought to hate, it is Jefferson. With Burr I have always been personally well. But the public good must be paramount to every private consideration."

It required five days and thirty-six ballots to settle the matter. The breakthrough came when Representative James Bayard of Delaware abstained. Bayard was a staunch Federalist who had supported Burr; his action took Delaware out of the Burr column, as he was the only representative from that state. Further abstentions in Vermont and Maryland then gave Jefferson ten votes, a clear majority that made him president. Allegations were subsequently made that Bayard's change of heart reflected a deal brokered between Jefferson and Samuel Smith of Maryland, acting on Bayard's behalf. Jefferson denied this. Whatever the truth might be, the election had come to a close.

These events have rightly been described as the Revolution of 1800. It was a remarkable peaceful transition from one ruling party to another in the wake of a series of deeply divisive political conflicts and an election where the choices were stark and profound. The Federalist Party that had dominated the first twelve years of the new nation's history was no longer in control. In its place came a Republican administration that espoused a radically different version of the American experiment.

Jefferson was sworn in in a ceremony that conspicuously did not include the participation of the man he defeated, who at 4:00 A.M. had boarded the coach that started him on his journey back to Massachusetts. Jefferson, however, took his oath of office from another individual he distrusted, John Marshall, who had been selected by Adams in the waning days of his administration to replace the retiring Oliver Ellsworth as chief justice of the United States.

For the time being peace reigned, at least publicly. In his inaugural address, Jefferson offered the reassuring words "We have called by different names brethren of the same principle. We are all republicans, we are all federalists." Privately, however, Jefferson wrote that he intended to "sink federalism into an abyss from which there shall be no resurrection." One of his primary targets was, unsurprisingly, the Bank. In October 1802 he complained to his secretary of the Treasury, Albert Gallatin, about the extent to which the Bank's stock was held by foreign nationals. And in July 1803 he informed Gallatin that he believed the Bank's monopoly on government deposits should be broken, couching his argument in blatantly political terms: "I am decidedly in favor of making all the banks republican, by sharing deposits among them in proportion to the dispositions they shew. If the law now forbids it, we should not permit another session of Congress to pass without amending it. It is material to the safety of republicanism to detach the mercantile interest from it's enemies and incorporate it into the body of it's friends. A merchant is naturally a republican, and can be otherwise only from a vitiated state of things."

Gallatin largely ignored these outbursts, but in December 1803 he recommended that the Bank be allowed to establish a branch in New Orleans in the wake of the Louisiana Purchase. Jefferson disagreed, declaring in an especially pointed letter, "This institution is one of the most deadly hostility existing, against the principles and form of our Constitution." The Bank, he argued, "penetrating by its branches every part of the Union, acting by command and in phalanx, may, in a critical moment, upset the government." It was then "the greatest duty we owe to the safety of our Constitution, to bring this powerful enemy to a perfect subordination under its authorities." The first step was to refuse to establish the branch office. That could in turn be followed by measures that placed the Bank "on an equal footing . . . with other banks, as to the favors of the government."

Gallatin did not agree, believing that the Bank had served and would continue to serve as a valuable resource for the government. In his reply to Jefferson he discussed at length the advantages realized from "Banks, and especially the Bank of the United States." He emphasized that "against this there are none but political objections, and those will lose much of their force when the little injury they can do us and the dependence in which they are on governments are duly estimated."

An indirect attack was in turn mounted in 1806 when Representative John Clopton of Virginia offered an amendment to the Constitution that would have added to the necessary and proper clause language declaring that it "shall be construed so as to comprehend only such laws as shall have a natural connexion with and immediate relation to the powers enumerated in the said section, or to such other powers as are expressly vested by this Constitution in the Government of the United States, or in any department or officer thereof."

Clopton was a member of a socially prominent family. He was also a Republican of the Jeffersonian school, with clear state rights credentials. He argued that the change was called for given the extent to which individuals had justified various federal measures as "expedient," a characterization that arguably fit the Bank. Two measures he mentioned in this regard were favorite state rights targets, the Alien and Sedition Acts, which had no "more connexion" with enumerated powers "than pitchy darkness has with the blaze of a meridian sun." His goal, he maintained, was simple and balanced. "It is no less incumbent on the Federal Government to confine itself within the sphere of its own appropriate powers, than it is incumbent on the States not to attempt the resumption of any of the powers which they have surrendered up to this Government."

Clopton's proposal did not pass, but the Bank's long-term future was far from secure. Its charter was scheduled to expire in 1811, and its supporters believed it important to secure early approval of an extension. In November 1807 they sought Gallatin's advice. He counseled caution, fearing that early action would be "blended with or affected by . . . extraneous political considerations." Early the next year he suggested that the Bank time whatever measure it wished to submit so that it could be discussed but not acted on before that session of Congress adjourned, thus keeping the measure from becoming an issue in the forthcoming presidential election.

The Bank heeded his advice, and in March 1808 the stockholders passed and forwarded to Congress a memorial, within which they argued for a renewal of the charter. That document stressed "the intimate connexion of the institution with the public credit and finances." It argued that the Bank "has enriched the Treasury," that it has "aided the Government to maintain inviolate the public faith and credit at home and abroad," and that it "has enabled the Government to collect its revenue, and to perform its pecuniary engagements, with ease, economy, and security." The stockholders stressed accordingly that they had "a duty to the Government and the commercial world as well as to themselves to submit the expediency of protracting the duration of their charter."

Both the House and the Senate referred the matter to Gallatin, with the Senate requesting that he report to it in the next session. The feared campaign issue did not accordingly materialize, and the matter lay dormant until March 1809, when Gallatin submitted an extensive report within which he outlined the Bank's structure and traced its history, observing that "it sufficiently appears from that general view, that the affairs of the Bank of the United States, considered as a moneyed institution, have been wisely and skillfully managed." He then described what he believed to be the "advantages derived by the Government from the bank," stressing its role as the institution within which public funds were kept, its ability to transmit public funds throughout the nation, its role in the collection of revenue, and the loans it had made to the government itself.

Gallatin conceded that state banks, which were being established in increasing numbers, might be in a position to assist in such matters. But he argued that "a national bank, deriving its charter from the National Legislature, will, at all times, and under every emergency, feel stronger inducements, both from interest and a sense of duty, to afford the Union every assistance in its power." He recommended that the Bank's charter be renewed, albeit with some modifications, including a substantial increase in its capital, from $10 million to $30 million.

James Madison took office as the fourth president in March 1809 with the Bank intact, albeit not with a renewed charter, which Congress refused to consider until 1810. The memorial was again referred to a House committee, which now had the benefit of the report Gallatin had prepared the previous spring. The committee supported renewal, and a bill to that effect was reported and debated by the House, which seemed favorably inclined. But it did not come to a vote, and the process continued into the fall, when the stockholders presented a second memorial, within which they emphasized that the Bank had also performed admirably as a central bank, a "general guardian of commercial credit" that "has fostered and protected the banking institutions of the States, and has aided them when unexpectedly pressed."

Unfortunately, although much had changed since 1791, much remained the same. Gallatin had convinced Madison that the Bank was necessary. Madison in turn was prepared to put his constitutional reservations aside, although he did not make any public statements to that effect. It became known, however, that Madison now viewed the constitutional question as "settled" by virtue of the initial decision to charter the Bank and the now almost twenty-year history of acquiescence and operations.

The response from die-hard Republicans was swift and predictable.

For example, on April 18, 1810, the *Baltimore Whig* printed remarks "From 'Tammany,'" in which the anonymous author characterized the argument as "sophistry [that] will turn the Constitution into a 'nose of wax,'" asking, "Is the Constitution 'like the cameleon, which changes its hue according to the times and positions in which it may be viewed?'" Tammany then declared, in a passage that linked the Bank debate with Madison's Virginia Resolutions and his report:

> JM "once thought and spoke differently." Time has not changed the validity of JM's earlier arguments on the bank question, and he is "committed in a thousand ways" on the subject; his speeches are "before the world" as is his report in the Virginia legislature. Should the present bank bill pass Congress and JM give it his sanction, his "fame will be blasted forever." No excuses about the question being *"settled"* will conceal his inconsistency or save him from "eternal odium and reproach." His change of opinion, moreover, could not be attributed to ignorance but only to "'corruption's soul-dejecting arts.'"

By early 1811, economic conditions had worsened. For many, this argued for an increasing government presence. In January 1811, for example, John Jacob Astor wrote Gallatin, declaring that "there was perhaps never a period when it was more in the power of government to do good than the present." But these sentiments were not universal. When the First Bank was established in 1791, it became one of only five banks in the nation. Since then, the number of banks had increased substantially, and in 1811 there were ninety in operation. Thus, while a substantial portion of the banking community argued for renewal, for some banks, especially smaller ones, the Bank represented unwelcome competition. And for some individuals, many of them influential, it was an unwelcome presence given the role it had played in bringing order and oversight to the economy.

These alterations in the economic and social climate clearly played a role in what happened. For example, Samuel Smith of Maryland was a Revolutionary War hero and a highly successful Baltimore merchant who in 1811 was one of the more influential members of the Senate. When the question of recharter came before that body, he was appointed to the committee created to consider it. Smith had considerable knowledge of banks and banking, both as a merchant who employed their services and as a member of the boards of two local banks, the Bank of Maryland and the Bank of Baltimore. He had reservations about the organization and operations of the Bank as then chartered but believed that the plan presented to the Senate in March 1810 would eliminate most of the defects. Like the House measure, that bill did not come to a final vote, and Smith returned to Baltimore in the summer of 1810 with a clear and consistent record of support for renewing the Bank's charter, provided the measure doing so contained the modifications he sought.

Unfortunately, the Baltimore branch of the Bank and its supporters had waged an ill-advised campaign to force the Baltimore business community to support recharter. As part of that process it tightened credit and withdrew funds it had deposited in local banks, provoking a recession in the area. Smith was furious and wrote Madison on August 8, 1810, demanding that federal funds be withdrawn from the Baltimore branch and placed in local banks. Smith declared that "if this course should not be pursued . . . there will be members of Congress who will attribute it to improper motives, and who will believe that the Secretary of the treasury was thereby favoring the institution." He suggested that if action was not taken, there would be severe repercussions, declaring that "we certainly had better have no such institution, if the consequence is that it can awe the government at it's pleasure."

Madison solicited Gallatin's advice on the matter, albeit without specifically mentioning Smith's charges. In his response Gallatin indicated that the fiscal situation was so dire that any changes in current policy would be disastrous. The actions Smith demanded were accordingly not taken. On August 29 Madison so informed him, stating that "any distributive transfer of [Treasury deposits] to the State Banks, would not be convenient to the public, and must soon become unimportant to them." As a result, when Smith returned to Washington for the final debates on the Bank, he fully opposed it.

The Bank's fate was sealed in January and February 1811. A bill to extend the charter was presented in the House on January 4, 1811. Various concerns were voiced, among which was the continuing issue of foreign ownership of approximately 72 percent of the Bank's stock. Opponents maintained that the Bank was subject to foreign manipulation, a charge whose full ramifications had perhaps been best expressed by Representative John Love of Virginia during the debates the previous April:

> King George the 3rd or the Emperor Bonaparte, may send their men, the ostensible owners of the stock, who may easily find, among the citizens of the republic, the friends and advocates of crowned heads. The former, it is said, owns a considerable portion of the bank, and the latter, should he ever deign a vital injury to this country, could in no way so successfully effect it, as by taking the management of our money matters. To buy this engine would cost him but the sum of twenty or thirty millions of dollars — nothing to a man who has in the hands the resources of the continent of Europe.

The Bank's supporters tried to counter this by arguing that foreign investments in the Bank had actually been for the good, a means by which "our own commercial capital has been created and our country improved." More to the point, these fears were arguably misplaced. Foreign shareholders could not cast votes in the election of the Bank's board, and at least that avenue of influence was not available to them. But the symbolic impact of a perception of either British or French influence was great in a nation that had fought a war to free itself of the English, remained concerned about the turmoil and excesses of the French Revolution, and was apprehensive about the power and intentions of Napoleon. Love's charges accordingly found a receptive audience in that part of the body politic that was either justifiably apprehensive about the state of international affairs or, as was too often the case, simply afraid of any hint of foreign influence.

Concerns were also raised about the structure and operations of the Bank. Some of these were justified. The Bank's record was not perfect, as virtually all its supporters recognized, a reality reflected in the various changes in the charter that were being proposed. But the single most consuming set of considerations were political, bound up in the ongoing dispute between the Federalists and Republicans, even as the power and influence of the Federalists were on the wane. The full extent of this reality became clear during discussions of the Bank's balance sheets. Some opponents of the Bank had charged that it had concealed its profits. As part of the attack, they characterized this accusation in ways that made the political underpinnings of much of what transpired obvious. "All the directors of the mother bank, at all times," Representative Robert Wright of Maryland complained, "have been Federalist or worse — many of them Tories or Monarchists — so that being under such control, I have ever doubted the statement of its funds."

The dominant issue became the question of constitutionality, which was itself an extension of the political conflict and debate. Discussion of renewal in the House began in earnest on January 16, 1811. The first individual to speak was Representative William A. Burwell of Virginia, who moved to strike the first section of the proposed bill, which contained the language granting the extension. He indicated very early in his statement that "the remarks I shall make are intended to show that Congress possesses no power to incorporate a bank; to show its effect on Government, and to satisfy the Committee [of the Whole] that the exercise of the power, even if possessed, is inexpedient." Burwell conceded, "I am well aware that I can add nothing new upon the Constitutional points. The subject was more thoroughly examined in 1791, and more ably elucidated than any other since the adoption of the Government." But he felt compelled to explore the issues at length in spite of the ultimate decision reached in those earlier discussions. "My conscientious belief is," he concluded, "that the law was unconstitutional, and I sincerely trust we shall destroy what has so long defaced its original purity, close up the breach which has been made, and cement it by a vote upon principle."

Burwell was the only one to speak that day. When debate opened on the seventeenth, Jonathan Fisk of New York attempted to shift the discussion to the importance of the Bank to the nation. But, inevitably, he turned to the constitutional concerns, stating that "if it is a question which Congress may discuss and decide, it was discussed and deliberately decided at the time this charter was granted. The decision it then received has met with the general approbation of the States and of the people." In particular, Fisk noted that in February 1804 Congress had approved, and President Jefferson had signed, a measure authorizing the Bank to establish branch offices "in any part of the territories or dependencies of the United States, in the manner and on the terms prescribed in the act to which this is a supplement." He observed, "If the original law was unconstitutional, this act extending the powers of the corporation was equally unconstitutional." But the 1804 measure "was passed by a Republican Congress, who did not believe that the original charter was unconstitutional." And Fisk declared that "it is but lately, very lately, that Constitutional difficulties have suggested themselves to some gentlemen. Even at this time, the Administration have no objections to the constitutionality of the measure."

Debate continued in this fashion. Both sides pressed their arguments about the constitutional questions, even as they admitted that they were simply repeating much of what had been said earlier. And, as we have seen, that debate was as old as the nation itself and included within its ambit virtually all the fundamental questions posed about the Constitution and the nature and scope of the federal government it created.

The bill came to a vote in the House on January 24, where it was defeated when a motion to indefinitely postpone was approved by one vote, 65 to 64. Debate began in the Senate on February 11 and followed virtually the same lines as the dialogue in the House. As had been the case there, Senator Richard Brent of Tennessee moved that the first section be stricken. After some minor procedural quibbles, William H. Crawford of Georgia observed, "After the most minute examination of the constitution, the majority of that committee were decidedly of opinion, that the Congress of the United States were clearly invested with power to pass such a bill." And so the battle was joined. William Branch Giles of Virginia admitted that he found it "peculiarly irksome to me to question the constitutionality of a law which has thus and so long been acquiesced in, because it tends to give the character of instability to the laws generally; and in my judgment, tends also, in some degree, to impair the sacred character of the laws, and of course, to lessen their efficacy." But he proceeded to do so, at length, in a statement within which traditional notions of the limited powers of the federal government and the residual sovereignty of the states formed the matrix for a detailed denial that Congress had the power to charter the Bank.

Senator Smith entered the fray in earnest on February 16, stressing that his prior support for the Bank must now give way in the face of the many defects he found in the measure before the Senate. Smith made it quite clear that recent events in Baltimore played an important part in his assessment. "Wherever [the Bank] extended its influence," he charged, "dissension commenced; wherever it placed its foot, it became absolutely necessary for the States to erect another ban to counterbalance its pecuniary and political influence." Three individuals from Baltimore whose judgment Smith trusted had informed him "that granting this charter would be a death-blow to the politics of the State of Maryland" and "would be injurious to them, for neither they nor many of the manufacturers of Baltimore had received much advantage from the branch bank; they had their own banks, from which they generally received accommodation." Toward the end of his remarks Smith sought higher ground, indicating that "the question never came before me on a constitutional argument before." But the "able arguments" of other senators "have made a very serious impression on me, indeed, and have almost brought me to think, that, if there were no other objections, I should vote against the bill on constitutional grounds alone."

The Senate voted on Brent's motion to delete the section authorizing the extension of the charter on February 20, with the final tally even, 17 to 17. This left the matter in the hands of Vice President George Clinton of New York, who had pursued the presidency in 1808, only to be opposed by both Madison and Gallatin. Clinton made a brief statement in which he emphasized that he sided with those who believed that Congress did not have the power to charter a bank, stating that "the power to create corporations is not expressly granted; it is a high attribute of sovereignty and in its nature not accessorial or derivative by implication, but primary and independent." Clinton maintained that if experience demonstrated that a bank was truly necessary the Constitution could be amended. He voted yes, and Brent's motion passed.

The Bank's fate was sealed. It asked for a temporary extension of two years, believing it essential to have that amount of time to conclude its affairs in an orderly manner. That request was referred to committees in the House and Senate, both of which refused to support it. The First Bank of the United States accordingly ceased operations on March 3, 1811.

Ultimately the fate of the First Bank was the product of a complex mixture of constitutional concerns, political considerations, and, in some instances, personal issues. Looking back on the events, Gallatin captured a portion of the mix when he wrote in 1830:

> In 1810 the weight of the administration was in favor of a renewal, Mr. Madison having made his opinion known that he considered the question as settled by precedent, and myself an open and strenuous advocate. We had the powerful support of Mr. Crawford in the Senate and no formidable opponent in either House but Mr. Clay, a majority of political friends in both Houses, and almost all the Federal votes on that question; with no other untoward circumstances but the *personal* opposition to Mr. Madison or myself of the Clintons, the Maryland Smiths, Leib, and Giles.

Given the closeness of the vote, Gallatin's assessment was telling. He did perhaps underestimate the extent to which local opposition played a role. Thus, while he was correct when he observed that "the opposition due to the jealousy or selfishness of rival institutions was confined to a few cities," those factors could well have been decisive.

Of course, if Gallatin was correct, the very fact that the vote was close requires further explanation. Representative Erastus Root, a Republican from New York, offered a second piece of the puzzle when he noted that at precisely the point that the Bank issue arose "this country was in the midst of its difficulties which resulted in [the War of 1812]. Great Britain had vexed us by the impressment of our seamen and by her orders in council blockading all the northern coast of continental Europe. France, too, under the pretext of retaliating the British orders in council, visited our commerce with the destructive influence of her Berlin and Milan decrees." These realities illustrate one of the reasons that concerns about foreign shareholders might well have mattered. Moreover, as Root observed, in some quarters the Bank was regarded as a "British" institution. "A majority of its directors were Federalists," he noted, "and under this circumstance, added to their British predilections, induced the whole Federal party to favor its recharter. Under such circumstances it is not wonderful that the great mass of the Republican party were opposed to the Bank."

Ultimately one of the most telling commentaries on the events of 1811 may be the one found in a letter that Timothy Pickering, a Federalist senator from Massachusetts, sent to Judge Richard Peters on January 30, 1811: "You will not be surprised if I should trace this opposition to the Bank to the 'origin of our (political) evil' — the philosopher of Monticello. He and Randolph perplexed the President with their plausible objections, which, at the last moment, were overthrown by Hamilton. Jefferson has never forgotten the signal defeat. Envy and hatred of his rival have ever since rankled in his bosom; and if he can now destroy the Bank, he will feel the final victory to be his own."

CHAPTER 3

The Rise of the Second Bank

The initial reaction to the loss of the Bank was somewhat muted. There was no public outcry, and the Bank's assets were quietly liquidated. Its absence nevertheless eventually proved troubling for a number of reasons. The United States still did not have a single, stable national currency, resulting in a pronounced preference for specie — gold and silver — as the medium of exchange. But specie was in short supply, and the gap was filled by notes issued by the increasing number of private banks, now in excess of 200. Unfortunately, these institutions tended to be reckless in this regard, issuing notes far beyond their ability to support or redeem them. The value of notes in circulation grew from just over $28 million to $45.5 million, while specie grew at a much smaller rate, from $15.4 million to $17 million. The foreign capital that had been invested in the Bank in turn left the country, a loss of some $7 million.

There was a natural cause-effect relationship in much of what happened. As Gallatin stressed:

> The creation of new state banks was a natural consequence of the dissolution of the Bank of the United States. And, as is usual under such circumstances, the expectation of great profits gave birth to a much greater number than was wanted. . . . That increase took place on the eve of and during a war which did nearly annihilate the exports and both the foreign and coasting trade. And, as the salutary regulating power of the Bank of the United States no longer existed, the issues were accordingly increased much beyond what the other circumstances mentioned rendered necessary.

The situation became so severe that even Jefferson was disturbed. In a letter to John Adams, with whom he had reconciled, he admitted,

"I have ever been the enemy of banks, not of those discounting for cash; but of those foisting their own paper into circulation, and thus banishing our cash." Characterizing what was happening as a "mania," Jefferson declared that "it has siesed by it's delusions and corruptions all the members of our governments, general, special, and individual." And he predicted glumly that there was little if anything that could be done. "You might as well, with the sailors, whistle to the wind, as suggest precautions against having too much money. We must scud before the gale, and try to hold fast, ourselves, by some plank of the wreck. God send us all a safe deliverance."

Jefferson wrote these words in 1814, when the problems caused by the loss of the Bank had been compounded by the outbreak of the War of 1812. Madison had become increasingly frustrated by the failure of his diplomatic efforts to reach any sort of accord with England, and he sent a war message to Congress on June 1. It responded with a declaration of war, which Madison signed on the eighteenth. Ironically, a few days later the British suspended their Orders in Council, an act that, had it come earlier, might have prevented a war.

Madison was overwhelmingly reelected to a second term that fall, but political success did not engender military triumphs. The low point came in August 1814, when a British force first defeated an untrained militia at the Battle of Bladensburg and then seized Washington and burned its public buildings, most notably both the Capitol and the White House. The severity of this setback was mitigated somewhat in September when the American forces in Baltimore were able to hold out in the face of the British bombardment of Fort McHenry, an event that inspired Francis Scott Key to draft what became known as "The Star-Spangled Banner." But victories were the exception rather than the rule, and the willingness of the British to seek a negotiated solution reflected their own troubles, as they had far more pressing concerns to attend to in Europe. These discussions took place in Ghent, where a treaty that essentially took everyone back to square one was agreed to on Christmas Eve, 1814. As the *National Intelligencer* observed, "The general principle of the treaty is a restitution and recognition of the rights and possessions of each party, as they stood before the war." Ironically, that treaty was negotiated prior to the most important American victory of the war, General Andrew Jackson's successful defense of New Orleans.

The war imposed incredible financial strains on the federal government. The full extent of the situation was captured by Representative Alexander Hanson, a Maryland Federalist, who wrote in November 1814:

> So completely empty was the Treasury and destitute of credit that funds could not be obtained to defray the current ordinary expenses of the different Departments. . . . the Department of State was so bare of money as to be unable to pay even its stationery bill. . . . the Treasury was obliged to borrow pitiful sums, which it would disgrace a merchant in tolerable conditions to ask for. . . . The Paymaster was unable to meet demands for paltry amounts — not even for $30. . . . In short it was difficult to conceive a situation more critical and perilous than that of the government at this moment, without money, without credit, and destitute of the means of defending the country.

There were a number of reasons for this situation. The 1807 Embargo and Non-Importation Acts had had a devastating impact on commerce, especially in New England. The major revenue sources available to the government, tariffs and importation duties, were producing little revenue because trade had declined precipitously. Government credit ratings were at their lowest point since the Revolution, and bonds and notes offered by the Treasury were at best unattractive investments. Tax revenue had also declined as a number of internal taxes had been abolished in 1802 when finances were in excellent shape.

In his annual report in December 1811, Gallatin asked to have the taxes restored. Congress refused. In December 1812 he estimated that expenses for the coming year would be on the order of $32 million, of which some $22 million would be to support the army and the navy. But projected income stood at $12 million, leaving a $20 million gap. Over time some of the needed funds were secured via new taxes on refined sugar, distillers, auctions, and stamps. But that revenue was not available until 1814, and in the interim it became necessary to finance the government and the war through loans.

Three financiers — two Philadelphians, David Parish and Stephen Girard, and John Jacob Astor of New York — formed a syndicate that agreed to purchase slightly over $9 million in government notes and thereby secure a $16 million loan. Additional loans were also eventually brokered by a fourth financial leader, Jacob Barker of New York. Meanwhile, John C. Calhoun of South Carolina led the fight in Congress for new sources of revenue with a degree of success that ultimately led the financier Alexander J. Dallas to describe him as "the young Hercules who carried the war on his shoulders."

Each of these individuals came to the conclusion that a new national bank was necessary. For Astor and Barker this represented a change in position, as they had clashed repeatedly with the directors of the First Bank and were pleased when its charter was not renewed. Their motives in these matters were mixed. There was a certain degree of patriotism involved, a belief that a new bank was necessary for the good of the country. But they also stood to profit because they held substantial amounts of government stock whose market value would increase if a bank were created. They also stood to benefit from the commissions they would realize from future stock sales, including those of the bank.

In January 1814, probably at the insistence of Astor, Congress received a petition from "a hundred and fifty inhabitants of the city of New York" requesting that a "National Bank" be created. In April a strong ally of the administration, Representative Felix Grundy of Tennessee, offered a resolution asking that "a committee be appointed to inquire into the expediency of establishing a National Bank; and that they have leave to report a bill or otherwise." Thomas Newton of Virginia argued that the measure should be indefinitely postponed, citing both constitutional concerns and a lack of time to thoroughly consider such a measure before Congress adjourned. Various others spoke for and against, and the attempt to postpone was eventually defeated. Grundy's motion then carried, and a committee of nine was appointed to take up the measure.

That decision both pleased the individuals seeking a new bank and provoked even more activity on their part. Their prior efforts had largely taken place behind closed doors in an attempt to forestall the criticisms that would inevitably have been voiced by the Bank's traditional opponents. The situation had now changed. Parish sent a letter to Astor, declaring, "We must now expect to see the subject fully & publickly discussed all thro' the Country. Secrecy is no longer necessary to be adhered to, but we ought on the Contrary to use all fair & proper means to make Proselytes and render the measures as popular as possible."

The bank's champions sought support from a large number of important political and business leaders. In particular they enlisted the aid of Dallas, who had been instrumental in the earlier loan negotiations and shared their opinion that a new national bank was necessary. Dallas was also an attorney and believed that the Constitution did in fact authorize Congress to issue a charter. He prepared an analysis of the constitutional issues with a view toward having it published in the *National Intelligencer.* In it he argued that the passage of time had resolved the matter. Conceding that various important figures had and would continue to disagree, Dallas stated:

> A diversity of opinion may honorably survive the contest; but upon the genuine principles of a representative government, the opinion of the majority can alone be carried into action. . . . When, therefore, we have marked the existence of a national bank for twenty years, with all the sanctions of the legislative, executive, and judicial authorities; when we have seen the dissolution of the one institution, and heard a loud and continued call for the establishment of another; when, under these circumstances, neither Congress nor the several states have resorted to the power of amendment, — can it be deemed a violation of the right of private opinion to consider the constitutionality of a national bank as a question forever settled and at rest?

These observations were prepared for public view. Privately Dallas was more blunt. In a letter to the acting secretary of the Treasury, William Jones, he maintained that the constitutional arguments were being pressed "by a few raving Printers and rival Banks. It may have been doubtful in 1792, but it is certain in 1814, that a National Bank is essential to the fiscal operations and credit of the Government. Then why is all put to risque, for want of the machinery which is best calculated to collect, to distribute & to anticipate the national treasure?"

It was at this point that Astor contacted various like-minded individuals to solicit their support and brought the financial leaders of New York together in a series of meetings held at his home. The end result was a proposal that would create a new national bank secured by real estate rather than specie, which remained in short supply. Astor circulated that plan, indicating that the actual means of financing the enterprise were subject to debate. In particular, in a letter to Dennis A. Smith, an official of the Mechanics Bank of Baltimore, Astor observed that "a Bank upon the plan of the last National Bank will pass most readily, & if it can be made to answer [the needs of the] Government it will do us."

Astor asked Dallas to forward the plan to his friend, Secretary of State James Monroe. Dallas did so, noting, "My principal inducement in troubling you with it arises from the suggestion that it is a result of a deliberate concert among the Capitalists; and perhaps, the Secretary of the Treasury may draw some useful hints from the plan, as well as from Mr. Astor's letter." The secretary in question was George W. Campbell, who had succeeded Gallatin and was now rumored to be planning to leave office. Dallas had previously been approached to fill the post but had declined, arguing that it required a financial sacrifice he was unwilling to undertake. But in a letter to Monroe that accompanied the Astor plan he intimated that he might be willing to reconsider. He made similar overtures to Jones in a series of letters, within which he indicated both that he now viewed these matters in the light of his obligations to the nation and that he had a specific set of goals in mind: "The state of public credit admits of no palliative remedy. There must be established an efficient, productive system of taxation. There must be established a National Bank to anticipate, collect and distribute the revenue."

Madison realized that Dallas both supported the administration and was well regarded in the business community. He nominated him on October 5, and Dallas was confirmed the next day. Dallas then wrote Jones, stating that "the Rubicon is passed. My head and my heart are not easy; but I will not look back." Astor was less restrained, declaring that with "Mr. Dallas at the Head there is no doubt we must do well."

Dallas quickly drafted his own plan for a new bank. The proposal seemed to have strong support. For example, on October 28, 1814, the House overwhelmingly rejected an amendment that would have deleted a provision authorizing the creation of branches in the states, a 138 to 14 vote that was regarded as an affirmation of the constitutional authority to create a bank. But there were nevertheless substantial concerns about many of the details, and a number of individuals voiced strong opposition to the measure. In the House, for example, John W. Eppes led a group of Republicans who championed the notion that currency needs could be met by the interest-bearing Treasury notes that would be issued under the Dallas plan. Eppes also believed that the Constitution did not authorize the creation of a bank, a position that was to be expected from Jefferson's son-in-law.

There were other concerns. Dallas had recommended a funding structure that would have authorized the Bank to lend the government $30 million in notes. That prompted many to fear that the Bank would not be able to make payments in specie. The remaining Federalists in turn believed that a government stake in the Bank would inure to the benefit of the Republicans. The tide of opposition prompted Calhoun to rethink his initial support for the Dallas proposal. He decided to offer a compromise, crafting a measure that (to assuage Eppes) would be capitalized at $50 million, one-tenth of which would be specie and the balance Treasury notes. His own allies would be reassured by a requirement that the bank maintain specie payments and would not be required to lend the government any money. And for the Federalists he proposed to eliminate any government role in the direction of the Bank.

Dallas was appalled and worked hard to derail the Calhoun plan, which was rejected overwhelmingly in the House, 104 to 49. But the Dallas measure also failed to gain a majority when it came to a vote on January 2, 1815. The tally was 81 in favor and 80 opposed, at which point the Speaker of the House, Langdon Cheves of South Carolina, offered his opinion on the matter for the first time, declaring that "the bill proposes a dangerous, unexampled, and, he might also say, a desperate resort." His "no" vote produced a tie, and the bill was defeated.

A new approach then surfaced, championed by Representative Daniel Webster, a Federalist from New Hampshire. Webster, in his first term, was already developing a reputation as a forceful, eloquent, and effective advocate. Like many from his region Webster was opposed to the war. He argued that "to look to a Bank as a source capable not only of affording a circulating medium to the country but also of supplying the ways and means of carrying on the war — especially at a time when the country is without commerce — is to expect much more than ever will be obtained." He was also a champion of hard money and was disturbed by the details of a plan he characterized as "a system of rank speculation, and enormous mischief, one that would found a bank on the insolvency of the government and create a paper department of government." He sarcastically described the proposed bank as "a wonderful scheme of finance" within which "the government is to grow rich, because it is to borrow without the obligation of repaying, and is to borrow of a bank which issues paper without liability to redeem it."

Webster accordingly advanced a plan that was eventually modified by Calhoun and William Lowndes of South Carolina. The new bank would be capitalized at $30 million, one-sixth of which would be specie, and the balance stock and Treasury notes. It would be privately controlled, would not be allowed to suspend payments in specie, and would not be obliged to lend any of its capital to the government. That measure was approved by the House by a substantial majority on January 7, 1815, and gained Senate approval on January 20.

This approach would have been effective in peacetime, but it did little if anything to meet the actual needs of a government that was still at war. Dallas was appalled: "I asked for bread and [Congress] gave me a stone. I asked for a Bank to serve the Government during the war; and they gave me a commercial bank to go into operation after the war." He recommended that Madison veto the measure. On January 30, 1815, Madison did just that.

Madison's veto message made it clear that his "deep and solemn conviction that the bill ought not to become a law" was not based on any objections to its constitutionality. Making public what he had privately concluded when the charter of the First Bank was up for renewal, Madison indicated that he was "waiving the question of the constitutional authority of the Legislature to establish an incorporated bank as being precluded in my judgment by repeated recognitions under varied circumstances of the validity of such an institution in acts of the legislative, executive, and judicial branches of the Government, accompanied by indications, in different modes, of a concurrence of the general will of the nation." The veto reflected instead his belief that the proposal before him did not do the sorts of things that made it either a necessary or a proper exercise of federal authority given the actual needs of the government at the time: "The proposed bank does not appear to be calculated to answer the purposes of reviving the public credit, of providing a national medium of circulation, and of aiding the Treasury by facilitating the indispensable anticipations of the revenue and by affording to the public more durable loans."

A new proposal that largely replicated the one made by Dallas was then quickly introduced. It was approved by the Senate on February 11 and sent to the House for what many believed would be a protracted debate. Three days later Secretary of State James Monroe gave Madison a copy of the proposed Treaty of Ghent. The news created a sharp difference of opinion about whether a bank was now needed. The House discussed the Senate bill on February 13, and a series of votes were taken on various proposed amendments. But when it returned to the issue on Friday the seventeenth, Lowndes moved "to postpone the bill indefinitely . . . not from any hostility to a National Bank, wishing, as [others] did, that a National Bank should be established, but because he wished it to be done at a time and under circumstances which would give the House the ability to decide correctly on the subject." Two individuals disagreed, expressing their belief that the issues had already been debated at length and their sense that the House could quickly deal with the matter. But the Lowndes motion was approved by one vote, 74 to 73, and the move to create a new bank in 1815 ended.

Discussions continued. In his seventh annual message in December 1815, Madison outlined various financial concerns and stated that if the state banks could not solve them — and Madison surely knew that they could not — "the probable operation of a national bank will merit consideration." Dallas followed up three days later in his annual report on the state of the finances, within which he argued that "the establishment of a national bank is regarded as the best, and, perhaps, the only adequate resource to relieve the country and the Government from the present embarrassments." Relying to a great extent on the widely shared belief that there was a pressing need for a "national circulating medium," Dallas outlined a noble vision for the proposed bank:

Established by the authority of the Government of the United States, accredited by the Government to the whole amount of its notes in circulation, and entrusted as the depository of the Government with all the accumulations of public treasure, the national

bank, independent of its immediate capital, will enjoy every recommendation which can merit and secure the confidence of the
public. Organized upon principles of responsibility, but of independence, the national bank will be retained within its legitimate
sphere of action, without just apprehension from the misconduct
of its directors, or from the encroachments of the Government.
Eminent in its resources, and in its example, the national bank will
conciliate, aid, and lead, the State banks in all that is necessary for
the restoration of credit, public and private. And acting upon a
compound capital, partly of stock, and partly of gold and silver, the
national bank will be the ready instrument to enhance the value of
public securities, and to restore the currency of the national coin.

Dallas's remarks found a receptive audience in Congress, especially
in Calhoun, now chair of the House Committee on the National Currency, who asked him to flesh out his vision. Dallas did so on December 24, sending Calhoun a lengthy letter within which he proposed a
bank that would have a twenty-year charter and be capitalized at $35
million (which could later be expanded to $50 million), with one-fifth
of the stock provided by the government and the balance by the public. One-quarter of the money subscribed would be in specie. There
would be twenty-five directors, all of whom must be citizens of the
United States, with five to be appointed by the president. The bank
would have branches, would not be required to lend money to the
government, and would not be allowed to suspend specie payments
unless "previously authorized by Congress."

Calhoun reported just such a bill on January 8, 1816, and on February 26 he was the first to speak when the House took up the subject. He indicated that there was no need to address the constitutional
question. That would "be an useless consumption of time" because
these had been fully aired, and "all had made up their mind on it."
The real issue, he averred, was "the cause and state of the disorders
of the national currency, and the question whether it was in the power
of Congress, by establishing a national bank, to remove those disorders." He maintained that it was and that Congress had an obligation
to "remedy" the "evil."

As in the past the proposal proved controversial. But unlike the
previous debates the participants this time largely ignored the consti-

tutional issues. Representative Robert Wright of Maryland, who opposed extending the First Bank's charter in 1811, offered one of the very few observations on this subject. It was both startling and informative, for Wright maintained that "the supreme judicial tribunal had decided on its constitutionality, by often recognizing it as a party, and it was too late to insist on the objection." That comment echoed Madison in his 1815 veto message, within which he included the judicial branch as one of the actors that had given "repeated recognitions under varied circumstances of the validity of such an institution." Neither Madison nor Wright pointed to specific decisions. Had they done so, they might well have cited *The Bank of the United States v. DeVeaux* (1809), which arose, ironically, when the First Bank refused to pay a tax that the state of Georgia attempted to levy on its stock. The Court did not address the constitutional questions in *DeVeaux*, disposing of the case on other grounds. It was accordingly ironic that one of the very few mentions of the constitutional issues in the 1816 debates took the form of a statement arguing that the Court itself had already settled the question.

Virtually all the discussion focused on the details of the proposal or what amounted to a generic opposition to any large federal institution that would meddle in the affairs of the states and the private sector. Most Republicans were in favor of the bill, which, in a change from the past, secured substantial support from the West and the South. The Federalists, in turn, again led by Daniel Webster, generally opposed it. Concessions were made. A firm limit of $35 million was imposed on the bank's capitalization, and the authority to appoint the bank president was given to the stockholders rather than the government. Congress would not be allowed to suspend specie payments, and Treasury notes would not be accepted in payment for bank stock.

Debate continued until March 14, when the House approved the measure, albeit by the somewhat narrow tally of 80 to 71. The Senate in turn gave it a wider margin of victory on April 3, 22 to 12. Madison then signed the bill on April 10, 1816, formally creating what would now be known as the Second Bank of the United States.

The Bank officially opened for business on January 7, 1817. As before, its main office was in Philadelphia. But unlike the First Bank, the Second Bank quickly established a large number of branch offices. Nineteen were opened in 1817, including one in Baltimore and two in Ohio. Some of these branches were eventually discontinued, and eight additional offices were opened from 1826 through 1830. What is important is that the Bank immediately established a presence in sixteen states (there were also two offices in Kentucky) and the District of Columbia. This allowed the Bank to fulfill one of its important functions, moving federal funds from place to place, but it also created numerous opportunities for local conflict, which soon materialized.

The most fateful initial development was the selection of the Bank's first president. Dallas had always intended that this position go to William Jones, who had been secretary of the Navy and had for a short time served as acting secretary of the Treasury. Dallas advanced Jones's cause in a number of letters to Madison that had their desired effect. Madison replied, "I am very glad to learn by your late letter that his prospects of being at the head of the institution have become favorable. . . . Besides the personal motives which make me wish his success, I am persuaded that it would accord much better with the interests of both the bank and the public than any other applicant in competition with it."

Unfortunately, this is in fact what happened, and Jones was selected by the board to serve as the first president of the Second Bank. But Jones was a weak individual who himself had recently declared bankruptcy, not a good sign in someone who was about to assume the responsibility for much of the nation's financial well-being. Dallas, who was otherwise so astute, was blindly loyal to Jones even as others expressed their alarm. In October 1816 Girard spoke of "intrigue and corruption [that] had formed a ticket for twenty directors of the Bank of the United States who I am sorry to say appear to have been selected for the purpose of securing the presidency for Mr. Jones." He voiced the same concerns the day the Bank opened, stating, "If I live twelve months more I intend to use all my activity, means, and influence to change and replace the majority of directors with honest and independent men."

Jones had numerous flaws, not the least of which was an unfortunate attitude toward the branch offices. The first mistake was to establish so many, a number of which were badly located, placed in areas that were poor and sparsely populated. More tellingly, Jones refused to closely monitor branch operations, which were generally not required to periodically settle their accounts. He also refused to assign each branch a specific amount of capital. In an especially brusque letter, he informed the head of the Charleston branch, "Your board will please observe, sir, that it is no part of the system of the parent board to give a definite capital to the respective offices, to be employed for the benefit of their several districts; but to extend or control their operations, as the exigencies of commerce, the requisitions of the Government, and the general interest of the institution shall from time to time direct." The net result was that many branches became irresponsible, replicating the conduct of state banks whose unrestrained issuance of unsecured banknotes had factored so greatly in the call for the creation of the Second Bank.

Jones also had an unfortunate conception of the Bank's role. In a July 1817 letter to Secretary of the Treasury William H. Crawford he indicated, "I am not at all disposed to take the late Bank of the United States as an exemplar in practice; because I think its operations were circumscribed by a policy less enlarged, liberal, and useful, than its powers and resources would have justified." The First Bank had had a largely exemplary record, characterized by a generally reserved approach to its tasks. Jones opted for a more aggressive stance, believing that the Bank should be operated for the benefit of its stockholders rather than as an instrument of national fiscal policy. Unfortunately, a number of other Bank officials and stockholders shared that attitude.

When the Second Bank began to do business, the economy was inflationary but generally sound. The problems caused by the War of 1812 were in the past. The trade blockades had ended. A hungry American market was now open, and other nations, in particular England, were eager to sell to individuals who wanted their goods. Both imports and exports increased and prices rose. The New York Stock Exchange opened its doors in March 1817, and the boom continued into 1818, fueled by speculation and by banks that were all too willing to provide the necessary means.

The Bank's desire to compete with established state banks and its aggressive rather than controlled approach to lending led it to make too many loans for paper currency, unbacked by specie. In May 1817 a Baltimore paper, the *Niles Weekly Register*, observed that "though our banks ostensibly pay specie, it is almost as rare as it was some months ago to see a dollar. 'Paper does the business still.'" This posed a real problem for the Bank. One of the arguments for its creation, after all, had been that a national bank would serve as an example to the state banks, a sound institution backed by and able to pay in specie. The Bank now was in the position where it labored under a legal obligation to pay specie for its notes, which it lacked, and was subject to a 12 percent penalty if it failed to do so, which would worsen an already problematic balance sheet. Moreover, the Bank was responsible for paying the debts of the government. One of those fell due in October 1818, a $2 million payment owed for the Louisiana Purchase that must be paid in specie. That equaled the Bank's entire stock of specie at the time, and the government was forced to yet again go abroad, to London, to satisfy the obligation.

The Bank realized that the situation had become untenable and began to curtail its expansionist policies. In the summer of 1818 it ordered its branches to have the state banks redeem the notes owed them. This forced the state banks to curtail their activities and seek repayment of their debts so that they might settle their accounts with the Bank. The money supply decreased dramatically, provoking a rapid and dramatic drop in prices. This in turn overwhelmed the system. Bankruptcies multiplied, and by 1819 more than 3 million individuals — one-third of the population — were feeling the effects of the resulting depression, which became known as the Panic of 1819.

Historians disagree about whether the Bank and its policies were the true cause of the panic or simply one of its major precipitating forces. At best the Bank's policies exacerbated an already tenuous situation. At worst they initiated the chain of events that produced one of the most severe economic dislocations in the young nation's history.

Ultimately it did not matter if the Bank was the actual cause or simply one of the contributing factors. Public perceptions of the Bank declined, and its traditional enemies had new ammunition to fuel the fires of their hostility. Newspapers in particular railed against the Bank. The attacks launched by William Duane, publisher of the Philadelphia-based *Aurora*, were especially sharp. Duane was a staunch Republican whose intensely partisan approach to his tasks in the 1790s had incurred the wrath of the Federalists, who secured his indictment under the Sedition Act. That charge was eventually dismissed when Jefferson became president and Duane became one of the nation's most important and influential Republican voices.

Predictably, part of that portfolio was his opposition to the Bank of the United States. In 1811 Duane and the *Aurora* strongly opposed the extension of the First Bank's charter, a decision and position that cost him the support of one of his most important financial backers, Thomas Leiper. And in 1818 he turned his attention to the Second Bank, observing in September, "It was long since imagined, even by those the least disposed to suspect ill, in men, whom they ought to have known incapable of better; that the measure of iniquity of the *paper bank managers*, was full, even to overflowing. It was deemed impossible, that they could go further, without rousing public indignation to an open and decisive rebellion against them, their corrupt bank, and their oppressive measures." But the Bank, Duane stressed, had now outdone itself. As part of its economy measures it had ended the requirement that each branch be obligated to redeem the notes of the other branches. This was designed to protect those branches that had embraced a conservative credit policy, mainly in the East, from those that had pursued unbridled expansion, mainly in the South and West. Duane was outraged: "For even the imagination revolts from the contemplation of an act, which implies that *last* and *blackest degree*, of turpitude and folly. What then was the astonishment, what the indignation, and the embarrassment of the public, without one exception of party, or social feelings, when the managers of this swindling bank, *refused to receive their own branch notes on deposit, or in payment of debts to the bank itself? When they refused to receive* THEIR OWN NOTES?"

Duane voiced these and similar concerns over the barely disguised pseudonym Brutus. The criticisms were continuous and savage. He declared, "In vain will this nefarious institution, attempt through the *connivance* of a corrupt administration, to shake off the overwhelming load of iniquity, that drags it down the channel of popular odium, to final ruin and disgrace." He lamented the impact the Bank was having on the people who had bought into it, "number[ing] the degeneracy of our minds, and the depravity of our morals, among the evil consequences that have so copiously flowed from the banking system."

Similar sentiments appeared in the *Niles Weekly Register*, published by another influential journalist, Hezekiah Niles. The *Register* was a different sort of publication, one of the few truly national newspapers of the period and devoted almost exclusively to politics and national affairs. It was accordingly both widely read and very influential.

On September 5, 1818, Niles stated, "It would seem that the point of time which every reflecting man has fearfully looked for, for several years, has nearly arrived. That the 'PAPER SYSTEM' would *blow up*, has been confidently expected as that the human body must die." A week later he declared that "the bank, like an *abandoned* mother, has most imprudently BASTARDIZED its offspring, and deserves not the countenance and support of honest people." The Bank, Niles observed, "has committed an act of *suicide;* — whether it will cause its death or not, the *doctors* at Washington city and in the seats of the several state governments, will soon have to determine." He subsequently softened the criticisms, denying that he sought "to destroy the banking establishments of the United States." Rather, he claimed, he hoped for "an extensive *pruning* — a careful retention of what is good, and a certain destruction of that which is evil." But the *Register* continued to monitor the Bank and its activities, with its pages presenting the picture of an institution that was increasingly unworthy of the public trust.

The newspapers were not the only bodies to go after the Bank. State legislatures also entered the fray, driven by both an inherent distrust of banks and a particular hostility toward the Bank itself. One of these measures predated the Second Bank. Indiana's first constitution, adopted in 1816, stated that "there shall not be established or incorporated in this State, any bank or banking company, or monied institution for the purpose of issuing bills of credit, or bills payable to order or bearer," other than a "State Bank," that the legislature was free to create. In 1818, in turn, the first Illinois Constitution declared, "There shall be no other banks or moneyed institutions in the State but those already provided by law, except a State bank and its branches, which may be established and regulated by the general assembly of the State as they may think proper."

Other states — each of which had at least one branch of the Bank within its borders — imposed new taxes that were at best thinly disguised assaults on the Bank. The first was Maryland, which in February 1818 passed "An act to impose a Tax on all Banks or Branches thereof in the State of Maryland not chartered by the Legislature." Institutions covered by the act were authorized to issue notes in certain stated denominations, but only on payment of a stamp tax that ranged from 10 cents to $20, depending on the value of the note. A bank wishing to avoid the tax could do so by paying an annual fee of $15,000. If it failed to do either, both it and its officers were subject to fines, respectively, of $500 or $100 "for each and every offense."

Tennessee followed suit in November 1818, imposing an annual tax of $50,000 on any bank in the state that did not hold a state charter. In December Georgia enacted a tax on bank stock that, by legislative resolution, was declared to apply only to branches of the Bank. North Carolina followed suit, albeit with a relatively modest tax of $5,000 on the Bank's branch in Fayetteville. Then Ohio and Kentucky significantly raised the ante. Ohio set the tax on each of the Bank's two branches in that state at $50,000 per year. Kentucky in turn imposed the highest tax of all, $60,000 per year, again to be levied on two branches.

Part of the opposition to the Bank was principled. Many people had deep-seated reservations about banks in and of themselves. These were also quite often the same individuals who worried about the implications of a nominally federal bank for states that viewed themselves as distinct and coequal sovereigns in a federal compact, rather than as constituent members of a national union. Equally important, however, were concerns about the Bank itself. Some of these were purely parochial, as the states took steps to protect their own banks. But the states were also legitimately concerned about the Bank's policies, especially those that factored into the emerging economic downturn that became the Panic of 1819. In addition, there were increasing rumors of corruption and mismanagement, the exemplar being the Baltimore branch of the Bank.

The constant criticism of the Bank could not be ignored, and on November 25, 1818, Representative John C. Spencer of New York offered a resolution in the House of Representatives asking "that a committee be appointed to inspect the books and examine into the proceedings of the Bank of the United States, and to report whether the provisions of its charter have been violated or not." Spencer stated, "As to the necessity of the inquiry proposed, he presumed there were few of those near him who were not aware of the agitation which exists in the public mind on this subject, and who did not perceive that, from one end of the country to the other, loud complaints were made against the conduct of the officers of the banks." He tied the need for an investigation to the fortunes of the Bank itself. "The friends of the bank," he thought, "ought to solicit the inquiry proposed," for a "full and fair view of the whole subject, thus obtained, would be attended with the most happy consequences to the nation and to the bank." He emphasized that "no one could doubt the utility of such an institution to the nation, if properly conducted."

Discussion carried over to November 30. There was some jousting between various representatives about the extent to which the Bank had fulfilled the roles promised by its supporters and about the details of the proposed investigation. Some of the numerous provisions contained in the original Spencer measure were eliminated, and the final motion was crafted in ways designed to give the committee the freedom to conduct "as broad and comprehensive" an investigation "as the nature of the subject would permit." It was approved, apparently without a formal vote. A five-person committee was then appointed, consisting of Spencer, William Lowndes of South Carolina, Louis McLane of Delaware, Burwell Bassett of Virginia, and a future president of the United States who would play an important role in the long-term fate of the Bank, John Tyler, also of Virginia.

The committee filed its report on January 16, 1819. It indicated that the members had conducted a thorough examination of the Bank's books and had "interrogated on oath" officers and officials of the Bank at its headquarters in Philadelphia and branch offices in Baltimore, Richmond, and Washington. The committee stressed that its focus had been on "the general management of the bank, and the conduct of its officers, and those which were connected with the question of a violation of its charter."

The first portion of the report contained a recitation of the events that provoked the investigation. The committee observed that the Bank had been in a position to "coerce" the state banks "into a moderate and reasonable reduction of their circulating notes." Noting that "when the bank began to call for specie, its demands were so considerable as to not only expose the local banks, but the citizens in their vicinity, generally, to very severe pressure," the committee placed much of the blame for the resulting economic problems on the Bank. "The committee think it evident . . . that the bank did not exercise, with sufficient energy, the power which it possessed, and might have retained, but rather afforded inducements to the State banks to extend the amount of their circulating notes, and this increased one of the evils it was intended to correct." It also criticized the conduct of the branches, singling out Baltimore in particular as one that "continued its drafts and discounts, and drained the specie from the Northern offices." Indeed, the committee came to the conclusion that the New York, Boston, and Philadelphia branches "were, in fact, made tributary to Baltimore; and all their means and energies were required to supply its extravagant issues."

The committee also made it clear that it was very much aware of the inappropriate manipulations that had occurred. It stressed that "the effect of these [actions] was, very obviously, to enable those who had made large purchases to retain their stock without paying for it, and to declare a benefit from its probable advancement in price." Large amounts of the Bank's capital were "placed beyond its control," and many of "the loans actually made were . . . unreasonable and excessive in their amount; they were not made to the merchant and trader, but to a few persons consisting of directors, brokers, and speculators; and have been renewed and continued, almost invariably, at the option of the borrower." Indeed, "many of the directors, as well those appointed by the Government, as those elected by the stockholders, appear to have been the most forward and the most active in trafficking in stock."

The committee concluded that substantial misconduct had occurred and that the Bank's charter had been violated in a number of ways. It did not, however, recommend any specific actions or sanctions, believing that "the salutary power lodged in the Treasury Department will be exerted, as occasion may require, and with reference to the best interests of the United States."

The report had an immediate and predictable effect. William Jones was forced out in January. The House in turn began formal consideration of the committee report on February 19, 1819, four days before the Court met to take up *M'Culloch*. Two resolutions were before it. The first called for the attorney general to issue a scire facias, a writ directed at the Bank "to show *cause* wherefore the charter, thereby granted, should not be declared forfeit." The second asked that the Committee on the Judiciary "be instructed to report a bill to repeal" the Bank's charter.

These provoked extended debate that ended on February 25, a point at which the Court was in the midst of the *M'Culloch* oral argument. All the Bank's sins were paraded before the House, as were the benefits that a properly administered Bank could bring to the nation. Many of the themes that emerged were familiar, including constitutionality and state rights. The House also indicated that it knew that it was not the only body judging the Bank at that time. On the twenty-fourth, for example, David Walker of Kentucky observed, "Have we not got reasons to believe, from the known complexion of a majority of the members of the United States Supreme Court, that the court will determine that the United States Bank have a right to extend her branches over every individual State in the Union, and that the States have no right to prune them?" The debates also showed that the members of the House recognized that the issues posed by the Bank were inextricably linked to those raised by another deeply divisive issue that had recently come before it, the Missouri question, with all its implications for the future of slavery.

Both resolutions were rejected by overwhelming margins on February 24. The focus then shifted fully to the Court, which was in the midst of oral argument in a case that arose when the cashier of the Baltimore branch of the Bank issued a series of notes on untaxed paper in the spring of 1818, an action that provoked application of the Maryland tax.

A Court for a Nation

The Constitution does not tell us very much about the Supreme Court. Article III, Section 1 indicates that "the judicial Power of the United States, shall be vested in one supreme Court, and in such inferior Courts as the Congress may from time to time ordain and establish." It also provides that "judges, both of the supreme and inferior Courts, shall hold their Offices during good Behaviour, and shall, at stated times, receive for their Services a Compensation, which shall not be diminished during their continuance in Office." Article III, Section 2 in turn lists the various types of jurisdiction the Court shall exercise, that is, the types of cases it is empowered to hear. Taken together these provisions indicate that the Supreme Court is the only federal court that the Constitution actually requires. They also show that many of the details of the Court's composition and jurisdiction were actually to be determined by Congress.

The First Federal Congress recognized the importance of the federal judiciary, and one of its first and most important actions was the passage of the Judiciary Act of 1789. Section 1 of that measure provided that "the supreme court of the United States shall consist of a chief justice and five associate justices, any four of whom shall be a quorum." It directed that the Court "shall hold annually at the seat of government two sessions, the one commencing the first Monday of February, and the other the first Monday of August." It imposed one additional duty on the justices by creating three circuit courts, to consist of "any two justices of the Supreme Court" and a district judge from the district in which the circuit court sat. This obligation, which became known as "riding the circuits," remained in place for a number of years and posed major problems, as many individuals were unwilling to serve on the Court given the demands that circuit duty imposed.

The Court initially played what can only be described as a minor role in the governing process. During the 1790s it decided at best a few cases of any significance. That changed in December 1800, when Chief Justice Oliver Ellsworth submitted his resignation to President John Adams. This posed a dilemma for Adams, who apparently had just lost the election to Thomas Jefferson. It was clear that any hope of preserving a strong Federalist presence on the Court required that Adams quickly identify and secure Senate approval of the new chief justice. He initially nominated John Jay, who had served as the nation's first chief justice, resigning in 1795 to become governor of New York. But he did so without first ascertaining that Jay was willing to serve. The Senate received that nomination on December 18 and approved it the next day. But in early January Adams received a letter from Jay that both declined the nomination and captured eloquently the reservations that many individuals had about the Court and the position it then occupied: "I left the bench perfectly convinced that under a system so defective it would not obtain the energy, weight, and dignity which was essential to its affording due support to the national government; nor acquire the public confidence and respect which, as the last resort of the justice of the nation, it should possess. Hence I am induced to doubt both the propriety and the expediency of my returning to the bench under the present system. Independently of these considerations, the state of my health removes every doubt."

Jay's decision, and Adams's response, changed the course of history. For Adams now approached one of his most trusted advisers, Secretary of State John Marshall, telling him, "I believe I must nominate you."

Marshall, a native of Virginia, was forty-five years old and a loyal Federalist. He had served with distinction in the Revolutionary War, forging a close relationship with both George Washington and Alexander Hamilton. In particular, he was part of the American force that wintered at Valley Forge in 1777–1778, an experience that taught him a great deal about both the human condition and the problems caused by a government that was either unwilling or unable to provide for its citizens. He then read law at the College of William and Mary and began a career marked by both distinction in the practice of law and a penchant for public service.

In 1788 Marshall was a delegate to the Virginia convention that debated and ratified the Constitution. It was here that Marshall first expressed many of the beliefs that became the hallmarks of his philosophy of government and the Constitution. In a response to Patrick Henry, a leading figure of the Virginia Anti-Federalists, he stated, "We are told that the Confederation carried us through the war." For someone who had endured the rigors of Valley Forge, that simply did not ring true: "Had not the enthusiasm of liberty inspired us with unanimity, that system would never have carried us through it. It would have been much sooner terminated had that Government been possessed of due energy." The problem was arguably a simple one: "The Confederation has nominal powers, but no means to carry them into effect. If a system of Government were devised by more than human intelligence, it would not be effectual if the means were not adequate to the power."

In the 1790s Marshall devoted most of his time to the practice of law, including one argument before the Supreme Court in *Ware v. Hylton* (1796), which he lost. He then agreed to serve as a member of the commission that attempted to settle various disputes that had arisen between the United States and the newly formed revolutionary government in France. That mission ended in failure but was a personal triumph for Marshall, who played an important role in exposing the duplicity of the French in what became known as the XYZ Affair. Marshall then represented Virginia in the House of Representatives for one term, during which he was a staunch defender of President John Adams and his administration. Adams rewarded this service in May 1800, making Marshall his secretary of state, the position from which Adams plucked him, in the waning days of his administration, to serve as the next chief justice of the United States.

Marshall was confirmed by the Senate on January 27, 1801. But he continued to serve as secretary of state until the new administration took office on March 4, when, in his capacity as chief justice, he administered the oath of office to Thomas Jefferson. The irony was profound. Marshall and Jefferson were old adversaries, a relationship that surely would not have improved had Jefferson known that Marshall had recently written Alexander Hamilton to express his belief that the new president was a man whose "foreign prejudices" — that is, his support for the French and their revolution — "seem to me to totally unfit him for the chief magistracy of a nation which cannot indulge those prejudices without sustaining deep & permanent injury." More tellingly, Marshall's strong Federalist philosophy, which he was now in a position to express in new and much more significant ways as the leader of the Court, made it unlikely that Jefferson included him in the group with whom he arguably sought reconciliation in his inaugural address, where he famously declared, "We have called by different names brethren of the same principle. We are all Republicans, we are all Federalists."

Over the next several years Marshall molded the Court in his image, transforming it from a bit player in the federal system into a major presence in the formation of a strong, vibrant nation under the terms of a Constitution that he interpreted with a strong nationalist cast. Ironically, one of the first and most important occasions for this arose when, as secretary of state, Marshall failed to deliver to one William Marbury his commission as a justice of the peace for the District of Columbia. Like Marshall, Marbury's appointment represented an attempt by Adams to place trusted Federalists in positions of authority before Jefferson assumed the reins of power. But Marshall failed to complete the process, and Marbury sought a writ of mandamus from the Supreme Court, an order directing that the new secretary of state, James Madison, deliver Marbury's signed and sealed commission. On December 18, 1801, Chief Justice Marshall announced that the Court would hear the case, setting it for argument during the next term of the Court, which was scheduled for the following June. But Congress had repealed the act authorizing that sitting, and the case was carried over until February 1803.

Speaking for a unanimous Court, Marshall delivered the opinion in *Marbury v. Madison* on February 24, 1803. The actual holding was that the Court did not have the power to hear the case. The Court's original jurisdiction, that is, the power to have a case filed directly with it, was controlled by the plain language of Article III, which limited that authority to cases involving "Ambassadors, other public Ministers and Consuls, and those in which a State shall be a party." But that clause dictated jurisdiction only for individuals who were officials of foreign nations, a class within which Marbury clearly did not fall. The provision of the Judiciary Act of 1789 that authorized the Court to issue a writ of this sort was accordingly unconstitutional, as it purported to expand the Court's power beyond the scope of what the Constitution conferred.

{ *Chapter 4* }

This seemed at first blush to be a victory for Jefferson, who would not have to place in office an individual whose beliefs were at odds with his. But the manner in which Marshall went about reaching the technical legal conclusion actually transformed victory into defeat. The holding of the case required at most a simple statement that the portion of the Judiciary Act authorizing the Court to issue the writ was unconstitutional. And while *Marbury* became the first case in which the Court actually held that a federal measure violated the Constitution, the notion that a court had the power to issue such a holding was hardly novel. It was not, then, the fact of judicial review but the manner in which Marshall expounded the doctrine that so offended his opponents.

Marshall approached the questions presented in *Marbury* in an order that allowed him to pen the first of a series of expansive opinions that articulated his vision of the Constitution and the nation it created. The authority of the Court to issue the writ was the third and final question considered. First came a discussion of the nature of the Constitution and the role of the judiciary in interpreting it. As a result, Marshall crafted an opinion announcing that this chief justice had every intention of seeing that the Court would fulfill its role as a coequal branch of the government. An "act of the legislature, repugnant to the constitution, is void," he declared. And the final responsibility for making such a determination fell to the Court: "It is emphatically the province and duty of the judicial department to say what the law is."

Marbury thus became the first of the decisions issued by what we now call the Marshall Court that placed the Supreme Court at the center of the American governmental and political systems. In virtually every one of these, Marshall wrote the opinion for the Court. That reality reflected a second Marshall innovation, the abandonment of the practice borrowed from the English under which each member of the Court expressed his individual view. This approach, known as speaking seriatim, had been the norm for the Court. In one of the very few truly important cases decided by the Court in the 1790s, for example, *Chisholm v. Georgia* (1793), there were five individual opinions, four holding that a federal court had the power to hear a suit against a nonconsenting state and one disagreeing. But Marshall believed that it was important for the Court to speak with a single voice whenever possible. And his adoption of the practice of a single opinion proved to be a further irritant for Jefferson and his allies, who complained bitterly that Marshall was squelching the voices of the other members of the Court and denying the nation the important knowledge of how each member actually felt about the issues before it.

The Court over which Marshall initially presided consisted of a chief justice, Marshall himself, and five associate justices, each of whom had been appointed by a Federalist president. Given that reality, a decision like *Marbury* was to be expected. The surprising thing was that subsequent appointments by Jefferson and his successor, James Madison, had no appreciable effect on Marshall's efforts to transform the Court and to take it in a decidedly nationalist direction.

In February 1819 there were seven individuals sitting on the Court, including the chief justice. One of them, Bushrod Washington, had also been placed on the Court by John Adams. Bushrod Washington was George Washington's nephew and heir, but his place on the Court reflected merit rather than patronage. Washington and Marshall became fast friends and close allies both on and off the bench. During the twenty-nine years they served together on the Court, they disagreed with each other only three times. The same could not be said of the first Republican appointed to the Court, William Johnson, who was nominated by Thomas Jefferson in 1804.

Jefferson had made it clear that loyalty to the Republican Party and Republican cause was a crucial characteristic for anyone who wished to be considered for the Court. He believed that Johnson was such a man, a South Carolina judge who was described by one supporter as "an excellent lawyer, prompt, eloquent, of irreproachable character, Republican connections, and of good nerves in his political principles." Johnson was both a brilliant and an opinionated individual and believed firmly that he had an obligation to express his own opinion. As a member of the Marshall Court he expressed his beliefs openly, tenaciously, and frequently, earning the sobriquet "the First Dissenter." During his twenty-eight years on the Court, Johnson wrote twenty-one concurring and thirty-four dissenting opinions. The next-highest totals for any justice during that period were five concurring opinions and twelve dissents.

In many instances Johnson's views, and his insistence that he be allowed to express them, put him at loggerheads with Marshall. But what he did not do, confounding his Jeffersonian supporters, was part company with the chief in virtually all the great national power cases. Indeed, in *Anderson v. Dunn* (1821), Johnson wrote one of the first post-*M'Culloch* opinions acknowledging the existence and importance of implied powers.

The next Republican confirmed was Henry Brockholst Livingston, a New York judge with a reputation as an active and effective member of the bench. Livingston had expressed pronounced Anti-Federalist sentiments in the past, and there was reason to believe that he would provide a strong voice for them on the Court. But he was also a congenial individual who, it is believed, was especially susceptible to Marshall's charm and leadership. He did not accordingly fulfill the promise that those who championed his appointment saw in him. That was also true of Jefferson's final appointee, Thomas Todd, an individual who largely agreed with Marshall's approach to most matters and made what little mark he did in cases involving real property and land titles, a reality that reflected the details of his law practice prior to becoming a judge.

Madison's first opportunity to influence the composition and direction of the Court came in 1811 when, after a series of false starts, he nominated Gabriel Duvall of Maryland and Joseph Story of Massachusetts. Duvall was confirmed and served for twenty-two years. But, like Todd, he made no mark on the Court. Hampered by increasing deafness, he contributed little beyond a reliable vote for Marshall's positions. Joseph Story, however, became one of the Court's most important and influential members. A brilliant individual with a seemingly inexhaustible appetite for work, he was thirty-one at the time he was appointed and is still the youngest individual to ever assume a seat on the Court. Jefferson was strongly opposed to Story's nomination, characterizing him in a letter to Madison as "unquestionably a tory" and "too young." But Madison refused to follow Jefferson's advice. Story served for thirty-four years and is appropriately remembered as one of the great justices of the Court.

Story became a close friend and dependable ally for Marshall. He also became one of the most productive members of the Court, second only to Marshall in the number of majority opinions written. Many of these were significant and, as matters unfolded, became important elements in developing and securing Marshall's national vision. One of these was *Martin v. Hunter's Lessee* (1816), in which the Court held that it did indeed have the power to review and reverse decisions of a state supreme court. John Marshall did not participate when the Court took up these matters because he had a personal interest in the case. It accordingly fell to Joseph Story to inform Virginia that "the constitution of the United States was ordained and established, not by the states in their sovereign capacities, but emphatically, as the preamble of our constitution declares, by 'the people of the United States.'" And in Article III, which "creates and defines the judicial power of the United States," we find "the voice of the whole American people solemnly declared, in establishing one great department of that government which was, in many respects, national, and in all, supreme." Appellate review had been expressly allocated in Article III and implemented by the people, speaking through Congress, in Section 25 of the Judiciary Act. "We dare not," Story concluded, "interpose a limitation where the people have not been disposed to create one."

Martin was not a Marshall opinion in the technical sense that he did not write it. But both the rhetoric and the result were very much in keeping with John Marshall's nationalist vision. Moreover, *Martin* provided further compelling evidence of the extent to which Marshall had transformed the Supreme Court into a unified and effective advocate for a national government that while limited in the scope of its powers would nevertheless be truly supreme in those areas where it acted.

The transformation of the Court from bit player to coequal branch was the product of both personality and circumstance. As indicated, one of the realities of life as a Supreme Court justice in the early part of the nineteenth century was that each member of the Court was expected to hear cases in the various circuit courts. The members of the Marshall Court spent a considerable portion of their time each year discharging that obligation and met as a group for only a brief period, generally for a single term that lasted about five to six weeks.

It was the practice of the justices to live together in the same boardinghouse during the time they were together in Washington. Marshall in particular valued this arrangement and worried when it appeared that it might not be possible. For example, when the British seized Washington in August 1814, they left much of the city in ruins. That December Marshall wrote Justice Washington to discuss two issues. The first was purely practical. The Capitol had been burned, and the Court's chambers in the basement of the north wing of that building were unavailable. The Court solved that problem for the forthcoming term by meeting at the Pennsylvania Avenue home of its clerk, Elias Caldwell. Marshall's second concern was arguably the greater. He informed Washington, "We must also rely on you to make enquiries, &, if in your power to make arrangements for our accommodation. If it be practicable to keep us together you know how desirable this will be. If that be impracticable we must be as near each other as possible. Perhaps we may dine together should we be compelled to lodge in different houses. Do me the favor to give me all the intelligence in your power on this interesting subject."

Communal living met both Marshall's needs and those of the Court. Marshall was a gregarious individual, someone who valued good company, good food, and good wine. He was also a practical person. He understood that the Court was together only for a brief time and that the issues it dealt with were complex, important, and often contentious. These realities made it especially important that the Court make effective use of its time together. Communal breakfasts and dinners became an important resource, as did the opportunity to quickly find and converse with each other. His colleagues also valued the arrangement. Shortly after joining the Court, Story wrote, "We live very harmoniously and familiarly." The justices of the Court, he told his wife, "live here with perfect harmony, and as agreeably as absence from friends and from families could make our residence. Our intercourse is perfectly familiar and unconstrained, and our social hours when undisturbed with the labors of law, are passed in gay and frank conversation, which at once enlivens and instructs."

The Court's time in Washington was not, however, an unrelenting exercise in legal drudgery. Contemporary accounts make it clear that the Court played an important part in the political and social life of the capital city. The Washington social season started each year when the Court term began, and the Court's sessions provided relief, entertainment, and a social focus in a city that was at the time still a very small place and, unlike the city of today, not a particularly pleasant one.

An early visitor, the Duc de La Rochefoucauld-Liancourt, characterized Washington in the 1790s as a town that might be "capable of growing to a point that could make it a bearable resting place for those fated to live in it." Twenty years later there was still much to be done in what Story characterized as the "wilderness of Washington." What passed for a city had actually been divided into a series of enclaves clustered around the major government facilities. The White House served as the magnet for the executive branch, and the Capitol for the legislative and judicial. The Navy Yard in turn became the focal point for the military establishment. Ironically, Georgetown, which is today regarded as the enclave of the elite and the establishment in Washington, was at the time a village at the far western end of the District that attracted few government officials, most of whom fled to locations closer to their work when the opportunity presented itself.

Part of the problem was simple geography. The city laid out by Pierre L'Enfant was large, and early residents complained of the substantial distances that must be traversed to go from one important place to another. One individual, for example, noted that "the house Mr. Gallatin has taken is next door to the Madisons' and three miles distant from us. I regret this circumstance, as it will prevent that intimate intercourse which I wished to enjoy." The area itself was in turn inherently unpleasant, a jumble of forests and swamps, with a creek, the Tiber, located between the Capitol and the White House that was prone to overflowing and frequently turned the major arterial, Pennsylvania Avenue, into an impassable quagmire. One diplomat, on departing the White House, described a coach sunk "to the axeltree," such that it became "necessary to leave the carriage, which had to be dragged out and scraped to remove the mud and slush which stuck to it like glue."

Perhaps the best characterization of the capital city in its early years is the one rendered by Charles Dickens, who visited in 1842. Like virtually every other tourist, Dickens and his wife admired the Capitol and White House. But it was the city in between that was the problem: "Spacious avenues that begin in nothing and lead nowhere; streets, miles long, that only want houses, roads, and inhabitants; public buildings that need but a public to be complete; and ornaments of great thoroughfares, which lack only great thoroughfares to ornament — are its leading features."

It is hardly surprising that in this sparsely populated, underdeveloped, and generally unpleasant place the one active industry, government, became the social focus. One early pillar of Washington society,

Margaret Bayard Smith, spoke of a city that "possesses a peculiar interest and to an active, reflective, and ambitious mind, has more attractions than any other place in America." One of these was Congress. "The house of representatives," she wrote, "is the lounging place of both sexes, where acquaintance is as easily made as at public amusements." The Court in turn provided a welcome source of companionship and entertainment when it was in session:

> Curiosity led me against my judgment, to join the female crowd who throng the court room. A place in which I think women have no business. The effect of female admiration and attention has been very obvious, but it is a doubt to me whether it has been beneficial, indeed I believe otherwise. A member told me he doubted not, that there had been much more speaking on this account, and another gentleman told me, that one day Mr. Pinckney had finished his argument and was just about seating himself when Mrs. Madison and a train of ladies enter'd, — he recommenced, went over the same ground, using fewer arguments, but scattering more flowers. And the day I was present I am certain he thought more of the female part of his audience than of the court.

Story's take on these matters was pointed yet gentle. "Abroad," he wrote, "our rank claims and obtains the public respect; and scarcely a day passes in Court, in which parties of ladies do not occasionally come in and hear for a while the arguments of learned counsel." The courtroom within which they gathered, however, did not reflect the status these observations arguably implied. L'Enfant's plans for the city had included a building for the Court, to be located halfway between the Capitol and the White House. But it was never built, and the Court met in various rooms in the Capitol until 1935, when it finally moved into a building of its own.

Its primary location, and the one it used for the 1819 Term, was in the basement of the Capitol's north wing. But, reflecting the relative status of the Court to that point, the room where it conducted its business was both out of the way and unimpressive. One newspaper account at the time indicated that "a stranger might traverse the dark avenues of the Capitol for a week, without finding the remote corner in which Justice is administered to the American Republic" in "a room which is hardly capacious enough for a ward justice." The courtroom was, as a result of the renovations and refurbishing required after the British burned the Capitol, "well finished." But it was "by no means a large or handsome apartment; and the lowness of the ceiling, and the circumstances of its being under ground, give a certain cellar-like aspect, which . . . tends to create . . . the impression of justice being done in a corner." This stood in stark contrast to "the business of legislation [which] is carried on with . . . pride, pomp, and circumstance."

The Marshall Court nevertheless rose above its surroundings, seizing the opportunities presented to both articulate its vision of the Constitution and place itself at the center of the governing process. The Court may have been viewed by others as the runt of the government litter. But under Marshall it became an institution that understood its role and the significance of the cases that came before it. This was especially so as it prepared for its February 1819 Term, which was perhaps the most important that it had held to date and which remains to this day one of the most significant periods in the Court's history.

In December 1818, Story noted in a letter to the newly appointed reporter, Henry Wheaton, that "the next term of the Supreme Court will probably be the most interesting ever known. Several great constitutional questions, the constitutionality of the insolvency laws, of taxing the Bank of the United States, and of the Dartmouth College new charter, will probably be splendidly argued." Story was correct. The Court's decisions in the three cases he identified were significant in their own right and also marked the final steps in the transformation of the Court under Marshall from an occasional player to a major figure in the governance of the country.

Two of the decisions involved a provision that the Court had considered a number of times in the past, the contracts clause. Article I, Section 10 of the Constitution included a number of express limitations on state authority. One of these declared that "no State shall . . . pass any . . . law impairing the obligation of contracts." The nature and implications of this clause had been at issue in one of the first cases in which the Court had held that a state statute was unconstitutional, *Fletcher v. Peck* (1810), and had been explored in a number of subsequent decisions. It was also an area of the law, and a provision of the Constitution, about which Marshall cared deeply.

The first of the great 1819 cases to be decided was *Trustees of Dartmouth College v. Woodard*. It arose when the State of New Hampshire attempted to take over the private Dartmouth College, seeking to change its name to Dartmouth University and place it under the oversight and supervision of public officials. The trustees of the college challenged this action, arguing that the royal charter that established Dartmouth was a contract and that, as a private corporation, the college and its charter were protected by the clause. The Supreme Court of New Hampshire disagreed, and the case came before the U.S. Supreme Court in February 1818. But the Court was unable to agree on a result and announced on March 13, 1818, that the case would be carried over to its next term. In the meantime, one of the college's attorneys, Daniel Webster, initiated a parallel case, which he pursued before a federal circuit court that included Justice Story as one of its members. When the Court reconvened the following February, virtually everyone assumed that there would be further oral arguments. But on February 2, 1819, Marshall announced that the Court had reached its decision, which he proceeded to announce.

The contracts clause, Marshall observed, had been placed in the Constitution to limit the authority of the states, required by "a course of legislation [that] had prevailed in many, if not in all, of the States, which weakened the confidence of man in man, and embarrassed all transactions between individuals, by dispensing with a faithful performance of engagements." The clause was designed to "correct this mischief, by restraining the power which produced it." The college in turn was not "a civil institution to be employed in the administration of the government." It was rather "a private eleemosynary institution, endowed with a capacity to take property for objects unconnected with government, whose funds are bestowed by individuals on the faith of the charter."

It was possible, Marshall admitted, that the rights of corporations were not at issue when the clause was inserted in the Constitution. But that did not matter. A corporate charter was clearly the sort of binding legal agreement that fell "within the words of the rule." To hold otherwise would be to propose a "literal construction so obviously absurd, or mischievous, or repugnant to the general spirit of the instrument, as to justify those who experienced the constitution for making it an exception." The state legislature in turn might well enjoy certain inherent powers. Indeed, while "a repeal of this charter at any time prior to the adoption of the present constitution of the United

States" would quite possibly have been "an extraordinary and unprecedented act of power" it was nevertheless "one which could have been contested only by the restrictions upon the legislature, to be found in the constitution of the State." But the federal Constitution had been ratified, and New Hampshire was bound by it, in particular by the requirement that it could pass no measure " 'impairing the obligation of contracts.' "

Webster was ecstatic. Even as the opinion was being delivered he was writing his brother, stating that "all is safe. . . . The opinion was delivered by the Chief Justice. It was very able and very elaborate; it goes the whole length, and leaves not an inch of ground for the University to stand on." Joseph Hopkinson, his cocounsel, observed that "our triumph . . . has been complete" and indicated that "I would have an inscription over the door of your building, 'Founded by Eleazor Wheelock, Refounded by Daniel Webster.' "

Story recognized the importance of the decision, stressing in a letter to the noted New York jurist James Kent "the vital importance, to the well-being of society and the security of private rights, of the principles on which that decision rested." Interestingly, the decision did not draw the sustained wrath of the Court's adversaries, and there was surprisingly little public comment outside of a few newspapers. Most simply mentioned that the decision had been handed down, some observing that it was "learned" and "able." Commentary in the New England papers, a region that had a closer appreciation of the case, was more extensive. Federalist papers applauded it, and Republican ones expressed their displeasure. But the case did not become a national issue, and even the *Argus of Western America*, which was otherwise intent to pounce on Marshall Court transgressions, observed simply that "we hope our Legislature will not hereafter grant any charter whatever, without reserving the right to alter, amend or repeal as the public interest may require."

The second major case in the February 1819 Term was *Sturges v. Crowninshield*, which focused on a bankruptcy statute that the State of New York had passed in April 1811. Richard Crowninshield had borrowed money from Josiah Sturges in March 1811 and had then declared bankruptcy under the New York measure in November of that year, claiming that he was "an insolvent debtor." Sturges sued, maintaining that the state act violated the contracts clause. The case initially came before Justice Story in his capacity as a circuit justice. He and the district judge sitting on the case, John Davis, indicated that they were divided on the subject, setting the case for consideration by the Court.

The case was argued on February 8, with many individuals believing that the Court was deeply divided, perhaps evenly split. But on February 17 Marshall and his colleagues surprised these observers with a relatively brief unanimous opinion holding that the New York law was in fact unconstitutional. This surface agreement masked deep divisions in the Court. Story, for example, believed that federal power in this area was either exclusive or at least so extensive that it left little room for competing state regulation. Johnson, in turn, thought that the bankruptcy powers were concurrent, with the states retaining a role in this area.

Marshall's approach reflected that divide even as he tried to fashion an opinion that presented the unified front he believed so important in major constitutional cases. Marshall stressed that "when the terms in which a power is granted to Congress, or the nature of the power, require that it should be exercised exclusively by Congress, the subject is as completely taken from the State Legislatures as if they had been expressly forbidden to act on it." But the area in question involved what were arguably two different situations, bankruptcy and insolvency. The distinctions between the two did not allow one "to say, with positive precision, what belongs exclusively to the one, and not to the other class of laws." But distinctions did exist. "It is said, for example, that laws which merely liberate the person are insolvent laws, and those which discharge the contract, are bankrupt laws."

The real question, Marshall maintained, was what Congress intended, as "the power granted to Congress may be exercised or declined, as the wisdom of that body shall decide. If, in the opinion of Congress, uniform laws concerning bankruptcies ought not be established, it does not follow that partial laws may not exist, or that State legislation on the subject must cease." Marshall stressed, "It is not the mere existence of the power, but its exercise, which is incompatible with the exercise of the same power by the States." Congress had not yet indicated that it wished to occupy the field with a uniform law.

Accordingly, "the States are not forbidden to pass a bankrupt law, provided it contain no principle which violates the 10th section of the first article of the constitution of the United States."

In this particular instance "the defendant has given his promissory note to pay the plaintiff a sum of money on or before a certain day." That was a contract, and its obligation was binding. "Any law which releases a part of this obligation, must, in the literal sense of the word, impair it." The contracts clause was in fact implicated, and "the words of the constitution . . . are express, and incapable of being misunderstood." Marshall made it clear that this interpretation accorded with the intent of the framers. This was a matter of applying the "plain meaning of a provision" within which the individuals who wrote the text used a simple and straightforward term, "contracts." Any other reading did "violence" to the text.

Or would it? At the end of his opinion Marshall observed that the Court's holding was "confined to the case actually under consideration," a statement that might have been read to mean a situation within which the legislation was being applied to a contract that had been negotiated and agreed to prior to its passage. But on February 18, one day after *Sturges* was announced, a unanimous Court declared in *M'Millan v. M'Neill* (1819) that "the circumstances of the State law, under which the debt was attempted to be discharged, having been passed before the debt was contracted, made no difference in the application of the principle." *Sturges* controlled. It therefore appeared that the Court had indeed struck a compromise, under which the cases before it were resolved but the ultimate constitutional questions left open.

Sturges itself had come before the Court at a particularly delicate time. The economic contractions of 1818 were coalescing into the Panic of 1819, and bankruptcies were multiplying as the nation's financial conditions worsened. Since Congress had not yet put a bankruptcy measure in place, a decision denying the states any power to act in the area would have had severe repercussions. There was accordingly great interest in the case, and the fine lines that Marshall drew were lost on many in the wake of the opinion's announcement. Many read it — or at least the accounts of it that came to their attention — as denying the states any power to legislate in the area. The *Niles Register* observed that "this opinion has given much alarm to many persons; it is highly interesting to everyone." And one Boston newspaper stated, "The late decision has created much excitement and alarm in many States. Persons, we learn, who have been discharged many years from contracts by the laws of their States, and have since acquired property, have had it attached to pay their old debts." These and similar comments coalesced into a call for action on the part of Congress. The *Niles Register* captured the mood when it declared that "in every commercial community, such a law is necessary. The apathy that prevails in Congress on the subject is really surprising. How long will they shut their ears against the cries of distress? How long will they neglect the supplication of thousands?"

As matters developed, they waited for a number of years, as Congress did not pass a bankruptcy measure until 1841 and even then continued to struggle with the issue. The 1841 measure was itself repealed the next year, and it was not until 1898 that Congress put in place a system that provided for a permanent and systematic federal role in the area. *Sturges* did not accordingly have the immediate impact that some observers predicted. Nevertheless, if all the Court had done in 1819 was decide *Dartmouth College* and *Sturges*, it would have had a truly notable term. But there was one additional case that promised to be important that was yet to be heard.

CHAPTER 5

M'Culloch

The Case and the Argument

M'Culloch v. Maryland began when James William M'Culloh, the cashier of the Baltimore branch of the Bank, issued a series of notes on which he had not paid the tax imposed by the state of Maryland. Most historians agree that this was a test case, with the opposing sides cooperating to initiate a legal proceeding to determine both whether Congress had the authority to charter the Bank and what, if any, were the nature and scope of state authority over such an institution. Most historians also misspell M'Culloh's name, and the Court itself subsequently compounded its own error seven years later when it took up *Etting v. The President, Directors, and Company of the Bank of the United States* (1826), a case within which M'Culloh is mentioned repeatedly but is identified in yet another manner, as one James W. M'Cullough.

M'Culloh was born in Philadelphia on February 5, 1789. He was the son of John M'Culloh, a merchant and veteran of the Revolution who achieved the rank of major and commanded "the artillery of the Pennsylvania line in Washington's army." John M'Culloh's colleague in that endeavor was a Colonel Porter, whose sons became, respectively, the governor of Pennsylvania, territorial governor of Michigan, and secretary of war. John M'Culloh and Colonel Porter in turn married sisters named Todd, who were relatives of the woman who became Abraham Lincoln's wife.

James M'Culloh settled in Baltimore and like many men of his generation served as a volunteer in the militia during the War of 1812. This led him to the Battle of Bladensburg on August 24, 1814, a member of a group described accurately as one that "knew nothing of military service, and from their habits and pursuits were ill-fitted to endure so suddenly the hardships and exposures of war." The British force they confronted was vastly different and included numerous veterans of the Napoleonic Wars. It was a rout, memorialized by one puckish observer as the Bladensburg Races. The British then captured Washington and destroyed much of the city, leaving in their wake a wounded James M'Culloh, who spent the next seven years on crutches.

M'Culloh appears to have played an important role in the militia, one that earned him the respect of Samuel Smith, the businessman and politician whose life had been intertwined with that of the Bank. Smith was commander of the Third Militia Division with the rank of general and had been charged with the defense of Baltimore. In 1816 he sent a letter to the acting secretary of war, George Graham, within which he discussed various aspects of the conflict. In it he noted, "At my solicitations, Mr. James W. McCulloch was appointed in April, 1813, as acting Deputy-Quartermaster-General, and in that capacity was directed by General Armstrong to obey my orders." And he described some of the many occasions on which M'Culloh paid invoices and otherwise played a role in the events that led to the furbishing of Fort McHenry and the successful defense of the city.

M'Culloh returned to Baltimore and found employment in the financial house Smith and Buchanan, presumably as a result of his interactions with Smith. The firm, one of the most important in Baltimore, at that point was overseen on a day-to-day basis by James Buchanan, who became the president of the Baltimore branch of the Second Bank when it was established. M'Culloh left Smith and Buchanan and became cashier of the Baltimore branch, a position that paid him the then decent but hardly outlandish sum of $4,000 a year. He also met and married Abigail Sears, a seventh-generation member of a family that had settled in Yarmouth, Massachusetts, in the seventeenth century and may have descended from one of the Pilgrims.

James and Abigail M'Culloh had eight children, one of whom, Richard, both changed his name to McCulloch and became a noted chemist and physicist. In 1818 James purchased 511 acres in an area near Baltimore known as Taylor's Forest, a tract that included a working stock and grain farm and that eventually became known as Hilton. M'Culloh paid $35,000 for the property and made substantial improvements to an operation that at one point required the services of eight hired men, one hired woman, and six slaves. He was quite clearly at the time on a track toward prosperity, albeit one that seemed somewhat beyond his means given the modest salary he received as cashier. But he had found a way to supplement that stipend.

In 1818 James M'Culloh was twenty-nine years old and apparently had a boundless stock of both energy and ambition. In the Baltimore of that time — perhaps more so than in any other city in the fledgling nation — energy and ambition were virtues of the highest order, characteristics that led Buchanan and other financial and political leaders there to work closely with M'Culloh as they went about their business in a city whose rapid growth and increasing prosperity had made it an economic force.

At the time Maryland passed its anti-Bank legislation, the various enterprises in which M'Culloh and his colleagues were engaged had became the prototype for a city that John Quincy Adams described in his *Memoirs* as perhaps the most prosperous in the Union. One year later they labored under a cloud, as the first real intimations emerged of what became one of the most serious financial scandals of the era. As Adams stressed, prosperity and profligacy had become intertwined, in particular with regard to the affairs of the Baltimore branch of the Bank. For a number of individuals, notably Buchanan and M'Culloh, had seized the opportunities presented by the opening of the Baltimore branch and pursued personal riches at the expense of sound financial management.

The time was clearly ripe for such endeavors. The period immediately after the War of 1812 was one of expansion and economic growth. The war had wreaked economic havoc, a state of affairs compounded, ironically, by the absence of a central banking authority after Congress had allowed the charter of the First Bank to expire in 1811. But with peace came the beginnings of prosperity, facilitated initially by state banks, which, in the absence of a central banking authority, had become the principal depositories for currency and issued their own bank notes.

M'Culloh, Buchanan, and a third individual, George Williams, became partners in a company formed for the exclusive purposes of acquiring and trading the Bank's stock. But their approach to these matters was specious at best. Recognizing that Jones and his colleagues in the central office of the Bank were either unable or unwilling to oversee their activities, they began to manipulate the situation to their own advantage. George Williams, for example, acquired 1,172 shares of stock, each registered in a different name to evade the provision in the Bank's charter that gave each shareholder a maximum of thirty votes, no matter how many shares the individual might hold. This allowed him and others who used the same stratagem to wield disproportionate influence.

The three partners also used their positions to manipulate the price of the Bank's stock in the open market, fueling a process that saw the share price rise steadily. In many instances they did not actually pay for the stock in any meaningful sense, having been allowed to pledge other stock — also not paid for — as security for the new purchases. The three advanced their fortunes in other ways, making substantial loans to themselves, sometimes on the Bank's stock and sometimes with no collateral at all. Estimates of the scope of their activities vary. By one account they engaged in more than $3 million worth of unauthorized transactions. Other sources cited a lower sum, some $1.6 million. Whatever the actual number, the scope of their activities was staggering and the eventual losses to the Bank substantial.

As cashier, M'Culloh was the functional head of the Baltimore branch and a pivotal figure in what transpired. Aspects of both his personality and his views about the Bank can be found in his official correspondence, within which he excoriated the First Bank, pressed for a proactive stance by the Second, and criticized the conduct of others in ways that were at best disingenuous.

For example, one of the things that had made the First Bank a success was the degree of caution it showed in most of its affairs. But M'Culloh took issue with those policies in a March 17, 1817, letter to Secretary of the Treasury William Crawford:

> If arrangements are not made, I fear that very soon you will find it necessary to accelerate a state of things which is now slowly but certainly approaching; I mean the suppression of State banks established where commerce is insufficient to have justified their erection.
>
> The Bank of the United States must assume its stand, and supported by the Government, might improve the medium of the country very essentially. The old bank did much to injure it. A system of permanent loans was adopted toward individuals and likewise to banks. Instead of extending its operations so as to embrace every real demand of commerce; instead of expanding its views as the country and its trade grew, it pursued a timid and faltering course, and invited, by its measures, the erection of rival institutions

to share its business, and contaminate the character of this country's medium.

That bank had a glorious field before it; and this has one almost as much so, whilst it harmonizes with the Government and meets every real call of commerce.

As we have seen, these sentiments mirrored those of the Bank's president at the time, William Jones. As we have also seen, Jones's willingness to forsake the conservative approach taken by the First Bank played a major role in the development of the financial problems that confronted the Second Bank, and the nation, during the Panic of 1819.

M'Culloh also assumed the public posture of someone who was vigilant in the identification and pursuit of fraud and abuse. On July 19, 1817, he again wrote Crawford to comment on the conduct of the Bank of Somerset:

I have taken considerable pains to ascertain the situation of that bank, and the result of my inquiries I now give you.

The subscribers paid very little into bank; for the balance they gave bonds, and these bonds are chiefly in suit. The customers of the bank are called upon to pay up, and those who cannot are sued.

The bank has no specie, stock, or notes of other banks. My informants believe that all which the bank will ever be able to get from its customers and stockholders will not be enough to pay the debt to the Government and the holders of its bank bills. They believe that the capital of the bank, and more, will have been entirely sunk. The bank receives its notes and issues its bills bearing interest to all who present them.

M'Culloh recommended, correctly, that legal action against the Bank be undertaken, for if the situation was as he described, there had been a clear abuse of trust. The irony of course is that many of the same abuses about which he complained were at that very point being committed within the Baltimore branch of the Second Bank, and that James M'Culloh and his partners were central figures in that process.

Maryland had passed the statute authorizing the tax on the Bank's notes in February, but it was not to go into effect until May. Once it did, M'Culloh issued the untaxed notes, an action that brought a prompt legal response from the state. On May 18, 1818, John James, state treasurer for the Western Shore, brought an action of debt against the Bank to recover $2,500 in penalties owed on five notes. The case proceeded quickly through the Maryland courts, with M'Culloh as the named party on behalf of the Bank. The opposing sides agreed on a statement of facts, and the Baltimore county court found that the Bank did indeed owe the tax. That judgment was affirmed in June in an unreported per curiam decision by the Maryland Court of Appeals, the state's highest court. Then, on September 18, 1818, the Supreme Court of the United States placed the case on its docket, issuing a writ of error and setting it for argument in its February 1819 Term.

The Court that convened on Monday, February 22, 1819, had much in common with the Court today. It believed that the Constitution limited its authority to the resolution of "Cases," an Article III term the Court has treated as a constitutional command that it issue its judgments only in written form, generated through adversarial proceedings within which opposing parties present legal questions for a legal resolution. The focus then as now was accordingly on the opinion of the Court. And in *M'Culloch*, as was almost invariably true for important cases decided during his years as chief justice, that opinion was prepared and announced by John Marshall.

In 1819, however, the Court did not have the benefit of the extensive written arguments its now receives from opposing counsel well in advance of acting. Rather, in those cases where it was reviewing a lower court's decision — which then as now constituted the vast majority of the cases before it — the Court rendered judgment based on the records and opinions produced below, supplemented by oral arguments presented by counsel for the opposing parties. Those oral arguments tended to be both lengthy and elaborate. Today the Court in most cases allocates one hour of time for argument, divided equally between the sides and generally presented by one attorney for each. But in 1819 the parties enjoyed what amounted to an almost unlimited opportunity to present their views, subject only to a Court rule that limited the number of counsel appearing to two per side.

Press accounts at the time made clear both the importance of the case and the quality of the advocates and the arguments they presented. Early on, on February 25, the *National Intelligencer* observed, "The argument has involved some of the most important principles of constitutional law which have been discussed with an equal degree of learning and eloquence and have constantly attracted the attention of a numerous and intelligent auditory, by whom the final decision of this most important question from the Supreme Tribunal of the country is anxiously expected." Two days later, Hezekiah Niles's *Weekly Register* — which subsequently railed against the decision and the Court — stated that "the discussion has been very able and eloquent, it involves come of the most important principles of constitutional law and the decision is anxiously expected."

It was at the time the custom of the newspapers to note both the fact of oral argument and the identities of the parties appearing before the Court. But their treatment of *M'Culloch* was distinctive. For example, the account in the *National Intelligencer* on February 25 began with the otherwise routine observation that "the Attorney General and Mr. Jones continued the argument of the case of M'Culloh against the State of Maryland, involving the question of the right of the several states to tax the Bank of the U. States." Such notices were not unusual, especially in a city where the Court and its sessions were an important part of the social scene. But, as indicated, the article did not confine itself to simply reporting that a particular case was being heard and that specific individuals were presenting arguments on behalf of the parties. Rather, it went on to both describe the nature of the advocates' efforts and emphasize the significance of the case. And it ended — with what proved to be a profound understatement — with the observation that "it is supposed the argument will be continued for several days longer." Similar sentiments appeared in *Niles Weekly Register*, which characterized the arguments as "very able and eloquent" and the decision as "anxiously expected," for "*Much will depend upon it.*" In a term characterized by cases of great importance, *M'Culloch* was distinctive, a reality both participants and observers understood.

The oral arguments in *M'Culloch* lasted nine days and were presented to an attentive Court and an appreciative audience. As Justice Story noted in separate letters, the case involved a "great question" and was argued before "a crowded audience of ladies and gentlemen; the hall was full almost to suffocation, and many went away for want of room." The Court itself recognized that this was a "case involving a constitutional question of great public importance, and the sovereign rights of the United States and the State of Maryland" and "dispensed with its general rule, permitting only two counsel to argue for each party." Thus six individuals came to the podium. Each was regarded as one the very best advocates of the day. And each, either as a matter of basic temperament or recognizing the importance of the questions before the Court, took the opportunity to explain his position at length.

The first to speak was Daniel Webster, who framed the issues on behalf of the Bank. Did Congress in fact have the power to create the Bank? If it did, could the State of Maryland levy its tax? Webster was an imposing figure. Known in some quarters as the "Godlike Daniel" or as "Black Dan," he was a physically commanding individual with jet-black hair and a large head within which were set a pair of piercing eyes. Extremely conscious of his appearance, he generally came before the Court "attired in the height of fashion." His voice in turn was one of his greatest assets. One individual who heard him speak, the Englishman Dana Hamilton, said that it was "clear, sharp, and firm, without much variety of modulation; but when animated, it rings on the ear like a clarion."

In 1819 Webster was regarded as the emerging star of the small group of attorneys who regularly argued before the Court. These were men who generally were thoroughly prepared and understood that the arguments they made before the Court were also public performances, presentations that were eagerly anticipated by the crowds that often packed the Court and read with interest when they were published, as many were. The Court in turn gave them free rein. Today's oral arguments are compact affairs during which the various justices participate actively, peppering the attorneys before them with questions that are as often actually intended as much for their brethren as they are for the advocates. That was not the case in Marshall's time. In 1824, for example, Webster argued yet another of the more than 200 cases in which he appeared before the Court, *Gibbons v. Ogden* (1824). A newspaper account at the time captured both the nature of the occasion and the relationship that had developed between the Court and the advocates who argued before it:

The Court sits from eleven o'clock in the morning until four in the afternoon. It is not only one of the most dignified and enlightened tribunals in the world, but one of the most patient. Counsel are heard in silence for hours, without being stopped or interrupted. If a man talks nonsense, he is soon graduated and passes for what he is worth. If he talks to the point, he will be properly measured, and his talents, discrimination and industry reflected in the opinion of the Court. The Judges of the Court say nothing, but when they are fatigued and worried by a long and pointless argument, displaying a want of logic, a want of acuteness, and a destitution of authorities, their feelings and wishes are sufficiently manifested by their countenances and the manners which are displayed.

Webster began his presentation in *M'Culloch* with the observation that "it might have been hoped that" constitutionality "was not now to be considered an open question." The issue was, he maintained, "discussed, and settled, as far as legislative decision could settle it, in the first Congress." The Bank had also garnered the support of the other two branches: "The executive government has acted upon it; and the courts of law have acted upon it." Webster glossed over the manner in which the question was treated by Congress in 1811, arguing that "it cannot be shown that either branch of the legislature has, at any time, expressed an opinion against the existence of the power." That was, of course, technically correct. No formal vote to that effect had been rendered. The Court should not, then, Webster maintained, hold otherwise, "unless [the Bank's] repugnancy with the constitution were plain and manifest."

Webster then addressed the first specific question, whether the power to incorporate existed. He began with the obvious, that Congress had certain specific powers and "as to the objects, and within the scope of these powers, it is sovereign." He maintained that "the grant of powers necessarily implies the grant of all the usual and suitable means for the execution of the powers granted." He argued that accumulated experience demonstrated that Congress had consistently embraced this understanding. And he declared that the words " 'necessary and proper' . . . are probably to be considered as synonymous. *Necessary* powers must here intend such powers as are *suitable* and *fitted* to the subject; such as are *best* and *most useful* in relation to the end pursued." The Bank was a means, not an end, and the constitutional question was not whether the Bank was the best possible way to meet the nation's financial needs. It was rather whether it was "a proper and suitable instrument to assist the operations of the government." And that was a judgment to be made by Congress, not by the Court.

The states could not in turn levy a tax on the Bank or its activities. "If the States may tax it," he asked, "to what extent shall they tax it, and where shall they stop? An unlimited power to tax involves, necessarily, a power to destroy; because there is a limit beyond which no institution and no property can bear taxation." Such a power, Webster observed, also extended to other arms of the federal government, even its courts. It was a power that could not be countenanced: "To hold otherwise, would be to declare that Congress can only exercise its constitutional powers subject to the controlling discretion, and under the sufferance, of State governments."

Webster was followed by the first attorney for Maryland, Joseph Hopkinson, who spoke for the rest of the day and all of the next. Hopkinson was a Philadelphian and had been Webster's ally in the Dartmouth College case. He was now his opponent, something that was not uncommon given the relatively small number of individuals who routinely practiced before the Court at that time. Hopkinson was the opposite of Webster in many respects, "thoughtful and refined . . . quiet yet distinguished." He was also a skilled advocate with a "beautiful and highly trained mind, equipped with immense and accurate knowledge systematically arranged."

Hopkinson began by attempting to cast doubt on the picture of constitutional unanimity that Webster had tried to sketch. "The first question" before the Court, he declared, "has, for many years, divided the opinions of the first men of our country." It was moreover inappropriate to treat the creation of the First Bank as precedent: "The argument might have been perfectly good, to show the necessity of a bank for the operations of the revenue, in 1791, and entirely fail now, when so many facilities for money transactions abound, which were wanting then." Indeed, he observed, Hamilton himself argued for the need for and value of public banks, an approach to such matters that did not itself justify a Bank of the United States. And the record since the First Bank ceased operations demonstrated that state banks were eminently suited to the tasks required.

Hopkinson then attacked the need for and propriety of the Bank having branches. He characterized branches as "not necessary for any of the enumerated advantages" and alleged that they were directed rather toward "the interests of the stockholders," that is, toward profit rather than the needs of the nation. The need for branches should not be determined by the Bank, but rather by Congress, mindful of the reality that "the establishment of a bank in a State, without its assent, without regard to its interests, its policy, or institutions, is a higher exercise of authority, than the creation of the parent bank."

This brought him to the subject of taxation, which implicated "the highest attribute of sovereignty, the right to raise revenue; in fact, the right to exist; without which no other right can be held or enjoyed." Banks in and of themselves, Hopkinson noted, were not immune from taxation. Indeed, the United States itself levied taxes on the state banks. "Is it then exempt, as being a bank of the United States? How is it such? In name only." The point was a potentially telling one, for the Bank was in fact a private corporation, a status, Hopkinson stressed, that Hamilton himself characterized as necessary. "Strip it of its name," he said, "and we find it to be a mere association of individuals, putting their money into a common stock, to be loaned for profit, and to divide the gains."

Hopkinson then came to the heart of the matter: "The Federal Government is to hold a power by implication and ingenuous inference from general words in the constitution, which it can hardly be believed would have been suffered in an express grant." The Bank's case rested on the assumption that "obscure constructions of indefinite clauses in the constitution" authorized its creation. Having been created, the Bank further assumed that it could both insinuate itself into the states and then claim an exemption from their sovereign powers. But the threats the Bank perceived in Maryland's tax were imagined, not real, the products of "supposed dangers" and "fearful distrusts."

The Bank was not at risk, for "whenever the States shall be in a disposition to uproot the general government, they will take direct and speedy means; and until they have this disposition, they will not use" their sovereign power to tax. It was in fact the arguments for the Bank that posed the true threat. By maintaining that the Maryland measure was unconstitutional, the Bank risked "an end to the confederation, which is founded on a reasonable and honourable confidence in each other." To the extent that the government truly needed a bank, it could and should operate one in the District of Columbia, "where it holds an exclusive jurisdiction." By operating in the states, the Bank achieved nothing "but profits and large dividends to the shareholders, which are the real object in this contest."

On Wednesday, February 24, the Court heard from two people. The first was the attorney general of the United States, William Wirt. Wirt had been a prosecutor when Aaron Burr — accused of plotting to form a separate republic in the Southwest that he would head — was tried and acquitted for conspiracy and treason in 1807. He became attorney general in 1817, a post he held until 1832. Wirt was in some respects the captive of his appetites, a "portly and erect" individual who by his own admission had at times "dissipat[ed] my health, my time, my money, and my reputation." But he was highly regarded as an attorney and argued more than 170 cases before the Court. John Quincy Adams said of Wirt that he had "two faults which may have an influence in the affairs of this Nation — an excessive leaning to State supremacy, and to popular humors." But Wirt effectively pressed the case for the government and against Maryland.

Wirt began by stressing, as had Webster, that "this exercise of power must be considered as ratified by the voice of the people, and sanctioned by precedent." The power in question was in turn appropriately implied, "because the end involves the means necessary to carry it into effect." The Bank, Wirt emphasized, was not simply a constitutionally authorized institution; it had also proved to be an extraordinarily effective one. The First Bank had been a success and had been sorely missed during "a period of war, the calamities of which were greatly aggravated by the want of this convenient instrument of finance." The question was not, he emphasized, whether the Bank was "indispensably" necessary. That interpretive approach would "render every law which could be passed by Congress unconstitutional . . . since a different law could be imagined, which could be enacted tending to the same object, though not equally well adapted to attain it."

Rather, Wirt declared, " 'Necessary and proper' are . . . equivalent to *needful and adapted.*" That was consistent both with the common understandings of the terms and with the manner in which the Constitution intended such matters to be treated. "To make a law constitutional," Wirt stated, "nothing more is necessary than that it should be fairly adapted to carry into effect some specific power given to

Congress." The means selected were for Congress to determine. This goal was "a natural connection," and the argument that state banks might be equally appropriate given the goals to be achieved, or that branch banks were inappropriate, "presents a mere question of political expediency, which, it is repeated, is exclusively for legislative consideration."

The state power to tax in turn could not be assessed only in the light of the prohibitions set forth in Article I and the reservation of state power confirmed by the Tenth Amendment. The supremacy clause must also be considered when assessing "a bank, as ordained by Congress, [that] is an instrument to carry into execution its specified powers; and in order to . . . operate effectually . . . must be under the direction of a single head." That head was the national government. And "surely," Wirt concluded, "the framers of the Constitution did not intend that the exercise of all the powers of the national government should depend on the discretion of the State governments. This was the vice of the former confederation, which it was the object of the new constitution to eradicate."

Wirt was followed by Walter Jones, an attorney in private practice from Washington, whose presentation carried over to Thursday. Jones was the least prominent of the six men who argued but had a reputation as a "legal genius." He began by characterizing past practice as "a manifest usurpation" rather than as an expression of constitutional faith. He insisted that the Constitution is "a compact between the States, and all the powers which are not expressly relinquished by it, are reserved to the States." The fact that the Tenth Amendment did not speak in terms of powers "expressly" granted did not matter. There is "an inherent sophism in the opposite argument, which depends on the conversion and ambiguity of terms." The Bank did not in fact exercise directly any of the enumerated powers offered as justifications for its existence. The Bank "may, indeed, facilitate the operation of other financial institutions; but in its proper and natural character, it is a commercial institution, a partnership incorporated for the purpose of carrying on the trade of banking." To hold otherwise, Jones declared, was to authorize all manner of constitutional violations, "chang[ing] the subordinate into fundamental powers."

Jones then tried to invert the analysis regarding what is necessary and proper, arguing that "many means may be *proper* which are not *necessary;* because the end may be attained without them." The appropriate inquiry was "whether the establishment of a banking corporation *be indispensably requisite* to execute any of the express powers of the government?" It was not. And banking and the power to create corporations were matters that the people had left to the states. Those states were sovereigns, whose powers were "co-equal and co-extensive" with those of the nation, and the Constitution expressly barred only state imposition of "imposts and tonnage duties, which the States cannot lay, unless for the purpose of executing their inspection laws." And, even if the states could not tax the property of the United States, a limitation Jones did not accept, how could it "follow, that this corporation, which is a partnership of bankers, is also exempt?"

The final argument against the Bank and for Maryland was presented by Luther Martin, the attorney general of Maryland. Martin was seventy-one and nearing the end of a long and distinguished career. He had served as a delegate in the Constitutional Convention, where he had been a vocal opponent of a strong federal government, a position he subsequently changed when his animosity toward Jefferson drove him to the Federalist Party. Martin served two terms as Maryland's attorney general, from 1778 to 1805 and 1818 to 1822. Roger Brooke Tawney, who succeeded Marshall as chief justice, said of Martin that he had an "iron memory" and a "fullness of legal knowledge." But he also noted a reality that dominated Martin's life, his fondness for drink, observing that Martin "often appeared in Court evidently intoxicated." *M'Culloch* represented Martin's last moment of glory. In August 1819, while "zealously engaged in making out 60 presentations against our famous bank gentry"—James M'Culloh and his colleagues—Martin suffered a major stroke that initially paralyzed him and effectively destroyed his intellectual capabilities. But his performance before the Court in *M'Culloch* was both memorable and, as was his wont, lengthy.

Martin began with an extensive discussion of the debates surrounding the drafting and ratification of the Constitution that is not in fact recorded in Wheaton's report of the case, which contains at best a skeletal outline of Martin's argument. In it, he "read several extracts from *the Federalist,* and the *debates of the Virginia and New-York Conventions,* to show that the contemporary exposition of the constitution by its authors, and by those who supported its adoption, was wholly repugnant to that now contended for by the counsel" for the Bank. He adopted the same technique at the end of his presentation, arguing that "the debates in the State conventions show that the power of State taxation was understood to be absolutely unlimited, except as to imposts and tonnage duties."

One of the individuals he quoted was John Marshall, who as a delegate to the Virginia ratification convention had defended the Constitution in the face of Anti-Federalist opposition by insisting that the states retained substantial authority under it. "The powers not denied to the states are not vested in them by implication," Marshall observed in 1788, "because, being possessed of the antecedent to the adoption of the government, and not being divested of them, by any grant or restriction in the Constitution, the States must be as fully possessed of them as ever they had been." Martin's tactic initially worried Marshall. Story reported that at the point his name was mentioned, "Marshall drew a long breath, with a sort of sigh." When asked about this he replied, "Why to tell you the truth, I was afraid I had said some foolish things in the debate; but it was not so bad as I expected."

In the main part of his argument Martin mounted an extensive attack on the notion that there can or should be a doctrine of implied powers, which he characterized as a major issue in the ratification debates. "The danger was denied to exist," he stated, "but to provide an assurance against the possibility of its occurrence, the 10th amendment was added to the constitution." Martin then argued that the very structure of the text counseled otherwise: "That the scheme of the framers of the constitution intended to leave nothing to implication, will be evident from the consideration, that many of the powers expressly given are only means to accomplish other powers expressly given." As an example, he cited the power to wage war, an express power accomplished by means of other express powers, such as raising and supporting an army and a navy to wage it and securing the revenue to pay for it. "If then," he argued, "the Convention has specified some powers, which, being only *means* to accomplish the *ends* of government, might have been taken by implication; by what just rule of construction are other sovereign powers, equally vast and important, to be assumed by implication?"

In particular, Martin maintained that it was inappropriate to imply a federal power to create corporations. That was "one of the great sovereign powers of government." It had not been expressly conferred on Congress. And if a power to incorporate was to be inferred, it should be assigned to the states, which "have all the usual powers which belong to every political society, unless expressly forbidden, by the letter of the State constitutions, from exercising them."

Assuming for the sake of argument that Congress did in fact have the power to create a Bank, it did not follow that Maryland could not tax notes issued by a Bank in which the United States was at best "partially interested." The Bank was a private corporation, and Maryland had every right to tax its activities. The notion that the power to tax was a power to destroy could not be sustained in the light of the fact that Congress itself believed it appropriate to levy taxes on state banks. Both sovereigns enjoyed the power to tax. Indeed, "This was one of the anomalies of the government, the evils of which must be endured, or mitigated by discretion and mutual forbearance." The only limits on state authority to tax were in fact express, found in Article I, Section 10's declaration that "no State shall, without the Consent of Congress, lay any Imposts or Duties on Imports or Exports, except what may be absolutely necessary for executing its inspection Laws." This single limitation was clearly significant, Martin maintained, for "the States would not have adopted the constitution upon any other understanding."

The last individual to address the Court was William Pinkney, who spoke for three days. That was itself an ironic turn of events given his subsequent barely veiled disdain for the length of Martin's presentation. But Pinkney had a well-earned reputation as a self-centered individual who, in the words of his biographer, Henry Wheaton, "cared for nothing but what contributed to his individual vanity and self-gratification." He was a clotheshorse, described by Story as "as polished as if he had been taken right from the drawer." He was also simultaneously "one of the brightest and meanest of mankind," petty and vindictive. There was nevertheless no gainsaying his effectiveness as an advocate, and Taney said of him, "I have heard almost all of the greatest advocates of the United States, but I have seen none equal to Pinkney."

Pinkney began with an "exordium to the argument" which is not set out in the report of the case, but must rather be read in Wheaton's biography. He began by attacking the very notion that he was called on to argue: "In the catalogue of those petty vexations, which are said to constitute the miseries of life, I know of nothing more irksome than to be compelled to speak to a well informed tribunal upon topics that have lost all the grace of novelty, upon which genius and learning have been so often exercised, that he who seeks to be either smart or profound in the discussion of them, can scarcely fail to be accused of pilfering the felicities of expression of some predecessor in the argument." These "felicities" did not necessarily include the arguments of the attorneys for the state. These individuals had made "polished" presentations that displayed the "whole power" of their positions, albeit marked by "all the artifices of a cunning and disciplined logic more or less within the reach of learned counsel." But, steeling himself to the task ahead, Pinkney declared, "I meditate with exultation, not fear, upon the proud spectacle of a peaceful judicial review of these conflicting sovereign claims by this more than amphictyonic council."

He began the main portion of his argument by stressing that the answers to the questions before the Court were to be found in both "authority" and "principle." The Constitution had worked a fundamental transformation. "No topics to illustrate it could be drawn from the confederation," he stressed, "since the present constitution was as different from that, as light from the darkness." The appropriateness of a given federal measure did not in turn require the sort of perfect fit and detailed justifications for which the state argued. It was a question of "a natural relation and connexion with, the objects of that government." The specific issue before the Court, the constitutionality of the Bank, "is no longer an open question. It has long since been settled by decisions of the most revered authority, legislative, executive, and judicial." And, to the extent that doubts were entertained, they should be resolved in favor of the Bank: "A legislative construction, in a doubtful case, persevered in for a course of years, ought to be binding upon the Court. This, however, is not a question of construction merely, but of political necessity, on which Congress must decide."

Pinkney then explained at length the history of the Bank and the significance of what was found there. In doing so, he turned a central point in the state's case — the absence of an express provision in the text — against it.

The First Bank was the product of a Congress that included within its ranks many of the framers, who "must have understood their own work." It was this group that determined, appropriately, that there were two compelling reasons that the Constitution should not in fact contain express authorization for the creation of corporations. A general provision "would have been perilous; since it might have been constructively extended to the creation of corporations entirely unnecessary to carry into effect the other powers granted." A more specific grant, in turn, "might have been equally dangerous, by omitting to provide for others, which time and experience might show to be equally, and even more necessary."

Pinkney also denied that the Bank's opponents could find any comfort in subsequent discussions. He denied that the failure to renew the First Bank's charter had any bearing. "Political considerations alone might have produced the refusal to renew the charter in 1811; we know that they mingled themselves in the debate, and the determination." Madison's 1815 veto was predicated on "political considerations only," the Bank's former constitutional opponent having "waived" those concerns. In 1816 in turn "all branches of the legislature concurred in establishing" the Bank, a matter of some significance, since "Congress is, *prima facie*, a competent judge of its own constitutional powers." All three branches had now concurred. Judicial affirmation, he conceded, had come *"sub silentio."* The courts had not expressly ruled on the constitutional question. But they had heard cases in which the Bank was a party. And "it was the duty of the judges . . . to have raised the question; and we are to conclude, from this circumstance, that no doubt was entertained respecting it."

Pinkney did stumble once in this portion of his argument, for he alleged that "the repeated determinations of the three branches of the national" government had been "confirmed by the constant acquiescence of the State sovereignties, and of the people, for a considerable length of time." That was clearly not the case. Maryland was simply one of eight states that had either by legislation or constitutional amendment signaled their hostility toward the Bank. The "people" in turn were hardly united in their support, as the virtually constant criticism of the Bank over the years demonstrated.

Pinkney then stated that "all the objects of the government are national objects, and the means are, and must be, fitted to accomplish them." He provided an extensive list of the actions the federal government was authorized to undertake. He then observed, "Yet it is doubted, whether a government with such immense powers has authority to erect a corporation within the sphere of its general objects, and in order to accomplish some of these objects!" That was both wrong and a contradiction. "The State powers are much less in point of magnitude, though greater in number; yet it is supposed the States possess the authority of establishing corporations, whilst it is denied to the federal government." More to the point, "The power of erecting corporations is not an end of any government; it is a necessary means of accomplishing the ends of all governments. It is an authority inherent in, and incident to, all sovereignty."

The federal government was sovereign and must certainly possess this power. The Tenth Amendment provided no shelter for those who denied this. Its reservation of powers to the states "is not confined to powers not *expressly* delegated," and the failure to list all possible means for fulfilling the objects of the national government was to be expected. "It was impossible for the framers of the constitution to specify prospectively all these means, both because it would have involved an immense variety of details, and because it would have been impossible for them to foresee the infinite variety of circumstances in such an unexampled state of political society as ours, forever changing and forever improving." Experience bore this out. "The statute book of the United States is filled with powers derived from implication."

Pinkney then discussed how the Bank fit within this scheme. "It is the duty of the Court," he began, "to construe the constitutional powers of the national government liberally, and to mould them so as to effectuate its great objects." And the determination that there was a connection between the end sought and the means adopted was to be made by Congress, for it "alone has the fit means of inquiry and decision." The Court "may, indeed, and must, see that what has been done is not a mere evasive pretext, under which the national legislature travels out of the prescribed bounds of its authority, and encroaches upon State sovereignty, or the rights of the people." But it should not and could not judge "the degree of political necessity which will justify a resort to a particular means, to carry into execution the other powers of the government." The Court should accordingly defer to the judgment of Congress that the Bank was both necessary and proper given the myriad ways in which it helped the government execute its express powers, a list that Pinkney then detailed.

The constitutional status of the Bank's branches involved a similar set of considerations and required the same conclusion. That left only the question of Maryland's authority to levy its tax. Pinkney conceded that the Constitution did not expressly exclude "national institutions or national property from State taxation." But it did not need to. They must be exempt, "or it would be in the power of any one State to destroy their use. Whatever the United States have a right to do, the individual States have no right to undo." And "A power to build up what another may pull down at pleasure, is a power which may provoke a smile, but can do nothing else."

It was one thing to recognize a state's sovereign power to provide for the needs of its citizens. It was quite another to sanction what had been done here, a tax passed "for a political purpose," to "destroy a great institution of the national government." And if Maryland could do this, what of Kentucky, which had authorized an even greater exaction? The fact that Congress could tax state banks did not justify a different conclusion. "Congress exercises the power of the people. The whole acts on the whole. But the State tax is a part acting on the whole." The various states and their people were represented in Congress, but the people of the United States did not, as such, have a parallel place in the Maryland General Assembly.

Pinkney then summarized his argument and concluded that "no other alternative remains, but for this Court to interpose its authority, and save the nation from the consequences of this dangerous attempt."

Pinkney finished on Wednesday, March 3. It was a masterful performance. In a letter written that same day Justice Story conveyed his impressions of Pinkney's presentation in language that presaged the eventual result: "I never, in my whole life, heard a greater speech; it was worth a journey from Salem to hear it; his elocution was excessively vehement, but his eloquence was overwhelming. His language, his style, his figures, his arguments were most brilliant and sparkling. He spoke like a great statesman and patriot, and a sound constitutional lawyer. All the cobwebs of sophistry and metaphysics about State rights and State sovereignty he brushed away with a mighty besom."

CHAPTER 6

The Decision

Webster was confident that the Court would hold in his favor. In a letter sent before the arguments began, he declared, "I have no doubt of the result." Having finished, he repeated these sentiments, observing "of the decision I have no doubt." Webster also fumed repeatedly about the length of the argument. On February 24, only two days into what became a nine-day marathon, he wrote, "Our Bank argument goes on — & threatens to be long." On the twenty-fifth, he stated that "the Bank cause is not heard thro. yet. . . . I am grown impatient to be off." And on the twenty-eighth he complained, "We are not yet thro. the Bank question. Martin has been *talking 3 ds*. Pinkney replies tomorrow & that finishes. I set out for home next day."

He was wrong. He remained in Washington for several more days, unable to set out for Boston until March 12. But he presumably had no complaint about the speed with which the Court acted. For it took just three days for Chief Justice John Marshall to prepare his opinion for a unanimous Court, which he delivered on Saturday, March 6.

A number of individuals have argued that the length of the opinion and the speed with which it was rendered indicate that Marshall had both prejudged the case and prepared much of his opinion before the Court's term started. This was, after all, an era in which a written opinion was just that, a document prepared with pen and ink, and there is much to be said for the idea that Marshall had drafted at least the outline, if not the actual text, in advance. Marshall's opinion ran thirty-seven pages in the official Court reports, and it is both elaborate and thoughtful.

There is nevertheless every reason to believe that Marshall gave a full and fair hearing to the attorneys who appeared before him, even as he contemplated how their arguments fit within a framework that he arguably already had in mind. There are, for example, echoes of

Webster's presentation in the opinion and instances where the nature and scope of what Marshall wrote seems to have been influenced by Hopkinson and Martin. It also seems quite clear either that Marshall and Pinkney were largely of the same mind or, more likely, that Marshall was deeply impressed by Pinkney's argument, for much of the spirit, if not always the letter, of Pinkney's words is found in Marshall's work.

It is also important to recognize that Marshall was not writing on a blank slate. As George Washington's biographer, for example, he had paid considerable attention to Hamilton's fiscal program in the volume dealing with the early years of Washington's presidency. In particular, he devoted more than six pages of the main narrative to a discussion of the constitutional issues raised during the debates about the First Bank. And he appended to the volume a "Note" within which he devoted an additional eight pages to the constitutional questions, quoting at great length the written opinions that Washington received.

One aspect of that discussion was especially revealing. Marshall observed that "a bill conforming to the plan [Hamilton] suggested was sent from the senate, and it was permitted to proceed, unmolested, in the house of representatives, to the third reading. On the final question, a great, and, it would seem, an unexpected opposition was made to its passage." He noted that one aspect of the ensuing debate dealt with the "general utility" of the Bank. He then emphasized that "the great strength of the argument was directed against the constitutional authority of congress to pass an act for incorporating a national bank."

Marshall's characterization of the protracted debate in the House as "unexpected" is telling. It certainly echoes Hamilton's take on these matters, as Hamilton found the attacks on his program "surprising," reflecting a "change in opinion" on the part of individuals who, he believed, shared his views on the financial problems confronting the nation. It also tracks in some respects what William Loughton Smith had to say about them in his 1792 pamphlet, *The Politicks and Views of a Certain Party, Displayed*, within which Smith mounted an extended argument that the debate was much more about the location of the permanent capital than it was about the Bank.

Marshall discounts that, stating that "the liberal mind which can review them without prejudice, will charge neither the supporters nor the opponents of the bill with insincerity, nor with being knowingly actuated by motives which might not have been sincere." But his choice of words is interesting. It may reflect Marshall's belief that his readers were familiar with the dispute and that he therefore had an obligation to address it. But it may also amount to a gentle reminder to one and all that there was at least a respectable argument that the constitutional concerns that surrounded the creation of the Bank were perhaps not as deeply felt as their advocates might have wished one to believe. This was especially appropriate in a volume written and published when one of the 1791 opponents of the Bank, Jefferson, was president and a second, Madison, was waiting in the wings.

A second background reality is that much of what Marshall actually said in his *M'Culloch* opinion had in fact been said before, by the Court, in opinions written by Marshall himself. One such case was *The Bank of the United States v. DeVeaux* (1809), which arose, ironically, when the Bank refused to pay a tax that the state of Georgia attempted to levy on its stock. In yet another Marshall opinion, the Court held "that the right to sue" conferred on the Bank in its original charter "does not imply a right to sue in the courts of the union, unless it be expressed," and that the citizenship of a corporation is determined by "the character of the individuals who compose" it. The Bank's attempts to avoid the tax were accordingly defeated.

The Court had no jurisdiction. The Bank could not bring a federal question action, and could not maintain one in diversity, given the strictures imposed by the rule of complete diversity. That rule required that in a diversity action, that is, one brought in federal courts between citizens of different states, no party from one side of the dispute could be from the same state as any of the opposing parties. The Court had announced that rule three years earlier in *Strawbridge v. Curtis* (1806), when it held that that is what Congress intended when it implemented diversity jurisdiction in the Judiciary Act of 1789.

Marshall did not discuss whether the Bank itself had been constitutionally created in *DeVeaux*. But he did lay the foundations for key aspects of what was to follow in *M'Culloch*, observing that "a constitution, from its nature, deals in generals, not in detail. Its framers cannot perceive minute distinctions which arise in the progress of the nation, and therefore confine it to the establishment of broad and general principles."

That formulation did not, obviously, have the ring or staying power of Marshall's subsequent admonition that "a constitution" cannot "partake of the prolixity of a legal code." But it does add telling force to the idea that much of the constitutional thought set forth in *M'Culloch* is not original. For that matter, in another early decision, *United State v. Fisher* (1805), Marshall outlined much of what followed regarding the nature and reach of the necessary and proper clause.

Fisher was a bankruptcy action, and the specific question before the Court was "whether the United States, as holders of a protested bill of exchange, . . . are entitled to be preferred to the general creditors, where the debtor becomes bankrupt?" The use of the plural here ("United States . . . are") is interesting. One of the major debates of the time, and a central element in the post-*M'Culloch* dialogue, was about whether the Constitution created a nation or simply a confederation of sovereign states. Marshall's use of the plural here is arguably at odds with the position he subsequently staked out in *M'Culloch* and defended vigorously in its wake.

The debtors in *Fisher* contested the preferred position given the government, arguing that "if the act of congress gives the preference claimed, it is unconstitutional, and not a law." Marshall's discussion of this issue in *Fisher* reads like a primer for *M'Culloch*. He began by noting that "in the case at bar, the preference claimed by the United States is not prohibited; but it has been truly said that under a constitution conferring specific powers, the power contended for must be granted, or it cannot be exercised." His response, which is quoted at length for reasons that will become obvious, was as follows:

It is claimed under the authority to make all laws which shall be necessary and proper to carry into execution the powers vested by the constitution in the government of the United States, or in any department or officer thereof.

In construing this clause it would be incorrect and would produce endless difficulties, if the opinion should be maintained that no law was authorized which was not indispensably necessary to give effect to a specified power.

Where various systems might be adopted for that purpose, it might be said with respect to each, that it was not necessary because the end might be obtained by other means. Congress must possess the choice of means, and must be empowered to use any means which are in fact conducive to the exercise of the power granted by the constitution.

Marshall then dismissed the argument that the federal measure "interfere[s] with the rights of the state sovereignties respecting the dignity of debts." This was, he declared, "an objection to the constitution itself." And, he stated, "The mischief suggested, so far as it can really happen, is the necessary consequence of the supremacy of the laws of the United States on all subjects to which the legislative powers of congress extends." The Court reversed the decision of the circuit court. Justice Washington, while noting that "I take no part in the decision of this cause," explained at length why he believed the lower court's construction of the applicable statutes was correct. He did not, however, address or dispute Marshall's discussion of the constitutionality question.

Marshall began the *M'Culloch* opinion on a suitably solemn note. "In the case now to be determined," he declared, "the defendant, a sovereign State, denies the obligation of a law enacted by the legislature of the Union, and the plaintiff, on his part, contests the validity of an act which has been passed by the legislature of that State." He then stressed just how important the issues were:

> The constitution of our country, in its most interesting and vital parts, is to be considered; the conflicting powers of the Union and of its members, as marked in that constitution, are to be discussed; and an opinion given, which may essentially influence the great operations of the government. No tribunal can approach such a question without a deep sense of its importance, and of the awful responsibility involved in its decision. But it must be decided peacefully, or remain a source of hostile legislation, perhaps even of hostility of a more serious nature; and if it is to be so decided, by this tribunal alone can the decision be made. On the Supreme Court of the United States has the constitution of our country devolved this important duty.

Marshall has here done a number of things. He has put us on notice that the questions before the Court are both fundamental and constitutional. As such, they are to be decided by the Court. He has also made it quite clear that this is about more than the Bank. It is about the nature and sanctity of the Union itself.

Marshall was of course aware of just how deeply certain segments of the body politic resented the Bank and all it stood for. It is nevertheless hard to believe that he thought the Bank itself represented an issue on which the fate of the nation rode. But there was of course another issue being actively discussed at the time within which a doctrine of implied federal powers would be viewed with alarm by individuals quite willing to argue in response that they had a right both to defy the nation and, if necessary, to leave it. That issue was slavery, and the particular manifestation of that divisive matter at that time was the question of the status of Missouri.

Congressional debate about the future of that territory was being conducted even as the Court considered the Bank case. The South harbored deep concerns about the ability of Congress to both condition admission on an end to slavery and bar slavery from national territories. Neither power was mentioned in the Constitution. But both presumably fell within the ambit of any expansive reading of the text, in particular one sanctioning the existence of implied powers and the notion that such matters were best left to the political process. *M'Culloch* accordingly struck fear into the hearts of the pro-slavery factions on both counts, and in the very first paragraph of his opinion Marshall seems to be acknowledging these fears and their implications.

Marshall then entered the main part of the opinion with an observation that tracked closely what the attorneys for the Bank had argued: "It has been truly said, that this can scarcely be considered as an open question, entirely unprejudiced by the former proceedings of the nation respecting it." He made it clear that the discussions and affirmations he had in mind were undertaken by each of the three coordinate branches. He placed special emphasis on the legislative proceedings and the public response to the creation of the First and Second Banks, noting that "an exposition of the constitution, deliberately established by legislative acts, on the faith of which an immense property has been advanced, ought not to be lightly disregarded." He stressed the significance of the fact that the Second Bank was created after "a short experience of the embarrassments to which the refusal to revive [the First Bank] exposed the government," observing that "it would require no ordinary share of intrepidity to assert that a measure adopted under these circumstances was a bold and plain usurpation, to which the constitution gave no countenance."

The fact that Marshall included the judicial branch within the list of those that have given their assent to the Bank is especially note-worthy. As indicated, he was not alone in this belief. Both Madison in his 1815 veto and Representative Robert Wright of Maryland during the 1816 debate had alluded to judicial approval of the Bank, each without specifying what decisions they had in mind. And as Pinkney noted during his argument, that judgment, if indeed it had been made, had not been express. Marshall now confirmed what the others had said: prior recognition of the Bank as a proper party in cases before the Court offered tacit recognition that Congress did indeed have the power to charter the Bank.

Marshall next confronted and dismissed a key assumption in the state's case, one that was central to the state rights position in virtu-ally all matters: the belief that the Constitution itself did not "emi-nat[e] from the people," but was instead "the act of sovereign and independent states." That was not true, Marshall said, given that the Constitution was in fact ratified by the people speaking through their individual state conventions. Approval by the people as a whole was clearly impractical, and state conventions provided an appropriate and workable means toward the essential end. The fact that ratification took place state by state was not, however, a sign that the states them-selves created that document. "The government proceeds directly from the people; it is 'ordained and established' in the name of the people," and "it required not the affirmance, and could not be nega-tived, by the State governments. The constitution, when thus adopted, was of complete obligation, and bound the State sovereignties."

Marshall then admitted the obvious, that the federal government "is acknowledged by all to be one of enumerated powers." He also conceded that the "question respecting the extent of the powers actu-ally granted, is perpetually arising, and will probably continue to arise, as long as our system shall exist." Stressing his belief that the issue "must be settled," Marshall then outlined his nationalist vision: "If any one proposition could command the universal assent of mankind, we might expect it would be this — that the government of the Union, though limited in its powers, is supreme within its sphere of action. This would seem to result necessarily from its nature. It is the government of all; its powers are delegated by all; it represents all, and acts for all." That government is, in turn, supreme. "The nation, on those subjects on which it can act, must necessarily bind its component parts," a doctrine expressly recognized by the Constitution in Article VI, which declares in no uncertain terms that "this Constitution, and the Laws of the United States which shall be made in Pursuance thereof . . . shall be the supreme Law of the Land; and the Judges in every State shall be bound thereby, any Thing in the Constitution of Laws of any State to the Contrary notwithstanding."

The next question was, then, whether that same Constitution authorizes Congress to charter a bank. Marshall acknowledged that "among the enumerated powers, we do not find that of establishing a bank or creating a corporation." But, he stressed, there is nothing in the Constitution that limits the federal authority to those powers specifically mentioned. The Tenth Amendment, he noted, "omits the word 'expressly'" and the question accordingly will "depend on a fair construction of the whole instrument." And that document, by its very nature, cannot and should not do what counsel for the State of Maryland have demanded:

> A constitution, to contain an accurate detail of all the subdivisions of which its great powers will admit, and of all the means by which they may be carried into execution, would partake of the prolixity of a legal code, and could scarcely be embraced by the human mind. It would probably never be understood by the public. Its nature, therefore, requires, only that its great outlines should be marked, its important objects designated, and the major ingredients which compose those objects be deduced from the nature of the objects themselves.

It is at this point that Marshall declared, "In considering this question, then, we must never forget, that it is a *constitution* we are expounding." The point is telling, for it affirmed what we have already seen in chapter 1, that the Constitution was by design an outline for a plan of government that developed over time, rather than a detailed exposition of precisely how the Compound Republic was structured and would function.

Marshall then noted the many things that were expressly listed in the text, observing "that a government entrusted with such ample powers . . . must also be entrusted with ample means for their execution." He observed, "It is not denied, that the powers given to the government imply the ordinary means of execution." That statement is of course an expression of Marshall's national vision rather than of the collective views of the parties to the dispute before the Court. State rights advocates had long denied that the federal government possessed implied powers. But for Marshall the existence of such authority was an intrinsic aspect of what it meant to be sovereign. And "The government which has a right to do an act, and has imposed on it the duty of performing that act, must, according to the dictates of reason, be allowed to select the means."

This was especially the case, Marshall explained, when the question involves the chartering of a corporation. That power, he stressed, "is never used for its own sake, but for the purpose of effecting something else." Congress in turn had been expressly given the authority to make "all Laws which shall be necessary for carrying into Execution" the powers expressly granted. Marshall rejected a narrow, Jeffersonian reading of that clause. "To employ the means necessary to an end, is generally understood as employing any means calculated to produce the end, and not as being confined to those single means, without which the end would be entirely unattainable." And, consistent with what he has stressed regarding the nature of a constitution, "To have prescribed the means by which government should, in all future time, execute its powers, would have been to change, entirely, the character of the instrument, and give it the properties of a legal code."

Marshall illustrated the point by discussing the many ways in which Congress had in fact used implied powers to effectuate those expressly granted. He noted, for example, that Article I, Section 8, Clause 7 grants the power "to establish Post Offices and post Roads." And that "from this has been inferred the power and duty of carrying the mail along the post road, from one post office to another. And, from this implied power, has again been inferred the right to punish those who steal letters from the post office, or rob the mail." He then criticized the "narrow construction" urged by Maryland, one that cannot be maintained "without rendering the government incompetent to its great objects."

It is at this point that Marshall outlined an approach to these matters that had extraordinary ramifications. The necessary and proper clause, he stated, is "placed among the powers of Congress, not among the limitations on those powers." That clause was considered carefully by those who wrote and ratified it, and "its terms purport to enlarge, not to diminish, the powers vested in the government." Congress in turn has "the right . . . to exercise its best judgment in the selection of measures to carry into execution the constitutional powers of the government." Marshall stressed that those powers are limited, but in two key passages he both granted wide latitude to Congress and seemed to restrict the scope of any judicial inquiries about whether Congress did in fact have the power to act.

Marshall first observed that "we think the sound construction of the constitution must allow to the national legislature that discretion, with respect to the means by which the powers it confers are to be carried into execution, which will enable that body to perform the high duties assigned to it, in the manner most beneficial to the people." He described the first step, the extent of legislative authority, in one of the decision's most famous passages: "Let the end be legitimate, let it be within the scope of the constitution, and all means which are appropriate, which are plainly adapted to that end, which are not prohibited, but consist with the letter and spirit of the constitution, are constitutional." He then carefully limited the role of the Court in judging the results: "Where the law is not prohibited, and is really calculated to effect any of the objects entrusted to the government, to undertake here to inquire into the degree of its necessity, would be to pass the line which circumscribes the judicial department, and to tread on legislative ground. This court disclaims all pretensions to such a power."

These passages proved especially controversial. It is enough for now to stress two things. First, Marshall's statement is carefully couched. It is clearly not a rule within which the end justifies the means. Rather, it seems to impose on Congress an obligation to consider carefully what it does and make certain that the resulting legislation is both necessary and proper. Whether or not Congress has proceeded in that manner in a given instance is of course another matter entirely. But Marshall's approach in these matters is fully consistent with that voiced by a future chief justice, Harlan Fiske Stone, who spoke of the need for legislatures to exercise "the sober second thought of the community, which is the firm basis on which all law must ultimately rest."

Second, Marshall has here carefully qualified the seemingly absolutist position embraced in the opening passages of the opinion, within which he seemed to reserve for the Court the role of constitutional guardian. It is quite clear that Marshall sees the Court as the ultimate arbiter of the text in those instances where its words are subject to dispute. But that does not mean that the other two branches have no role in this process. Congress in particular must be given wide latitude in making appropriate judgments about the nature and scope of its powers. And if the power is clearly vested in Congress, and if Congress has in fact exercised its collective judgment, the Court can and should defer to the conclusions Congress has reached.

Marshall concludes the first part of the opinion with the observation that the legislation creating the Second Bank fits comfortably within the framework he has erected, observing that "were its necessity less apparent, none can deny it being an appropriate measure." He makes it clear that this was a judgment that many of the First Bank's key opponents now share: "All those who have been concerned in the administration of our finances, have concurred in representing its importance; and so strongly have they been felt, that statesmen of the first class, whose previous opinions against it had been confirmed by every circumstance which can fix the human judgment, have yielded those opinions to the exigencies of the nation."

Congress had the power to charter the Bank and, by necessary implication, its branches, including the one in Baltimore. This leaves only the question "Whether the State of Maryland may, without violating the constitution, tax that branch?"

Marshall started by stressing that "the power of taxation is one of vital importance" and that "it is retained by the States." Nevertheless, "such is the paramount character of the constitution, that its capacity to withdraw any subject from the action of even this power, is admitted." As Luther Martin had argued, there are provisions in the Constitution that directly address the question of state taxation, clauses that did not mention a tax of the sort at issue in this case. But that does not end the inquiry. "The constitution and the laws made in pursuance thereof are supreme," and from that axiom follow three "corollaries": "1st. that a power to create implies a power to preserve. 2nd. That a power to destroy, if wielded by a different hand, is hostile to, and incompatible with these powers to create and preserve. 3d. That where this repugnancy exists, that authority which is supreme must control, not yield to that over which it is supreme."

Marshall then embraced both the themes and the rhetoric employed by Webster and Pinkney. "That the power of taxing [the Bank] by the States may be exercised so as to destroy it, is too obvious to be denied. States have the authority to tax and that is an essential attribute of their sovereignty." But "It is of the very essence of supremacy to remove all obstacles to its action within its own sphere, and so to modify every power vested in subordinate governments, as to exempt its own operations from their own influence." In the normal course of events an abuse of the taxing power is corrected by the people who authorized and are subjected to it. "But," Marshall emphasized, "the means employed by the government of the Union have no such security, nor is the right of a State to tax them sustained by the same theory."

Both Hopkinson and Martin had argued at length that the state power to tax was a sovereign prerogative that must be respected, especially in the light of the notion that the states predated the union. But Marshall emphasized that the Bank represented the exercise of a power vested by the people in their national government and that this authority was distinct from that possessed by the people of any single state. As such, it was the product of a phenomenon that did not exist prior to the ratification of the Constitution. "We find, then, on just theory, a total failure of this original right to tax the means employed by the government of the Union, for the execution of its powers. The right never existed, and the question whether it has been surrendered, cannot arise."

Maryland had also alleged, Marshall noted, that "taxation . . . does not necessarily and unavoidably destroy," and that the Court can be "confident" that the states would not in fact treat the Bank in that manner given the safeguards inherent in a system of representative government. He then declared that this does not follow, for "In the legislature of the Union alone, are all represented. The legislature of the Union alone, therefore, can be trusted by the people with the power of controlling measures which concern all, in the confidence that it will not be abused." Moreover, "If the States may tax one instrument, employed by the government in the execution of its powers, they may tax any and every other instrument." That, Marshall stressed, "was not intended by the American people. They did not design to make their government dependent on the States."

Marshall concluded with the assurance that "the Court has bestowed on this subject its most deliberate consideration." The Court, he emphasized, is "not depriv[ing] the States of any resources which they originally possessed." Maryland had rather presumed to levy "a tax on the operations of the bank, and is, consequently, [taxing] the operation of an instrument employed by the government of the Union to carry its powers into execution." But "the States have no power, by taxation or otherwise, to retard, impede, burden, or in any manner control, the operations of the constitutional laws enacted by Congress to carry into execution the powers vested in the general government. This is, we think, the unavoidable consequence of that supremacy which the constitution has declared." The Court was, he stressed, unanimous. "Such a tax must be unconstitutional."

As indicated, Marshall announced the opinion for the Court on Saturday, March 6, 1819. Story wrote his wife the next day, indicating that "this decision excites great interest, and in a political view is of the deepest consequence to the nation. It goes to establish the Constitution upon its great original principles." A few weeks later Webster stated in a letter to Story that "the opinion in the Bank cause is universally praised."

Story was correct. *M'Culloch* did in fact "excite great interest" and is today recognized as one of the greatest expositions of the Constitution and the principles for which it stands. But Webster was wrong. The subsequent praise was hardly universal, and there were trying times ahead for both the Court and the Bank. Indeed, it took several years before *M'Culloch* itself secured the place it now enjoys in constitutional doctrine.

CHAPTER 7

The Decision Defended

One of the most interesting aspects of *M'Culloch* is that Marshall's opinion for the Court was only the first part of an extended debate within which Marshall himself was an active participant. These events began when Thomas Ritchie, the editor of the *Richmond Enquirer*, printed a series of essays attacking the decision.

Ritchie presented a stark contrast to many journalists of the time. He was by birth and upbringing a member of the Virginia elite. Indeed, his mother, Molly Ritchie, was the sister of another important Virginian, Judge Spencer Roane, a connection that eventually took him from a teaching career into journalism. In 1804 Roane and Jefferson were looking for a way to enhance the Republican voice in Virginia and the nation and believed that an appropriate-minded newspaper was one of the best means to that end. They accordingly induced Ritchie to purchase a failing newspaper, the *Richmond Examiner*, which was then renamed the *Richmond Enquirer*. Ritchie edited the paper for the next forty-one years and in the process became one of the most influential journalists in the nation.

Ritchie was both a staunch Republican and a dedicated southerner. For example, he trod a delicate line on the question of slavery, observing that "we protest in our own name and that of so many others, that we do not vindicate servitude; we wish no slave had touched our soil; we wish it could be terminated. As Republicans, we frankly declare before our God and our country, that we abhor its institution." The path toward abolition could not, however, be one dictated by an overbearing national sovereign. In 1820, for example, Ritchie wrote the preface to John Taylor's extensive attack on *M'Culloch* and the Court, the book *Construction Construed, and Constitutions Vindicated*. He opened that essay with the declaration that "the crisis has come, when the following work 'may do the state some service.'" He made it clear that one aspect of that dislocation was "the *Missouri Question*," part of a process by which "the first principles of the government and some of the dearest rights of the states are threatened with being utterly ground into dust and ashes."

Ritchie offered his own criticisms of *M'Culloch* when the decision was announced. He noted on March 12 that the opinion had come down, using the same summary that had appeared in the *National Intelligencer.* He printed the entire decision on March 23, along with an appeal to "those firm Republicans of the Old School" to "rally round the banners of the constitution, defending the rights of the states against federal usurpation." But his most important role was to provide a conduit for others, rather than serving as an active individual advocate, although he had his opinions and expressed them. For it was in the pages of the *Enquirer* that the first salvo was launched in what proved to be one of the most remarkable battles of opinion in the history of the nation.

Ritchie initiated this process on March 30 when he penned a brief preface to the first of two essays on the decision written by an individual who used the pseudonym Amphictyon. "We cannot too earnestly press upon our readers," Ritchie wrote, "the following exposition of the alarming errors of the Supreme Court of the United States in their late interpretation of the Constitution. We conceive those errors to be most alarming, and this exposition most satisfactory. Whenever state rights are threatened or invaded, Virginia will not be the last to sound the tocsin. Again, we earnestly recommend the following to the attention of the reader."

Anonymous political writings were the norm for the time. Various justifications have been offered for the practice, the most important of which is that this forced the reader to concentrate on what was said rather than on the personality and perspectives of the author. In some instances the identity of the author was known or easily discovered. In others it remained hidden. At the time they were written, many believed that the Amphictyon essays were the work of Spencer Roane. But that was not the case, for as Marshall himself correctly surmised in an August 3, 1819, letter to Justice Bushrod Washington, Amphictyon was actually another Virginian, William Brockenbrough.

Brockenbrough was, unsurprisingly, yet another member of the Virginia elite, the son of a doctor who studied law and eventually entered politics. In 1819 he was a circuit judge in Richmond, an important post one step below the court of appeals on which Roane served. He was also Roane's first cousin and a member of the Richmond Junto, a powerful but secretive group that in effect controlled Virginia politics. Brockenbrough's views on these matters were accordingly important, as they formed one part of the canon of the "powerful party" that pressed the Republican cause in the pages of the *Enquirer* and elsewhere. The ultimate importance of Brockenbrough's essays nevertheless lay in the responses they provoked rather than their substance. For this attack on the Court led to a public albeit anonymous exchange of views within which John Marshall and Spencer Roane engaged in a detailed debate about the nature and scope of the Constitution, the role of the Court, and the appropriate division of authority between nation and states.

The two Amphictyon essays appeared in the *Enquirer* on March 30 and April 2, 1819. Two essays written by "A Friend to the Union" were in turn published in a Philadelphia paper, the *Union*, on April 24 and April 28, essays that noted in their very first sentence that they had been crafted in response to Amphictyon.

The identity of this new author was a closely guarded secret. Arguably only John Marshall and two of his colleagues, Bushrod Washington and Joseph Story, knew for certain that Marshall himself penned these essays. Roane probably suspected this, and it is not surprising that he was moved to submit four essays to the *Enquirer* under the name Hampden, essays that took issue with Marshall, his opinion, and his defense of it. These responses in turn provoked Marshall to write another nine pieces, which were published in a Virginia newspaper, the *Gazette and Alexandria General Advertiser*, as the work of "A Friend of the Constitution."

The notion that any judge, much less a sitting chief justice, would take up the cudgels in a newspaper in a pointed debate about one of the Court's opinions strikes us today as at least extraordinary, if not in fact entirely inappropriate. The twin assumptions under which the Supreme Court works are that it speaks through its opinions and that the decisions it issues must be assessed as matters of law and reason. Political theory and debate are left to others. The Court, and its members, are to be above the fray. The same holds true for state court judges. These individuals might not agree with the holdings of the federal court. But the expectation is that any criticisms they voice will be found in comments made in the course of deciding cases before them, even as they adhere to the settled doctrine that the Supreme Court in particular has the final and binding say on matters of constitutional interpretation.

That was clearly not the perspective that either Marshall or Roane brought to these matters. Given the tenor of the times, one might expect that Roane would speak out, albeit, as he did, anonymously. But Marshall's "A Friend to the Union" and "A Friend of the Constitution" essays are truly unique in the history of the Court and its justices. Much of his thinking about the whys and wherefores of what he did may be found in a series of letters he wrote to his colleagues.

The dialogue that shaped these essays began on March 24, 1819, when Marshall wrote Story, indicating that "our opinion in the bank case has roused the sleeping spirit of Virginia — if indeed it ever sleeps. It will I understand be attacked in the papers with some asperity; and as those who favor it never write for the publick, it will remain undefended & of course be considered as *damnably heretical*." Three days later, he informed Justice Washington that "great dissatisfaction has been given to the politicians of Virginia by our opinion on the bank question. They have no objection to a decision in favor of the bank, since the good patriots who administer the government wished it, & would probably have been seriously offended with us had we dared to decide otherwise, but they require an obsequious, silent opinion without reasons. That would have been satisfactory, but our heretical reasoning is pronounced most damnable." He then came to the crux of the matter, noting, "We shall be denounced bitterly in the papers & as not a word will be said on the other side we shall undoubtedly be condemned as a pack of consolidating aristocrats. The legislature & executive have enacted the law but who have power & places to bestow will escape with impunity, while the poor court who have nothing to give & of whom nobody is afraid, bears all the obloquy of the measure."

Marshall was at this time back home in Richmond, where he presumably had the benefit of a close involvement in and understanding of the political scene. His predictions both were reasonable and proved to be correct. The *Enquirer* printed the first of the attacks on March 30. The solution to the problems they posed was obvious: Marshall himself would write in response.

Brockenbrough began the first Amphictyon essay with an attack on the manner in which the Court had decided the case. He stressed that the Court had issued a *"unanimous* and decided opinion." But, echoing earlier Republican attacks on Marshall's elimination of seriatim opinions, he noted, "We are not informed whether the whole court united in the course of reasoning adopted by the Chief Justice, nor whether they all accorded in the various positions and principles which he advanced." Having expressed his wish that the public should have had the benefit of the views of each member of the Court, Brockenbrough then launched a subtle but telling salvo at Marshall himself, noting that the case involved "a subject which has employed his thoughts, his tongue, and his pen, as a politician, and an historian, for more than thirty years." The opinion itself might be "very able, [as] every one must admit." And Marshall might be "a man of . . . gigantic powers." But the seed had been planted that *M'Culloch* should be viewed as a political rather than a legal resolution of the important issues it addressed.

Brockenbrough's greatest concerns revolved around the threat to state rights posed by the doctrines the Court had embraced and the powers it had confirmed in Congress:

> There are two principles advocated and decided on by the supreme court, which appear to me to endanger the very existence of state rights. The first is the denial that the powers of the federal government were delegated by the states; and the second is, that the grant of powers to the government, and particularly the grant of powers "necessary and proper" to carry the other powers into effect, ought to be construed in a liberal, rather than a restricted sense. Both of these principles tend directly to the consolidation of the states, and to strip them of some of the most important attributes of their sovereignty. If the Congress of the United States should think proper to legislate to the full extent, upon the principles now adjudicated by the supreme court, it is difficult to say how small would be the remnant of power left in the hands of state authorities.

These arguments were a continuation of the debate that had raged since 1787. The Court's contention that "the powers of the federal government are not delegated by the states" was both irrelevant and wrong, Brockenbrough stressed. The real question was the nature and scope of the powers actually given. The states in turn were the source of the powers conferred, and their independent, sovereign existence was both an essential part of and limit on federal authority. "The states not only gave birth to the constitution, but its life depends upon the existence of the state governments." The lessons learned as a result of the Alien and Sedition Acts confirmed this. "The doctrine" that the states were not essential "parties to the federal compact . . . was exposed and refuted, and I did not expect that it would be brought forward at this day under the supposed sanction of the highest judicial authority." Indeed, Brockenbrough continued, the very notion that the Court itself decided these issues was startling: "There are many cases which can never be brought before that tribunal, and I do humbly conceive that the states never could have committed an act of such egregious folly as to agree that their umpire should be altogether appointed and paid by the other party. The supreme court may be a perfectly impartial tribunal to decide between two states, but cannot be considered in that point of view when the contest lies between the United States, and one of its members."

Brockenbrough ended the first essay with an extensive series of quotations from Madison's *Virginia Report* that provided support for his position. His second essay in turn focused on the doctrine of implied powers, the "danger" of which "has always been seen and felt by the people of the states." He discussed at length the nature and importance of the word "necessary," arguing that if " '*necessary*' means *convenient*, or *useful*, or *conducive to*, then it might have been totally omitted, because the word *proper*, would have conveyed the whole meaning." He then attacked the notion "that if Congress is not allowed to exercise its discretion in selecting such means 'as are appropriate and conducive to the end,' they cannot beneficially execute the great and important powers expressly delegated to them." He posed various examples of how this might play out, each of which encroached on the rights of the states. And he argued that both the "first principles" of a written constitution and sound political practice argued against simply trusting Congress to act wisely: "I cannot exclusively rely on my confidence in our representatives: if that were a sufficient guarantee for the preservation of our state rights, then there would be no necessity for a specific enumeration of granted powers."

The balance of the second essay explored two questions. The first was the nature of federal power, which Brockenbrough argued must largely be understood to extend only to "those cases where uniformity was desirable, in which cases the states fully surrendered the power." The "residuary powers" were in turn left to the states, in particular those that dealt with "the daily transactions of men" which should be exercised by entities — the states — that "have a regard to their interests, their feelings, even their prejudices."

Brockenbrough then conceded that the debates of 1791 and 1815 resolved the question of the Bank's threshold constitutionality in its favor. His quarrel with *M'Culloch* was rather with the principles for which the decision stood. "The consequences of giving an enlarged, or what is called a liberal construction to the grant of powers, are alarming to the states and the people." This doctrine meant, for example, that the federal government could "build universities, academies, and school houses for the poor . . . companies for the promotion of agriculture" and "churches [all of which] promotes the general welfare of the people." Those sorts of encroachments were intolerable. And while Brockenbrough agreed with the Court that if a Bank were indeed proper the states could not tax it, he believed it important that the states nevertheless voice their opposition to measures of that sort: "In Virginia no tax has been laid on the operations of the bank. Her course is more wise. When unconstitutional laws are passed, this state calmly passes her resolutions to that effect. . . . May this continue to be her policy, and may other states follow her example! I do most ardently hope that this decision of the supreme court will attract the attention of the state legislatures, and that Virginia will, as heretofore, do her duty."

M'Culloch did in fact "attract the attention" of the states. The Virginia House of Delegates, for example, lodged a "most solemn protest" against a decision that "undermine[d] the pillars of the Constitution itself." The Ohio legislature in turn approved and sent to Congress a lengthy attack on the decision within which it denied that a "contrived" action brought before the Court regarding Maryland's tax could in any way be seen as binding on Ohio. And it declared "that this General Assembly do assert, and will maintain, by all legal and Constitutional means, the right of the States to tax the business and property of any private corporations of trade, incorporated by the Congress of the United States, and located to transact its corporate business within any state."

The Court responded in a sense to both Virginia and Ohio in subsequent cases within which it reaffirmed both the doctrines it had articulated in *M'Culloch* and its place in the constitutional order. Brockenbrough's essays were in turn dealt with by Marshall himself, whose initial "A Friend to the Union" essays appeared in the *Philadelphia Union* on April 24 and April 28. Marshall sent these pieces to Justice Washington, who arranged for their publication. Unfortunately, the editor of the *Union*, Enos Bronson, botched the assignment. As Marshall complained in a subsequent letter to Washington, Bronson had "cut out the middle of the first number to be inserted in the middle of the second; & to show his perfect impartiality, has cut out the middle of the second number to be inserted in the first. He has thrown these disrupted parts together without the least regard to their fitness & made a curious mixture . . . which, however good the ingredients may be, when compounded as he has compounded them, are rather nauseous to the intellectual palate." Marshall accordingly asked Washington to have the errors corrected and the essays republished. Washington did so, and they appeared as Marshall intended them in three installments in the *Gazette and Alexandria General Advertiser* in May.

The *Union* essays are nevertheless worth noting. As indicated, Marshall stated at the outset that he was writing in response to "mischievous errours contained in the [Amphictyon] essays," articles that seemed intent on resurrecting a spirit of opposition to the federal government that had become dormant. The decision that provoked Amphictyon, he stressed, is that of the whole Court. It could hardly be otherwise, he argued, as it is unlikely that "the judges of the Supreme Court, men of high and respectable character, would sit by in silence, while great constitutional principles of which they disapproved, were advanced in their name, and as their principles." Marshall also discounted the attack on a chief justice who "is a federalist" and "who was a politician of some note before he was a judge" by noting that the decision is that of "all the judges, — four of whom have no political sin upon their heads; — who in addition to being eminent lawyers, have the still greater advantage of being sound republicans."

Marshall agreed with Brockenbrough that the actual source of the federal power was arguably irrelevant. But he stressed that "if Amphyction means to assert, as I suppose he does, that the powers of the general government were delegated by the state legislatures, then I say his assertion is contradicted by the words of the constitution, and by the fact; and is not supported, even by that report, on which he so confidently relies." He emphasized that the true focus must be on the wishes of the people, comparing that with what he took to be Brockenbrough's fixation on the "state governments, as contradistinguished from the people of the states." Indeed, he argued that a close and careful reading of both Madison and Brockenbrough established the opposite of what Amphictyon alleged, that "the powers of the general government were not delegated by the state governments, but by the people of the several states."

In the second essay he then stressed that the people have spoken through the Constitution and that the Court has opted for "the fair sense of the words used in" that document, rather than the "restricted interpretation" that Brockenbrough proposed. He noted that both Amphictyon and counsel for Maryland advanced the same reading of the term "necessary," an approach that the Court considered carefully and rejected. "Every case presents a choice of means. Every end may be attained by different means. Of no one means can it be truly said, that, '*without it,* the end *could not* be attained.'" The logical conclusion, Marshall argued, is then that "the rule laid down by Amphyction is impracticable, and consequently an erroneous rule." The truth of that proposition is evident, he asserted, in the numerous practical examples of how an implied power to, for example, "punish those who rob the mail" was a necessary corollary of the express power "'to establish post offices, and post roads.'"

Marshall stressed that "if the rule contended for would not absolutely arrest the progress of the government, it would certainly deny to those who administer it the means of executing its acknowledged powers in the manner most advantageous to those for whose benefit they were conferred." And he observed, in what for him is the most telling indictment of Brockenbrough's position, that "the principles maintained by the counsel for the state of Maryland, and by Amphyction, would essentially change the constitution, render the government of the Union incompetent to the objects for which it was instituted, and place all its powers under the control of the state legislatures. It would, in a great measure, reinstate the old confederation."

As indicated, Marshall discovered that these essays were not printed in the form he intended and had Washington place them in the correct sequence in an Alexandria, Virginia, newspaper, the *Gazette and Daily Advertiser.* He also continued his exchanges with Story and Washington on the nature of the threats posed by the pieces appearing in the *Enquirer.* On April 28 he wrote Story, declaring that "the opinion in the Bank case has brought into operation the whole antifederal spirit of Virginia. Some latent feelings which have been working ever since the decisions of Martin & Hunter have found vent on this occasion & are working most furiously." He also complained that "the offence would have been equally great had we pronounced the law unconstitutional," an observation that accurately reflected state resentment about the power of the Court to undertake inquiries of this sort.

On May 6, in turn, he wrote Washington, noting, "It is understood that this subject is not to drop. A very serious effort is undoubtedly making to have it taken up in the next legislature." He observed, "It is said that some other essays written by a very great man are now preparing & will soon appear." That man was Spencer Roane.

Roane was a leading figure in the Virginia bar. He was the son of a prosperous planter and businessman and had studied law at the College of William and Mary and in Philadelphia. As a member of the Virginia ruling class, Roane had extensive contacts among that state's elite. He was especially close to one of Virginia's leading Anti-Federalists, Patrick Henry, and married one of Henry's daughters.

Roane opposed the adoption of the Constitution, believing both that in some respects the nation it proposed would be "too loosely banded together" and that the federal government had been given certain powers that should have been reserved to the states. His sense that the new government was too weak was ironic to say the least given his views on the Bank, as that critique reflected his belief that the new nation should have the ability to raise the revenue required for its defense and should not be dependent, as had the Confederation, on the sufferance of the states.

Roane became a judge in 1789 and in 1795 was elected to the Virginia Court of Appeals, where he spent the rest of his life and in particular championed two causes: judicial review and state rights. His

opinion in *Kamper v. Hawkins* (1793) was an important early endorse-
ment of both the power and the obligation of a court to overturn a
legislative act that violated a constitution. His staunch Republican
beliefs in turn both permeated his opinions as a judge and led him to
found the *Richmond Enquirer* in 1804, believing it necessary to have
in Virginia a newspaper espousing the Republican philosophy of a
limited national government and the sovereignty of the states.

The positions Roane took in his critique of Marshall and *M'Culloch*
were actually an extension of an earlier dispute with the Court, as
Roane had written one of the key opinions in the *Martin v. Hunter's
Lessee* litigation. There he stated bluntly that "it is not for [this court]
to regard political consequences, in rendering its judgments." The case
before him required adherence to a central premise of the Constitution, "that the government of the United States is not a sole and consolidated government." The danger, he warned, was posed by the fact
"that there is a Charybdis to be avoided, as well as a Scylla; that a cen-
tripetal, as well as a centrifugal principle, exists in the government; and
that no calamity would be more to be deplored by the American people, than a vortex in the general government, which should ingulph
and sweep away every vestige of the state constitutions."

The Supreme Court's initial order in *Martin* was a "plain case of the
judiciary of one government correcting and reversing the decisions of
that of another." That, Roane believed, was improper. The courts of
Virginia were precisely that: state courts that existed independent of
the federal judiciary and were not, accordingly, subject to the superin-
tending power of the Supreme Court. "The jurisdiction granted to a
government, is confined to the courts of that government. It does not,
naturally, run into and affect the courts of another and distinct government." The mere fact that a state court — a court of a distinct
government — might construe the Constitution or a federal law or
treaty did not make its decisions and orders fodder for the federal
courts. To argue otherwise meant that, for example, "the Supreme
Court of Calcutta [would become] a part of the judicial system of the
United States, when enforcing the laws of this country in that."

Roane entered the *M'Culloch* fray on June 11, when the *Enquirer*
published the first of the Hampden essays. He began with the claim that
this was not a political matter: "I address my fellow citizens without any
distinction of parties." Some might disagree with what he had to say,

but "none can hear . . . with indifference." And none, he believed, "can be prepared to give a Carte Blanche to our federal rulers, and to obliterate the state governments, forever, from our political system." Roane reminded his readers that they enjoyed the "happiness to believe, that in the partition of powers between the general and state governments, the former possessed only such as were expressly granted, or passed therewith as necessary incidents, while all the residuary powers were retained by the latter." There were two problems now, he complained. The first was that "that legislative power which is every where extending the sphere of its activity and drawing all power into its impetuous vortex, has blinked even the strong words of [the Tenth Amendment]." The second was the judicial power, which in England had "always [invaded] on the side of arbitrary power" and now "has also deemed its interference necessary, in our country."

Roane characterized what had occurred as a "judicial *coup de main*" that gave "a *general* letter of attorney to future legislatures of the union." The scope of the authority conferred, he maintained, was staggering: "That man must be a deplorable idiot who does not see that there is no earthly difference between an *unlimited* grant of power, and a grant limited in its terms, but accompanied with *unlimited* means of carrying it into execution." And it ran counter to every principle for which the Constitution ought to be understood to stand for, as "that court had no power to adjudicate away the *reserved* rights of a sovereign member of the confederacy, and vest them in the general government."

Roane expressed some doubt about the likely effect of his sallies. "My fellow citizens," he stated, "are sunk in apathy . . . sodden in the *luxuries* of banking. A money-loving, funding, stock-jobbing spirit has taken foothold among us." But he pressed ahead, arguing in the second installment that the historical record supported his belief that federal powers were few and carefully limited. That was the position taken, he declared, by both Madison and Marshall at the time the Constitution was drafted and ratified. Settled doctrines of the common law — that is, the body of law developed by judges — in turn "conclusive[ly] . . . favour[ed] . . . a restricted construction of the incidental powers. — They shew that nothing is granted but what is *necessary*. They exclude every thing that is only *remotely* necessary, or which only *tends* to the fulfillment." Indeed, the words " 'necessary and proper' . . . add nothing to the powers given to the general gov-

ernment. They were only added (says the Federalist) for greater caution, and are tautologous and redundant, though *harmless.*"

The third Hampden essay stressed that "the constitution is a *compact* between the people of each state, and those of all the states, and it
is nothing more than a compact." Roane denied that either Congress
or the Court had the authority to change the terms of that compact,
declaring that "the adjustment of those powers made by the constitution, between the general and state governments, is beyond their
power, and ought to be set aside." In a similar vein, it was for the people to adopt a "means" toward a specified end. "If this criterion be inadequate to the true interests of the union, let the supreme court shew
it to the *people*, or to the next convention, and these means will be
enlarged." The Bank itself was not "necessary," at least as that term
should be understood, to achieve any power actually given. And its
constitutionality should not be deemed as settled by the record. Congress had approved two bills chartering a national bank. But it had
also rejected two, and in Hampden's eyes at least President Washington had at best reluctantly approved the First Bank against the advice
of a majority of his cabinet.

In the final Hampden essay, which appeared on June 22, Roane
confronted directly one of the central elements in the ongoing debate
about the origins and nature of the Constitution. That document, he
maintained, "was not adopted by the people of the United States, as
one people. It was adopted by the several states, in their highest sovereign character, that is, by the people of the said states, respectively;
such people being competent, and *they* only competent, to alter the
pre-existing governments in the said states." He then argued that the
Court should not be deemed the ultimate arbiter. Rather, "the *parties*
themselves must be the rightful judges, whether the compact has been
violated, and that, in this respect, there can be no tribunal above their
authority." Roane declared, "The supreme court is but one department of the general government. A department is not competent to
do that to which the whole government is inadequate. The general
government cannot decide this controversy and much less can one of
its departments. They cannot do it unless we tread under foot the
principle which forbids a party to decide his own cause."

Hampden concluded with the observation that "I invoke no revolutionary or insurrectionary measures. I only claim that the people

should understand this question. The force of public opinion will calmly rectify the evil." Roane believed that the true evil was the concentration of power in the national government at the expense of the states and the people. In particular, it was the mistaken notion that the Supreme Court should be allowed to serve as the arbiter in these matters, especially when it acted in an "extrajudicial manner" and promulgated "abstract doctrines" that in effect gave virtually unfettered discretion to Congress.

Marshall was clearly aware of and concerned about what Hampden had to say. In May he wrote Story, noting that a movement was under way to do precisely what Roane subsequently suggested in the fourth Hampden essay: "An effort is certainly making to induce the legislature which will meet in December to take up the subject & to pass resolutions not very unlike those which were called forth by the alien & sedition laws in 1799." He characterized much of the criticism of the decision as "gross misrepresentations." But, he declared, "prejudice will swallow anything. If the principles which have been advanced on this occasion were to prevail, the constitution would be converted into the old confederation."

A few weeks later he informed Washington that "the storm which has been for some time threatening the Judges has at length burst on their heads & a most serious hurricane it is." He indicated that the Hampden essays must be dealt with. "I find myself more stimulated on this subject than on any other because I believe the design to be to injure the Judges & inpair the constitution. I have therefore thought of answering these essays & sending my pieces to you for publication in the Alexandria paper." He accordingly forwarded his responses to Washington for publication in the *Gazette*, but he insisted that precautions be taken to keep his identity as the author a secret. For example, as a check against further mistakes by the printers, he asked that Washington secure two copies of his essays as they were published, which should be "directed to T. Marshall, Oak Hill Fauquier. I do not wish them to come to me lest some suspicion of the author should be created." And he asked, albeit too late to have it accomplished, that the name of the anonymous author be changed to "A Constitutionalist," noting that "A Friend of the Constitution is so much like a Friend of the Union that it may lead to some suspicion of identity."

The results began to appear in the *Gazette* on June 30. Marshall initially believed that he could cover these matters in five essays. But nine would actually be written, a total that reflected both Marshall's enthusiasm for the task and the degree of thoroughness he believed essential.

In the first one Marshall indicated that he wrote as someone sensitive to the fact that the judiciary was arguably the "weakest part" of the government, and that his work was a response to "the systematic efforts which certain restless politicians in Virginia have been for some time making, to degrade that department in the estimation of the public." As he had in the "A Friend to the Union" papers, Marshall emphasized that the federal government was a creature of the people, and that they had a vested interest in seeing that it was able to fulfill the important responsibilities entrusted to it: "In fact, the government of the union, as well as those of the states, is created by the people, who have bestowed upon it certain powers for their own benefit, and who administer it for their own good. The people are as much interested, their liberty is as deeply concerned, in preventing encroachments on that government, in arresting the hands which would tear from it the powers they have conferred upon it, as in restraining it within its constitutional limits."

In the second essay Marshall attempted to distance himself from what he perceived to be the tone of the Hampden articles: "I gladly take leave of the bitter invectives which compose the first number of Hampden, and proceed to a less irksome task—the examination of his argument." He reduced it to what appeared to be two "propositions": that the federal government had limited powers, and that to the extent it enjoyed any authority beyond that expressly listed, that power was confined to those acts that "were *fairly incidental* to them." But, Marshall replied, "The power to do a thing, and the power to carry that thing into execution, are, I humbly conceive, the same power, and the one cannot be termed with propriety 'additional' or 'incidental' to the other." The federal structure must in turn be viewed in the light of the nation's history: "Under the confederation congress could do scarcely any thing, that body could only make requisitions to the states." But the Constitution was different, as "the powers of government are given in terms which authorise and require congress to execute them. The execution is the essence of the power."

Marshall spent the balance of the second essay and much of the third responding to Roane's invocation of Emer de Vattel's *The Law of Nations* and his appeal to the common law. Roane had argued that Vattel, a major eighteenth-century figure, should be read in support of his position. But Marshall maintained that Roane had turned Vattel around, for Vattel had clearly stated that " 'a nation has a right to every thing which can secure it from such a threatening danger, and to keep at a distance whatever is capable of causing its ruin.' " And common-law rules of interpretation — assuming for the sake of argument that Roane had correctly identified them — were inapposite. The Constitution was not, for example, "a contract for a single object, every thing relating to which, might be recollected and inserted." Rather, he declared, in a lengthy passage that drew directly on his admonition in *M'Culloch* that "we must never forget, that it is a *constitution* we are expounding," that document

> is the act of a people. The powers of this government are conferred for their own benefit, are essential to their own prosperity, and are to be exercised for their good, by persons chosen for that purpose by themselves. The object of that government is not a single one which can be minutely described, with all its circumstances. The attempt to do so, would actually change its nature, and defeat its purpose. It is intended to be a general system for future times, to be adapted by those who administer it, to all future occasions that may come within its view. From its nature, such an instrument can describe only the great objects it is intended to accomplish, and state in general terms, the specific powers which are deemed necessary for those objects.

Congress then "direct[ed] the manner in which" the express powers "are to be exercised, the means by which the objects of the government are to be effected." That body was chosen by the people and, as Congress had done since the Constitution was ratified, routinely gave effect to the enumerated powers through the exercise of its discretion to adopt particular means not listed within the text. "The very business of a legislature is to select the means." And "if the means have a plain relation to the end — if they be direct, natural, and appropriate, who, but the people at the elections, shall, under the pretext of their being unnecessary, control the legislative will, and direct its understanding?" And, as Marshall emphasized in the fifth essay, the Court had not in fact embraced an "end justifies the means" approach to these matters:

In no single instance does the court admit the unlimited power of congress to adopt any means whatever, and thus to pass the limits prescribed by the constitution. Not only is the discretion claimed for the legislature in the selection of its means, always limited in terms, to such as are appropriate, but the court expressly says, "should congress under the pretext of executing it powers, pass laws for the accomplishment of objects, not entrusted to the government, it would become the painful duty of this tribunal, should a case requiring such a decision come before it, to say that such an act was not the law of the land."

Marshall then explored the question of whether the national government should be viewed as "consolidated" or "federal." The key fact for him was that there is a body politic consisting of the "people of the United States." Those people have created "a government, and not 'a league.'" That marked a fundamental change from the approach embraced under the Articles of Confederation, within which "congress was a corps of ambassadors" from the several sovereign states "to be recalled at the will of their masters." The Court in turn properly exercised its jurisdiction to consider and resolve the dispute that had been brought before it. Hampden's objection to this, Marshall contended, "proceeds from the fundamental error, that our constitution is a mere league, or compact, between the several state governments, and the general government." But that is not the case. "This government has all the departments, and all the capacities for performing its various functions, which a free people is accustomed to bestow on its government." One of these is the judiciary, which "is not a partial, local tribunal, but one which is national."

Marshall then emphasized a fundamental precept of the federal system, within which each branch of the national government exercised those powers entrusted to it by the Constitution. Article III created the Court and authorized it to hear "cases and controversies." "On a judicial question then, the judicial department is the government, and can alone exercise the judicial power of the United States." Common sense dictated that result:

To whom more safely than to the judges are judicial questions to be referred? They are selected from the great body of the people for the purpose of deciding them. To secure impartiality, they are made perfectly independent. They have no personal interest in aggrandizing the legislative power. Their paramount interest is the public prosperity, in which is involved their own and that of their families. — *No* tribunal can be less liable to be swayed by unworthy motives from a conscientious performance of duty. It is not then the party sitting in its own cause. It is the application to individuals by one department of the acts of another department of government. The people are the authors of it all; the departments are their agents; and if the judge be perfectly disinterested, he is exempt from any political interest that might influence his opinion, as imperfect human institutions can make him.

Marshall concluded the final essay with the observation that Roane and his allies are seeking "the utter subversion of the constitution. Let Hampden succeed, and that instrument will be radically changed. The government of the whole will be prostrated at the feet of its members; and that grand effort of wisdom, virtue, and patriotism, which produced it, will be totally defeated." That is clearly a result that Marshall could not countenance, and by writing his essays he obviously hoped to prevent it.

The Roane and Marshall essays are fascinating, both for the fact that they were written at all and for their content. Two of the foremost figures in the history of American law engaged in a detailed and often eloquent assessment of one of the Supreme Court's most important decisions. During the course of that debate they explored in detail many of the questions that had perplexed the nation since the Constitution was conceived and ratified. They sketched out the conflicting positions of those who believed in the need for a strong national government and those who feared the implications of such an entity for the sovereignty of the states. These were not the words of judges, constrained by the facts of a particular case or the conventions of legal discourse, although those worlds informed what they said. They were rather essays written by statesmen at the height of their powers, offered anonymously in a form that freed them from the constraints they might otherwise have experienced had they spoken, as they usually did, from the bench.

CHAPTER 8

The Nation Reacts

The dialogue between John Marshall and his Virginia opponents was clearly important, but it was only part of a larger public reaction to the decision that was intense and in most respects entirely predictable. Those of a nationalist bent were pleased, sensing correctly that the Court had both accepted a broad construction of federal authority and sharply limited the ability of the states to act in those areas where national powers had been appropriately exercised. State rights advocates were in turn appalled, believing that the Court had struck a deadly blow against the states and that the implied powers doctrine served as the license for all manner of federal abuses.

Initial press accounts of the ruling were sketchy. Most newspapers simply announced the result and perhaps some of the details. The first mention in the *National Intelligencer* came on Monday, March 8, when the paper reported that

> Mr. Chief Justice Marshall delivered the unanimous opinion of the Court in the case of McCulloh against the State of Maryland.
>
> 1st. That Congress had, constitutionally, a right to establish the Bank of the United States.
>
> 2dly. That the Bank has authority to establish Branches in such States of the Union as it thinks fit.
>
> 3dly. That the State of Maryland has no right to tax the Branch of the Bank established in that state.

The following Saturday the paper became more pointed, in keeping with its nationalist sentiments: "The Supreme Judicial authority of the Nation has rarely, if ever, pronounced an opinion more interesting in its views, or more important as to its operation, than that recently given, as to the right of a state of the Union to tax the National Bank. We have therefore taken some pains to procure a copy of this interesting and elaborate opinion for publication, and have the pleasure today of presenting it to our readers."

The Federalist press picked up this theme. On March 14 a writer in the *Boston Daily Advertiser* stated, "It is one of the most able judgments, I will venture to say, ever delivered in this Court, and when read it will satisfy all minds." Six days later the *Kentucky Gazette* observed, "This interesting decision cannot be too highly appreciated, and it will furnish a happy lesson to local politicians against their right to infringe upon the National Constitution or the laws of Congress. We hope to see no more interference by State Legislators." But the Republican press saw the decision as both a betrayal of the Constitution and a blow to state rights. Their condemnation was lengthy and bitter, attacking both a decision "that prostrates the State sovereignty entirely" and a "Court, above the law and beyond the control of public opinion." The "spirit" of the Constitution, the *Natchez Press* observed, "has been murdered," with the "last vestige of the sovereignty and independence of the individual States composing the National Confederacy . . . obliterated in one fell sweep." It was a decision that reflected "the aristocratical character of the Court," one that "must sooner or later bring down on [its] members . . . the execration of the community."

Comments of this sort were typical and in many respects no different from those engendered by other major decisions of the Marshall Court. But as the weeks passed the nature and scope of both the public and the private commentary intensified in ways that made it clear that *M'Culloch* was indeed different. Some of the ensuing dialogue was a reprise of issues that had been sharply contested during the Constitution's framing and ratification, questions involving the respective rights and authority of nation and states. But these old wounds were exacerbated by an issue that soon engulfed the nation, slavery, with *M'Culloch* serving as a catalyst for pro-slavery factions who feared that the federal government now believed it had the implicit approval of the Court to either limit the scope of that "peculiar institution" or perhaps even eliminate it altogether.

The decision also alarmed those who believed that banks were the tools of the powerful and the source of many evils, not the least of which was the ongoing Panic of 1819. As indicated, the Second Bank at the time had an unfortunate record. The Spencer Report and the lengthy debates in the House that followed it had placed the Bank and banking in the public eye, opening a dialogue within which general opposition to banks was reinforced by the emerging story of the abuses that had taken place, especially in the Baltimore branch. The public was then already inclined to be critical of the Bank. Marshall's opinion was accordingly grounds for concern, given the extent to which it appeared to endorse an institution that seemed unworthy of the trust the Court appeared to invest in it.

Three individuals played especially important roles in generating and structuring the press commentary: William Duane, the editor of the Philadelphia-based *Aurora General Advertiser* and the *Weekly Aurora;* Amos Kendall of Frankfort, Kentucky, the editor and part owner of the *Argus of Western America;* and Hezekiah Niles, the owner and editor of the *Niles Weekly Register.*

William Duane was a bitter foe of the Bank. But his position in these matters was nuanced, for he believed that a national bank under complete government control was a positive force for economic development. That was of course not how either the First or the Second Bank was structured, and Duane had been a harsh critic of the movement to create the Second Bank. In July 1815 he observed in the *Weekly Aurora* that "on the subject of a *national bank,* that is a *bank really national,* we shall be glad to give full room for discussion; but if by a *national bank,* be intended a scheme of *public corruption,* like that which expired a few years ago; we shall consider it our duty to *expose it in the most direct and nonreserved manner.*" The First Bank, Duane argued, had been "falsely denominated the United States Bank." And what was called for was "a bank *truly national,* in which the national interests should predominate, *founded on the domain of the nation, and the public exchequer of treasury.*"

It was accordingly no surprise that Duane was bitterly disappointed when Madison signed the measure creating the Second Bank. "By this act Mr. Madison places his character among the too great number of men, who have, in the decline of years, forfeited all their early claims to an honorable reputation in the affections of the country, or the respect of posterity." The Second Bank in turn became a special source of concern for Duane, both for the fact that it existed and the policies it pursued. Writing as Brutus in September 1818, Duane argued that "the accumulative progression of vice, like the divisibility of matter, seems to expand beyond the power of conception and to surprise us into fresh horror upon every new step, which it makes, toward final punishment and retribution." The Bank was a positive evil, and "in vain will this nefarious institution, attempt through the *connivance* of a corrupt administration, to shake off the overwhelming load of iniquity, that drags it down the channel of popular odium, to final ruin and disgrace."

Duane devoted a substantial number of pages to the Bank as the events of 1819 unfolded. The Spencer Report confirmed what Duane suspected, that the Bank was a "fetid and monstrous abortion of private avarice and political prostitution." The responsibility to act had accordingly passed to Congress. But the report "was eventually entombed in the grave of liberty, by the corrupt and murderous hands or slaves of Mr. Monroe, and the *livery men* of his court." A second major blow was struck when the Court decided *M'Culloch*, a decision Duane denounced on March 22 as "determined by causes disconnected with and wholly foreign from the intrinsic merits of the question."

Duane had discussed the constitutional issues at length in January and February, ostensibly as part of his review of the Spencer Report but likely in anticipation of the Court's consideration of *M'Culloch*. His remarks made it clear that he adhered to the narrow Jeffersonian position, within which the Bank's "necessity" was to be understood as meaning that "those operations [of government] could in no efficient way be accomplished, without its aid and subservience." Duane believed that experience had shown that this was simply not the case. In his estimation the nation had, for example, been able to successfully prosecute the war against Great Britain without the assistance of the Bank. This meant that there must be some other ground for the Court's decision. And while Duane "did not intend to *insinuate* that the judiciary were openly and impudently bribed upon the bank question," it was nevertheless clear to him that "it was self-interest, sir, that wrought this judgment of the *supreme court* against the RIGHTS OF THE PEOPLE and against the LIBERTIES OF THE STATES."

That self-interest was clearly not a financial one. Marshall, for example, had sold the few shares of Bank stock he owned once the case was placed on the Court's docket. The lodestar was rather political, "a judgment in favor of their own passions in this decree of death to our *republican constitution:* for if this bank be constitutional, the suspicion of which alone excites our mockery and derision, this government is neither *free* nor *republican* — neither pure nor popular: It is a *monarchy* — It is a government of gold and ambition — it is any thing evil and may be styled by any evil appellation."

Duane nevertheless saw some hope, for he argued that the Court exercised only a judicial power that in this instance "only terminates all legal disputation between the individual states, and the general government." This was "a mere decision *in law* and nothing more. The *great political* question of the constitutionality of this bank is still open for discussion; or rather, it is to be determined in opposition to the judgment of this *supreme court*." Congress and the people could yet decide for themselves that the Bank was not an appropriate exercise of the national power and, presumably by repeal of the charter, rectify the Court's grave error.

Duane continued the discussion in subsequent issues, offering familiar arguments about the "independence of the several states" and extent to which this was "brought into jeopardy by this vital circumscription of their power." The Constitution, he maintained, would never have been approved had the sorts of federal authority now affirmed been contemplated. And it could not possibly be true that the states, who were in Duane's eyes the source of the very limited sovereign prerogatives delegated to the federal government, "have granted to the *union* a power to destroy them."

These themes were repeated by other Republican critics of the decision. But Duane's critique was notable for the extent to which his rhetoric brought to mind the extreme positions taken by Jefferson on the subjects of the First Bank and the Alien and Sedition Acts. As indicated, in 1792 Jefferson had suggested that if the First Bank opened a branch in Virginia, that constituted "an act of *treason* against the state." In 1798, in turn, in his Kentucky Resolutions he posed the specter of "revolution & blood" as an appropriate response by the states to the Alien and Sedition Acts.

Duane embraced a similar view of *M'Culloch*. "The crime of treason to the *constitution*, and enmity to the country," he wrote, "is sufficiently infamous and derogatory — but to have the sin of ignorance and stupidity to answer for, in addition to this stigma, is a degree of humiliation, which by causing self-debasement, renders the heart callous, and somewhat mitigates the pangs which we naturally feel for prostrated liberty, and a violated constitution." The decision had in turn brought the nation to a precipice:

> The predicament to which the states and the people, are now reduced by this judgment of the supreme court, at the instigation of Mr. Monroe, fairly brings the people, and the government to an issue on the question of *power* and *right — prerogative and liberty!* The government and the people, are now upon this point at open war. One party must succumb — and one party must conquer — both have gone too far to recede. The *revolution* speaks for the people — the usurpations and ambition of Monroe, speaks for the government! It is for the people, and the states to act, once for all — they cannot be reclaimed, when once lost, without the effusion of blood, or a disjunction of the union. The precedent of slavery will be eternally recorded on the passions of the executive — the corruptions, and servility of congress — the opinions of the judiciary, and the debasement of the people — may Heaven avert from the country a disaster so unparalleled in the annals of the world! A disaster so fraught with misery and disgrace to us; and everlasting bondage to our descendants!

Duane was not the only individual to connect *M'Culloch* and the question of slavery, an issue that was very much alive in February and March 1819 as Congress initiated the process that eventually produced the Missouri Compromise. Nor did he stand alone in suggesting that the position the Court embraced risked serious conflicts with the states, perhaps even secession, if taken to its logical conclusion by a Congress emboldened by the Court's recognition of broad and arguably unreviewable federal legislative authority. The commentary in the *Aurora* was nevertheless unique in both its breadth and depth, and certainly conveys a sense of the passions that the decision ignited.

A second major critic was Amos Kendall, the part owner and editor of the *Argus of Western America*, which was published in Frankfort, Kentucky. Kendall was the son of a poor Massachusetts farmer who, in typical American fashion, overcame his origins. He graduated first in his class from Dartmouth College in 1811 and was elected to the honor society Phi Beta Kappa. He studied law for a time but eventually decided to abandon that profession and seek his fortune in the West. He made his way to Kentucky and ultimately settled in Frankfort in 1816, having been persuaded by William Gerard to acquire a half interest in and assume the editorship of the *Argus*.

Kendall subsequently described the decision as a difficult one, "in effect a proposal to abandon all his plans of life and adopt a purely literary and political career." He noted that "political strife had no charms for him; but just then party spirit had died away, and the time was called 'the era of good feelings.'" This seemed to mean, accordingly, that Kendall "would be allowed to indulge his literary taste, without encountering the personality and asperity which had for many years characterized newspaper discussions." But his decision to accept Gerard's offer ultimately had the opposite effect, placing Kendall in the midst of an intensely political landscape within which his editorial voice became prominent and from which he eventually progressed to a series of important positions in the national government.

Gerard was a director of the Bank of Kentucky, and one of the reasons he had for hiring Kendall was his desire to secure the services of someone who could help him counter the plans of the Second Bank to open branches in the state. Kendall was his man. During an earlier stint as editor of the *Georgetown Patriot*, Kendall had supported the creation of the Second Bank, expressing his belief that it was an essential tool for the government. But the Bank's role in precipitating the Panic of 1819 caused him to change his mind, as the resulting depression was especially severe in Kentucky. In October 1818 he delivered a stinging indictment of the Bank, condemning its officials as "brokers, stock-jobbers, and shavers," individuals who administered a "monster" that pursued private profit rather than the national good.

The following January Kendall noted that the Kentucky legislature had passed the measure imposing a tax on the Bank's branches and observed that "after this decisive expression of the wishes and determination of Kentucky, we cannot but hope that the President and Directors of the United States' Bank will promptly take measures to withdraw their Branch from this state." In February in turn he indicated that an application had been filed to prevent the law from going into effect and speculated about what the proper response should be:

If an injunction should be presented, ought the Sergeant of the Court of Appeals to obey it?

Would it not be the duty of the executive to defend the Sergeant in the execution of that act, particularly as he approved it, and is sworn to see the laws executed?

These are solemn questions. We cannot believe, that the branches will have the madness to struggle against the state, nor that their friends will have the madness to aid them in it. But let the people prepare their minds even for this!

Interest in the Kentucky litigation faded as it became clear that the Court would determine the Bank's fate. And on April 2, 1819, when the *Argus* announced that *M'Culloch* had been decided, Kendall declared:

> The broad grounds assumed in this opinion, must be truly alarming to all those who hold sacred the *reserved powers* of the states and the people. It amounts to this — if Congress think it "*convenient*" to clothe the citizens of the states with corporate powers for the collection of the revenue, for the regulation of commerce, or the execution of any other power mentioned in the constitution, they are entirely above the control of the states. In fine, whatever is thought "convenient" by Congress becomes perfectly constitutional.

Kendall believed that this power was subject to abuse: "Some excuse, some pretense of conveniency in carrying into effect specified powers, may be found to justify the incorporation of companies with a monopoly of trade, of individuals for the purpose of farming out the revenue, of companies for the purchase of public lands, and perhaps even of a national church to correct and maintain morality among the people without which none of the specified powers of the constitution could be carried into effect."

Kendall maintained that "the principles assumed in this decision must raise alarm throughout our widely extended empire. They strike at the root of states rights and state sovereignty. The people must rouse from the lap of Delilah and prepare to meet the Philistines." But his proposed response was measured and, certainly by comparison to that of Duane, temperate:

> There must be a fixed, a determined resistance to these encroachments, not of arms, but of the moral energy of a free people. . . .
> We can bear the present usurpation under the continuance of the

bank charter. — But let it not be repeated or extended. — The constitution must be amended, and this should be the substance of such amendment: Congress shall have no power to establish a corporation except within the District of Columbia. This would cut up the evil by the roots. No Bank or other corporation could then be established except by state authority.

Kendall's views in these matters ultimately proved to be extraordinarily important, as he eventually cast his political lot with Andrew Jackson and became one of Jackson's trusted advisers. It is accordingly both significant and hardly surprising that Kendall felt compelled to offer an extensive commentary on the decision and its implications. Those essays appeared under the title "STATE RIGHTS OR A REVIEW of the Opinion of the Supreme Court of the United States on the constitutionality of the Bank of the United States and the right of the states to tax it."

There were eleven essays in all, with the first appearing in the *Argus* on May 7, 1819. In that installment Kendall provided an "introduction" to a discussion "of the highest importance," one that involved "no less than the extent of the powers granted to the nation as well as those reserved to the states under that glorious system of government, the noblest monument of patriotic wisdom, under the influence of which we have so long been peaceful and happy." But the national government, Kendall observed, "is the instrument of the states; its sole object is their preservation and protection." The Court had spoken and misconstrued both the text and its implications. "From the Supreme Court" there was nevertheless "an appeal to the people." And in the essays that followed Kendall structured that appeal, pointing out the errors in the decision and framing the contexts within which they should be assessed.

In the second essay, published on May 14, Kendall traced the history of the dispute, noting that "there was a party in the convention and the country who were favorable to a more energetic system of government than that which was adopted. The proposition to give congress the power to establish corporations and many others of a similar nature, were a part of their system. But every attempt to destroy the sovereignty of the states and establish a more energetic government, was met and defeated by those who better understood the true and permanent interests of the American people." He then argued that a purported Federalist failure to shape the text in the manner they wished carried over into the Washington administration: "Thwarted in the convention they carried their principles into the administration of the government and attempted to effect by the aid of congress, that which they could not accomplish with the consent of the people. At an early period of our government, they obtained an ascendency in every department, and commenced the execution of their plans with confidence and zeal. Hence the original bank, the alien and sedition laws, a standing army, unnecessary taxes, and all the arbitrary measures of the 'reign of terror.'"

These actions, Kendall maintained, produced the Revolution of 1800. Hamilton and his allies "advanced with too rapid strides. The people were alarmed; and driving them from power, intrusted the administration to those who interpreted the constitution, according to the intentions of the parties to that compact." Unfortunately, Kendall observed, that transformation did not extend to the Court, where, as we have seen, Adams had successfully installed John Marshall in the waning days of his administration. And the fruits of that victory remained to this day. "The judiciary could not be so easily and speedily reformed. The principles of the energy system had taken deep root in that department where they still continue to flourish with unabated vigor. Hence the United States Courts have sanctioned every encroachment which congress have made."

Like many others, Kendall argued that the reading the Court now embraced — if it had been known in 1787 — would have made ratification impossible. "Had the constitutionalists in the conventions of New York, Pennsylvania, Virginia or any other state, declared boldly, that Congress would possess the right to exercise implied powers which could neither be defined nor imagined, does any man believe that the federal constitution would ever have been ratified?" He criticized Marshall in particular as someone who was complicit in what was in effect a conspiracy of silence, if indeed the Federalists had actually contemplated such a reading of the text. As part of this he compared Marshall's stance during the Virginia ratification debates with that of Patrick Henry, the state's most ardent Anti-Federalist:

But the difference between the two men was this: Henry wished the state sovereignties preserved — Marshall wished them destroyed;

Henry boldly and frankly declared his position — Marshall was silent; Henry opposed the constitution because he believed Congress might exercise implied powers — Marshall advocated it having the same opinion, although he did not declare it; he heard what he must have believed a false construction put upon this section by its friends, and he would not open their eyes — he wished to see the people deluded and subsequently to take advantage of that delusion.

Kendall also attacked the status now conferred on the Bank. "The creature is clothed with greater powers than the creator, and the states must bow in silence to the authority of the bank in cases where they might rightfully withstand the usurpations of the government." The fact that the Bank was arguably national in character did not impress him: "It is difficult to distinguish between bankers whose business is regulated by the states and those whose business is regulated by the Union. *Banking* is still *their business*, and private gain *their end*." The response to these realities must nevertheless be a peaceful one. "*Disunion* and *consolidation* are the *Scylla* and *Charybdis* which it should be equally our care to observe and avoid." This meant, accordingly, that "as the attempt by congress has been sanctioned by judicial authority, we now have no remedy but a peaceful acquiescence & a speedy amendment to the constitution."

The third major figure in the newspaper responses was Hezekiah Niles, who had also been a consistent critic of the Bank, an institution he believed "deserves not the countenance or support of honest people." Part of this hostility derived from Niles's opposition to paper money, which he believed bore "no kind of proportion to the solid wealth of the nation — nor to the real wants of the people." The "Paper System" was, moreover, closely intertwined with banks, which could make "enormous gains" at the expense of "the miserable dupes" who believed that paper notes had value and were willing to accept them. Niles was also deeply opposed to the Bank itself and applauded when Madison vetoed the first measure presented to him in 1815.

Niles wrote privately, "I doubt both its constitutionality and its expediency." These reservations deepened in 1818 when the Bank began to pursue its policy of contraction, in particular through the refusal of the branches to accept notes issued by other branches. Niles was appalled. On February 28, 1818, he declared, "It was expected that such drafts might always be had — *it was one of the considerations on which the bank was chartered;* the people have a right to *insist* upon it — and they ought to insist upon it, and to have it, 'peaceably if they can, violently if they must.' " Indeed, perhaps aware of the fact that seventeen days earlier Maryland had passed the law that would lead to the *M'Culloch* litigation, he explained this statement in terms that proved prophetic: "By 'violently,' *I mean that the* STATES *should take it up; and tax the mother bank and the branches out of every resting place except* [Washington, D.C.]. In this right of the states is the only hope of safety against the power of the mammoth; and it is well, indeed, that the right exists."

Niles subsequently indicated that he was not unalterably opposed to either the Bank or banking. The true evil, he maintained, lay in the manner in which the system had been implemented. But his support for the notion that the states retained the authority to tax the Bank was clear. In November 1818 he wrote, "We never had any doubt of the right and power of the states to tax the bank of the United States, and should be sorry to doubt it, because in it lies the best, or only, hope of safety." He noted both that Maryland had passed such a tax and that "a suit, we are informed, is about to be carried at once before the superior court of the United States, to test the law of Maryland."

That suit was of course *M'Culloch.* And when the Court announced its decision in March, Niles became one of its most ardent critics. His initial comments appeared on March 13 in the first of a series of articles, "Sovereignty of the States," which began with the declaration that "an insidious dilapidation or violent dismemberment of the American union, together with a consolidation of the reserved rights and powers of the states, is the darling hope that the enemies of liberty, at home and abroad, have hugged to their heart with demoniac fervor and constancy." Writing in the familiar terms of confederacy and limited national authority, Niles declared: "A deadly blow has been struck at the *sovereignty of the states,* and from a quarter so far removed from the people as to be hardly accessible to public opinion — it is needless to say that we allude to the decision of the supreme court, in the case of McCulloh *versus* the state of Maryland, by which it is established that the states cannot tax the bank of the United States." He conceded that "we are yet unacquainted with the grounds of this alarming decision." But, he declared, "of this we are resolved — that nothing but the tongue of an angel can convince us of its compatibility with the constitution of the United States, in which a power to grant acts of incorporation is not delegated, and all powers not delegated are retained."

The Court, Niles observed, consisted of "great and learned men; *but still, only men.*" He believed that these individuals had not simply approved the Bank, but also certain general principles that, while appearing reasonable, nevertheless threatened to undo all the Constitution stood for. "Where are these things to end, and what will be the consequences of them? Every person must see in them a total prostration of the state rights, and the loss of the liberties of the nation, unless the decision turns upon some *point of common* (not CON-STITUTIONAL) law, in the special case that has been before the supreme court." But that did not appear to be the case. This was not the decision of a judge about arguably mundane matters embracing positions and voicing impressions that could and likely would change. It was, rather, one declaring that this was indeed what the Constitution commanded. The only proper response was accordingly a constitutional amendment, to the effect that *"Congress shall not have power to grant articles of incorporation, or vest monopolies, in any person or persons, for any purpose whatsoever, except within the district of Columbia."*

In his next issue Niles published the text of the decision, which he characterized as "more important than any before pronounced by that exalted tribunal." But he also criticized both the Court and Marshall. The former he averred had become "so far removed from the people, that some seem to regard it with a species of that awful reverence in which the inhabitants of Asia look up to their princes." As for Marshall, he declared, "We frankly confess *our* opinion, that the writer of the *opinion* in question, has not added any thing to his stock of reputation by writing it — *it is excessively labored.*"

The second of the *Sovereignty* essays appeared on April 3. "History," Niles observed, "will bear us out that there is a constant disposition in rulers to increase their power and extent of their jurisdiction; and that, if the people do not watch carefully, and sometimes compel a recurrence of the *first principles of government,* by a change of rulers, their liberties will naturally expire." Again disclaiming any intent to "impeach the integrity of the judges of the supreme court," Niles nevertheless made it clear that he believed that *M'Culloch* was "far more dangerous to the union and the happiness of the people of the United States, than anything that we have ever had to fear from *foreign invasion*." He argued that the latitude the decision gave Congress meant that virtually no act, even the most appalling, was beyond contemplation, so long as it could be deemed somehow " 'necessary and proper.' "

In the final installment, published on April 24, Niles opined, "It cannot be believed, that there is a man in the United States who will venture to assert that the constitution would have been ratified, if it had been understood that congress might grant monopolies, or deprive the states of their right to tax property, except as to imports and exports." He noted in some detail the requests made by various states for amendments to the proposed text to make clear the limited nature of federal authority, requests that eventually led to the ratification of the Tenth Amendment. He argued that Hamilton in particular had assured the nation in *Federalist 33* and *Federalist 34* that the Constitution did not in fact limit state authority to levy the sort of tax at issue in *M'Culloch*.

The commentaries in the pages of these three newspapers were typical of the criticisms lodged against the decision. There were, as indicated, individuals and publications that praised *M'Culloch*, but their offerings were neither as frequent nor as detailed as those that opposed it. And in the words of Duane, Kendall, and Niles, one sees both the nature and the extent of the public hostility expressed against the Court and a decision that many believed both preserved an institution unworthy of life and violated certain fundamental principles, the most important of which was the supposed sovereignty of the states.

But as important as these exchanges are, they cannot and should not be considered the last word in these matters, for the decision also provoked the interest of two individuals who had played key roles in the debate about the constitutionality of the First Bank of the United States, James Madison and Thomas Jefferson.

Madison's observations were especially telling. He devoted very little time or space to the Bank itself, preferring instead to focus on an issue that ultimately proved to be far more important, the role of the Court in assessing the validity of federal statutes. In a September 2, 1819, letter to Roane, Madison observed:

But what is of most importance is the high sanction given to a latitude of expounding the Constitution which seems to break down the landmarks intended to by a specification of the Powers of Congress, and to substitute for a definitive connection between the means and ends, a Legislative discretion as to the former to which no practical limit can be assigned. In the great system of Political Economy having for its general object the national welfare, everything is related immediately or remotely to every other thing; and consequently a Power over any one thing, if not limited by some obvious and precise affinity, may amount to a Power over every other.

This was deeply troubling because Madison in particular believed in the importance of checks and balances, the need for the respective departments of government to operate in ways that prevent each other from abusing the powers they were given. He asked accordingly, "Does not the Court also relinquish by their doctrine, all controul on the Legislative exercise of unconstitutional powers? According to that doctrine, the expediency and constitutionality of means for carrying into effect a specified Power are convertible terms; and Congress are admitted to be Judges of the expediency. The Court certainly cannot be so; a question, the moment it assumes the character of mere expediency or policy, being evidently beyond the reach of Judicial cognizance."

Madison's remarks bore directly on one of the major current constitutional disputes, the nature and scope of judicial review. For *M'Culloch*'s importance is not confined to the question of implied powers, as important as that might be. It is also a key element in the debate about the Court's role in our democratic system of government and, in particular, the extent to which it can or should serve as a check on Congress.

Jefferson in turn praised Roane's contributions. In a September 6, 1819, letter to Roane he noted, "I have read in the Enquirer, and with great approbation, the pieces signed Hampden. . . . They contain the true principles of the revolution of 1800, for that was as real a revolution in the principles of our government as that of 1776 was in its form." He criticized the Court's holding, observing that "the Constitution, on this hypothesis, is a mere thing of wax in the hands of the judiciary, which they may twist and shape into any form they please." Jefferson also made it clear that he was unwilling to accept the notion that the Court should have the final word on constitutional questions. "My construction of the Constitution is very different from that you quote. It is that each department is truly independent of the others, and has an equal right to decide for itself what is the meaning of the Constitution in the cases submitted for its action; and especially, where it is to act ultimately and without appeal."

Jefferson wrote Roane again on June 27, 1821, noting that "I have read with great satisfaction Colonel Taylor's book of 'Constructions Construed,' and I will say, with edification; for I acknowledge it corrected some errors of opinion into which I had slidden without sufficient examination." That book, he declared, "is the most logical retraction of our governments to the original and true principles of the Constitution creating them, which has appeared since the adoption of that instrument. I may not perhaps concur in all its opinions, great and small; for no two men ever thought alike on so many points. But on all its important questions, it contains the true political faith, to which every catholic republican should steadfastly hold."

John Taylor was an ardent state rights advocate and prolific spokesman for that position. As indicated, in the 1790s he had taken Jefferson's side in the quarrel with Hamilton about the First Bank and had written a pamphlet that both denied the authority of the government to create that institution and criticized it as an entity. He eventually wrote a number of important books examining the Constitution and explaining at considerable length the Republican theory of state rights. One of them, *An Inquiry into the Principle and Policy of the Government of the United States* (1814), has been described as "brilliantly express[ing] the conception of American politics that had emerged from the Revolutionary era." Unfortunately, his writing style left much to be desired. Indeed, one supporter lamented that Taylor seemed unable to express himself in English.

The book Jefferson praised, *Construction Construed, and Constitutions Vindicated,* was nominally about *M'Culloch* and examined the decision at great, albeit often tedious, length. But as Thomas Ritchie, the editor of the *Richmond Enquirer,* made clear in prefatory remarks that appeared in the volume, Taylor also had a wider aim, to combat any inference that *M'Culloch* meant that Congress could appropriately resolve the questions posed by slavery.

Taylor's general philosophy was that of Jefferson and his Republican allies. He complained, for example, of the "habit of corrupting our political system, by the instrumentality of inference, convenience and necessity." Sovereignty resides with "the people of each state, by whom it has been and may be exercised" and does not belong "to the people of the United States, by whom it never has been nor can be exercised." Banks in turn are evil, and "A catalogue of the immoral tendencies of banking ought to be awful to a republican government, which many great writers assert to be incapable of subsisting long, except by the preservation of virtuous principles."

Taylor's attacks on the Court were sharp and contained echoes of positions previously embraced by Jefferson and Duane. He asked, "Which can do most harm to mankind, constrictive treasons or constructive powers? The first takes away the life of an individual, the second destroys the liberty of a nation. The machine called inference can act as extensively in one case as in the other." And he excoriated Marshall and his colleagues for sanctioning the notion of implied powers, observing:

> As ends may be made to beget means, so means may be made to beget ends, until the co-habitation shall rear a progeny of unconstitutional bastards, which were not begotten by the people; and their rights being no longer secured by fixed principles, will be hazarded upon a game at shuttlecock with ends and means, between the general and the state governments. To prevent this, means as well as ends are subjected by our constitution to a double restraint. The first is special. In many instances, the means for executing the powers bestowed, are defined, and by that definition, limited. The other is general, and arises necessarily from the division of powers; as it was never intended that powers given to one department, or one government, should be impaired or destroyed, by the means used for the execution of powers given to another. Otherwise, the indefinite word "means" might defeat all labour expended upon definition by our constitution.

Taylor's observations on the subject of slavery were especially telling, both for their support of each state's right to determine that issue and the extent to which he connected it to the Bank and banking. He declared that "one portion of the union is afflicted by negro slavery; therefore, make it tributary to capitalists. Cultivation by slaves is unprofitable; therefore, make it tributary to capitalists. The freedom of labour deprives it of the benefit of being directed by intelligence; therefore, subject it to capitalists. Taxation is preferable to economy; therefore, enhance it for the nourishment of capitalists, and the gratification of avarice." He predicted the logical outcome of these matters in a passage that proved tellingly prescient: "Let us recite the succession of events. The great pecuniary favour granted by congress to certificate-holders, begat banking; banking begat bounties to manufacturing capitalists; bounties to manufacturing capitalists begat an oppressive pension list; these particularities united to begat the Missouri project; that project begat the idea of using slavery as an instrument for effecting a balance of power; when it is put in operation, it will beget new usurpations of internal powers over persons and property, and those will beget a dissolution of the union."

The public exchanges about *M'Culloch* were sharp and protracted and far more extensive than this brief summary indicates. In them the participants revisited and in many instances advanced a dialogue that had been virtually continuous since the Constitution was proposed, debated, and ratified. As such, they provide ample evidence of the importance of the decision to both the people who participated in fashioning it and those who were then and are today subject to the rules of law it imposed.

CHAPTER 9

The Second Bank

Redemption and Ruin

In March 1819 the Second Bank was at a crossroad. Marshall and his brethren had handed it an important victory, holding both that it was a necessary and proper exercise of federal authority and that the states could not interfere with it as it went about its business. A second but no less notable reprieve had been granted by Congress. The report of the Spencer Committee had detailed a number of crucial failings on the part of the Bank and many of its officials. But the House as a whole rebuffed attempts to revoke the Bank's charter, and the committee's instinct that corrective action could be achieved within the system eventually proved to be entirely correct.

It was clear that reforms were called for. The first critical decision was to replace the weak and unfortunate William Jones with a strong and respected new president, Langdon Cheves, who was confirmed as president of the Second Bank on March 6, 1819, the same day Marshall issued his opinion in *M'Culloch*.

The situation when Cheves took office was dire. The policies pursued by Jones had brought the Bank to the brink of financial and political ruin. Irresponsible decisions by many branches, especially in the South and West, had drained the Bank of most of its specie and imposed financial obligations it could not possibly meet. As Cheves noted in 1822 in *Exposition*, a document he prepared on these matters, "The southern offices were remitting tardily and the western offices not at all. All the resources of the bank would not have sustained it in this course and mode of business another month!!" What Cheves characterized as "stupendous fraud" committed by a number of directors and officers — especially in the Baltimore branch — had come to light, confirming the suspicions of the Bank's critics that it was a thoroughly corrupt institution.

Cheves moved aggressively to cure the problems and eventually placed the Bank on a sound financial footing. As he subsequently observed:

> These measures, simple and obvious as they are, and some of them so strangely overlooked so long, lifted the bank in the short space of 70 days (from 6 March to 17 May) from the extreme prostration which has been described, to a state of safety and even some degree of power, enabled it to cease its curtailments, except at points where it had an excess of capital, to defy all the attacks upon it, and to sustain other institutions which wanted aid and were ascertained to be solvent; above all, to establish the soundness of the currency which had just before been deemed hopeless; and, in a single season of business (the first) to give every office as much capital as it could advantageously employ.

Cheves's assessment of the economic consequences of his initial actions was sound. Under his leadership the Bank began to pursue a systematic and responsible course of action that allowed it to fulfill the financial promise envisioned by the individuals who sought its creation. But his judgment that the measures he undertook would also allow the Bank to "defy all the attacks upon it" was misplaced. There were two principal reasons for this: the consequences of the frauds committed, and the continuing hostility exhibited by various segments of the body politic.

The Spencer Report made it quite clear that various directors and officers of the Bank had abused their positions of trust and pursued individual financial gain, often in ways that constituted fraud against the Bank. In Baltimore, in particular, James M'Culloh used his position as cashier to mask the activities of him and his partners, James A. Buchanan and George Williams. Cheves knew when he took office that there were problems and that they were especially acute in Baltimore. In his *Exposition* he noted, "In the office at Baltimore of which James A. Buchanan was president, and J. W. M'Culloh was cashier, there were near three millions of dollars discounted or appropriated, without any authority, and without the knowledge of the board of the office, or that of the parent bank!" But he professed that when he became president, "I had not the faintest idea that [the Bank's] power had been so completely prostrated, or that it had been thus unfortunately managed or grossly defrauded."

Cheves purged the Bank of many of the individuals who either were unable to discharge their duties appropriately or who viewed their positions as an opportunity for personal enrichment. M'Culloh, for example, was dismissed from his post in May 1819, having engaged in frauds that, as Cheves put it, were at "the immense sum of 1,671,221 dollars 87 cents." That reality prompted Luther Martin, perhaps smarting from his defeat in *M'Culloch*, to initiate an investigation into these matters, which eventually resulted in indictments in Maryland state court against M'Culloh, Buchanan, and Williams. Martin was not able to bring the case to trial, having suffered the massive stroke that effectively ended his legal career. Nor did the legal proceedings, which became known as the Conspiracy Trials, come to a successful conclusion, unless of course one embraced the position of M'Culloh and his colleagues. For in 1823 the three were acquitted.

As important as these matters were, they were nevertheless simply one subset of the wider story of the affairs of the Second Bank in the wake of *M'Culloch*. For while the Supreme Court had spoken, and had pronounced the Bank both "necessary and proper," its political enemies refused to accept that verdict. With one notable exception, that of Hezekiah Niles (whose change of heart did not come until at least 1828), the major opponents of the Bank continued to wage a campaign against it.

Some of these responses were political. In Virginia the House of Delegates approved a measure that expressed its "concern and alarm" about *M'Culloch* and summoned "the spirit of 98." It characterized the decision as one "calculated to undermine the pillars of the constitution itself, and sap the foundations and rights of the state governments." The resolution indicated that "the General Assembly denies to the supreme court of the United States the right to impair or construe away the sovereign authorities reserved to the states or the people." It stated that the House might have remained silent if the Court had sustained the continuation of the Bank as a matter of financial expediency. But the Court had not done so. Rather, Marshall had articulated "principles of such universal extent, and such alarming tendency, not called for by the particular case, but calculated to open a door, through which the dearest rights that belong to the states, may be *invaded*." The resolution therefore asked that Virginia's two U.S. senators secure an amendment to the Constitution that would "create a separate tribunal for the decision of all questions, in which the powers and authorities of the general government and those of the states . . . are in *conflict*." It urged them to resist the passage of any measures that were inconsistent with "the resolutions and report adopted by the General Assembly of Virginia in their sessions of 1798 and 1799."

The proposed amendment did not materialize. But the nature and identity of the sorts of measures that the House of Delegates contemplated became quite clear in a second resolution that secured the support of the full General Assembly on February 1, 1820. That measure expressed the belief "that the effort, which is now making, to impose upon [the people of Missouri], as one of the conditions of their admission, an unalterable inhibition of slavery, is forbidden, by good faith, by the constitution of the United States, and by considerations intimately connected with the tranquility and welfare of the nation." It made it clear that there was a distinct connection between this issue and *M'Culloch*, noting that the "general grant of power, to make all laws necessary and proper to carry delegated powers into effect, has been resorted to, for the purpose of sustaining the right" to impose conditions on Missouri's admission. It declared that if Congress were to proceed as proposed, that would "be attended with serious and extensive evils . . . pervading the whole confederacy."

Ohio also joined the fray, albeit in a more proactive manner. As indicated, Ohio was one of the states that had passed measures designed to force the Bank to cease operations within that state, imposing a tax of $50,000 a year on each of the Bank's two branches. That act passed on February 8, 1819, just before *M'Culloch* came to the Court. Ohio officials initially seemed to proceed with caution and did not attempt to collect the tax. But public hostility toward the Bank was such that the state auditor, Ralph Osborn, was eventually ordered to collect the tax when it became due on September 15, 1819. Two days later, three state agents appeared at the Bank's branch in Chillicothe and confiscated more than $100,000 in cash and bank notes, funds that were eventually deposited in the state treasury in Columbus.

The Bank knew that these events were in the offing and went to federal court to secure a temporary injunction against enforcement of the state act. In doing so, it relied on a provision in its charter that "made [it] able and capable in law . . . to sue and be sued, plead and be impleaded, answer and be answered, defend and be defended in all

State Courts having competent jurisdiction, and in any Circuit Court of the United States." An order was issued requiring that the state return the money, which it refused to do. Osborn was then arrested and the keys to the treasury confiscated, with federal agents entering that facility and seizing the Bank's funds. Ohio appealed the circuit court order, arguing to the Supreme Court that both the presence of the Bank in the state and its various actions had violated the state's sovereignty.

The evolving state position in these matters was expressed in an article that appeared in the *Steubenville Herald* in October:

> The doctrines set up by the court, on that occasion, are such as the people of this state, so long as they determine to preserve their rights, cannot recognize as correct. If a case decided, an agreed case, — in which this State is not a party, can be considered binding upon this State, if such a decision is to suspend the force and operation of our laws legally, regularly and constitutionally enacted, what are our boasted privileges? . . . We complain that in the case of *M'Culloch v. Maryland*, matters have been conceded by the latter, or rather, many of the strongest grounds were relinquished or not brought into view, on which this State meant to reply. The State of Ohio does not admit that a case between two parties, collusively or ignorantly agreed upon, is or ought to be binding on any other party.

This political position became the official posture of the state in December, when a committee of the Ohio legislature issued a report declaring that "upon the promulgation of [*M'Culloch*], it is maintained that it became the duty of the State and its officers to acquiesce, and to treat the act of the Legislature as a dead letter. The Committee have considered this position, and are not satisfied that it is a correct one."

The matter was formally litigated in February 1820, when Supreme Court justice Thomas Todd, sitting as a circuit judge, held that the injunction was proper — that is, that the Bank did indeed have the authority to bring the legal action — and that Ohio did not have the authority to tax the Bank. The inevitable appeal was initially set for argument before the Court in its February 1823 Term. But another case involving the state of Georgia had arisen, prompted by a state act that barred the redemption of state bank notes for specie in most circumstances. That had the effect of preventing the Bank from redeeming any of the state notes that it held. The Bank sued when one state bank, the Planters' Bank of Georgia, refused to redeem notes that the Bank held. Georgia argued the Eleventh Amendment in defense, maintaining that the Bank's status as holder of the note had been derived from and was in essence that of a citizen of Georgia, making this the sort of suit between private parties that seemed to fall within the prohibition voiced by the amendment.

Recognizing that the Planters' Bank case had implications for the Ohio proceeding, the Court asked that it be reargued on March 10 and 11, 1824. The Court then issued its decision on March 19, 1824. The opinion in *Osborn v. The President, Directors, and Company of the Bank of the United States* was written by Chief Justice Marshall and had the support of all members of the Court except Justice Johnson. A portion of it was devoted to the question for which the case is now studied, whether the Bank could actually bring the action. That authority was affirmed given Article III's express recognition that federal courts had jurisdiction in cases "arising under this Constitution, the Laws of the United States, and Treaties made, or which shall be made, under their Authority." Since the Bank had been created by an act of Congress, and since Congress had expressly empowered the Bank to initiate legal proceedings, Marshall held that the federal courts had the power to hear the case. The fact that the heart of the dispute involved a question of state law did not matter.

Marshall then turned to the Eleventh Amendment issue, one that had not been raised or discussed in *M'Culloch* but had been considered three years earlier in another Marshall opinion, *Cohens v. Virginia* (1821). That case arose when Philip and Mendes Cohen brought a test case against a Virginia statute when they sold tickets for a national lottery at the Norfolk branch office of a Baltimore firm. The Cohens admitted that they sold the tickets and that this action violated state law. But they argued that in 1802 Congress had authorized lotteries in the District of Columbia and that the federal statute barred enforcement of the Virginia measure, since the tickets in question were for a lottery whose proceeds were for the construction of a city hall in Washington.

The case in some respects presented a reprise of *Martin v. Hunter's Lessee*, the 1815 decision in which the Court held that it had the authority to consider and reverse a decision of the Virginia courts. But it was also different in fundamentally important respects, for *Martin* had involved the comparatively simple matter of appellate review of a civil law question. *Cohens* posed a much greater threat to state sovereignty, as the state court decision that Virginia now tried to defend involved a matter of criminal law, an area within which state prerogatives were especially pronounced.

Once again, Virginia argued that the Court did not have jurisdiction. And once again, this time speaking through John Marshall, the Court rejected that claim. Marshall noted that Article III clearly granted jurisdiction in "all Cases, in Law and Equity, arising under the Constitution." This was just such a case. Neither Virginia's general claim of immunity nor its invocation of the Eleventh Amendment as a bar to the suit could be accepted. The Constitution had been conceived and ratified as a means of preserving the nation. As part of that process, the states had surrendered certain aspects of their sovereignty. And the federal courts had an essential role to play in this process. The federal judiciary "is authorized to decide all cases of every description, arising under the constitution or laws of the United States. From this general grant of jurisdiction, no exception is made for those cases in which a State may be a party."

In *Osborn*, in turn, Marshall argued that the approach taken by the state, if accepted, would hamstring the federal government. He stressed that it was appropriate to "pause for a moment, and reflect on the relative situation of the Union with its members, should the objection prevail." If that happened, "Each member of the Union [would be] capable, at its will, of attacking the nation, of arresting its progress at every step, of acting vigorously and effectually in the execution of its designs, while the nation stands naked, stripped of its defensive armour, and incapable of shielding its agent or executing its laws, otherwise than by proceedings which are to take place after the mischief is perpetrated, and which must often be ineffectual, from the inability of the agents to make compensation." Phrased in this manner, Marshall's nationalist conclusion was obvious. The Eleventh Amendment should not serve as a bar. More to the point, the action had been brought against the agents of the state rather than the state itself. As such, it did not implicate the state and its sovereignty.

The key question in *Osborn* was, then, the question of constitutionality. Marshall noted that "a revision of [*M'Culloch*] has been requested; and many considerations combine to induce a review of it." One of these was the argument that the Bank was in fact a private corporation. But Marshall maintained that was not the case. "The Bank is not considered a private corporation, whose principal object is individual trade and individual profit; but as a public corporation, created for public and national purposes." Indeed, the "whole opinion" of the Court in *M'Culloch* was "founded on, and sustained by, the idea that the Bank is an instrument which is 'necessary and proper for carrying into effect the powers vested in the government of the United States.'"

Marshall discussed in some detail the ways in which the Bank was "an instrument . . . for carrying on the fiscal operations of government." He then emphasized, "If the trade of the Bank be essential to its character, as a machine for the fiscal operations of the government, that trade must be as exempt from State control as the actual conveyance of the public money." The Bank was both an appropriate instrument of federal policy and protected from the interference of the states:

> Considering the capacity of carrying on the trade of banking, as an important feature in the character of this corporation, which was necessary, to make it a fit instrument for the objects for which it was created, the Court adheres to its decision in the case of *M'Culloch* against *The State of Maryland*, and is of the opinion, that the act of the State of Ohio, which is certainly much more objectionable than that of the State of Maryland, is repugnant to a law of the United States, made in pursuance of the constitution, and, therefore, void.

The *Osborn* decision did not provoke the sort of response that followed *M'Culloch*. The Court entered a decree ordering that the funds be returned, and the attorneys for the two sides consulted and agreed on a way to implement the Court's mandate. The Ohio legislature then abandoned its objections and passed a measure appropriating the necessary amount of money. Other cases involving the Bank came before the Court over the next several years. None of them, however, posed the sort of challenge that came with *Osborn*, and with that decision the Court ceased to be a major player in the life and story of the Second Bank.

Cheves resigned in 1823 and was replaced by Nicholas Biddle, who stayed at the helm for the remainder of the Bank's life. Biddle was a native of Philadelphia, the son of a wealthy merchant and a member of an old, distinguished family. He was secure in his intellectual gifts and understood that he was neither a banker nor a businessman. But he believed that that sort of experience did not matter. Indeed, he thought that such a background might well be a burden. In a letter written in 1822 to one of the other directors of the Bank, Biddle stated that what he believed was called for was a "*talent* for business rather than what is commonly called a man of business." "The fact is," he observed, "that the misfortunes of the Bank which grew principally out of the injudicious extension of the Western Branches were actually occasioned by the men of business & their errors were precisely the faults into which men of business were likely to fall."

Biddle was strong-willed and intemperate, but he also had considerable intelligence and charm. These characteristics served him alternately badly and well over the next several years as he doggedly pursued what he believed to be the nation's best interests, above all, a strong Bank of the United States to settle the American economy, stabilize the currency, and counter what proved to be the inflationary pressures of an era of rapid growth and expansion. The Second Bank became Biddle's Bank. The 1820s, in turn, became a critical and positive period for a Bank that was widely seen as an essential part of the government's financial program. Unfortunately, the Bank also had an implacable foe who would soon be in a position to translate his hostility toward banking in general and the Bank in particular into official government policy. That man was Andrew Jackson.

Jackson ran for president in 1824 and secured the highest number of both popular and electoral votes. But there were four candidates — Jackson, John Quincy Adams, William Crawford, and Henry Clay — and none of them had secured a majority. That threw the election into the House of Representatives, where Adams, who had finished second in the vote, prevailed with the support of Clay. Jackson believed that his victory had been stolen from him. His anger carried over to the 1828 contest, which Jackson won, defeating Adams by a substantial margin. The campaign was a bitter one, within which personalities dominated over issues, and allegations of immorality and corruption formed the basis for much of what transpired.

With Jackson's election Biddle and the rest of the Bank's supporters understood that the government was now in the hands of a potential enemy, an individual who had on various occasions expressed constitutional, economic, and political reservations about the Bank. And they were correct, for the Bank became the defining issue of the Jackson presidency.

Jackson did not mention the Bank in his first inaugural address. But he did invoke the rhetoric of state rights, observing that "in such measures as I may be called on to pursue in regard to the rights of the separate States I hope to be animated by a proper respect for those sovereign members of our Union, taking care not to confound the powers they have reserved to themselves with those they have granted to the Confederacy." He repeated this theme in the first annual message. "That this was intended to be a government of limited and specific, and not general powers," he reminded everyone, "must be admitted by all, and it is our duty to preserve it for the character intended by the framers." And, he declared, "Both the constitutionality and the expediency of the law creating this bank are well questioned by a large portion of our fellow-citizens, and it must be admitted by all that it has failed in the great end of establishing a uniform and sound currency."

Jackson's characterizations were telling. *M'Culloch* may have purported to settle the constitutional questions, but in Jackson's estimation these were now subject to "question." The Bank itself in turn was not "expedient." In particular, it had not over its thirteen-year life achieved perhaps the most important goal assigned to it, a sound and uniform currency. This was music to the ears of many key figures, for Jackson and a number of his close allies were fervent both in their support for hard money and in their disdain for the Bank. Congress did not agree and passed measures that signaled its strong support for the Bank. None of this mattered. Jackson dismissed two committee reports in this vein as "feeble" and the products of the Bank's pernicious influence. He then suggested, in his third annual message in December 1831, that the matter should now be left to an "enlightened people," which indicated quite clearly, for those who paid close attention, that the Bank was about to become a political football. Indeed, both sides in the impending presidential election clearly wanted that to be the case.

Henry Clay, Jackson's opponent in 1832, needed an issue on which he could draw a sharp contrast between himself and Jackson. The Bank clearly offered one, and Clay believed that the people were on his side in this matter. That judgment was not far-fetched, as the Bank enjoyed widespread support, consistent with its generally positive record. But Clay badly underestimated Jackson's appeal within the body politic, and his instincts in these matters proved fatal for both his candidacy and the Bank.

Clay pressed Biddle to seek early renewal of the Bank's charter. He believed deeply that the Bank was a necessary and appropriate part of a sound financial system. As the champion of what became known as the American System, Clay had argued that three things were essential to the economic welfare of the nation. The first was a protective tariff, that is, a tax on imported goods that would both shield American business and manufacturing and provide a source of revenue. The second was a program of internal improvement, through which the infrastructure necessary for commerce and manufacturing to flourish would be provided. The final ingredient was a national bank, which would both promote economic control and facilitate the development and maintenance of a sound national currency.

Clay told Biddle that "the friends of the Bank expect the application to be made," and Biddle refused to listen to those who counseled restraint. In January 1832, petitions seeking recharter were introduced in both the House and the Senate. The ensuing debate was protracted and bitter. The measure came to a vote in the Senate on June 11, 1832, passing by a vote of 28 to 20. The House in turn approved the bill on July 3, 107 to 85. Biddle stated at the time, "I congratulate our friends most cordially upon this most satisfactory result. Now for the President. My belief is that the President will veto the bill though this is not generally known or believed."

Biddle was correct. Jackson did plan to veto the measure, and the only open question was whether he would fashion that message in ways that would allow a different version of a bank bill to gain his support. Although a number of individuals in his cabinet urged that course, Jackson did not take it. It was initially believed that Roger Taney was the dominant force in drafting the veto message, but it is now clear that an old foe of the Bank, Amos Kendall, had that role. "Providence," Jackson told Kendall, "has had a hand in bringing forward the subject at this time, to preserve the republic from its thraldom and corrupting influence." Kendall and Jackson accordingly crafted the veto in a way designed to "leave the Subject *open* for the decision of the people at their next Election."

Jackson delivered his veto message on July 10, 1832. He conceded at the outset that "a bank of the United States is in many respects convenient for the Government and useful to the people." But "some of the powers and privileges possessed by the existing bank are unauthorized by the Constitution, subversive to the rights of the States, and dangerous to the liberties of the people." It was for these reasons, he observed, that he had at the beginning of his administration expressed those views and had sought the creation of "an institution combining all its advantages and obviating these objections." The measure now before him, however, did not fulfill those expectations. Instead, it preserved both a "monopoly" and "exclusive privileges" that represented a disservice to the people and an imposition on the states. In particular, it held open the possibility of foreign influence and control, a state of affairs that could become especially troubling in the event of a war with a nation that might be in a position to influence the conduct and policies of the Bank.

These and other structural indictments were important. But the key passages of the veto message dealt with the inevitable question, was the Bank constitutional? "It is maintained by the advocates of the bank that its constitutionality in all its features ought to be considered as settled by precedent and by the decision of the Supreme Court." But, Jackson declared, "Mere precedent is a dangerous source of authority, and should not be regarded as deciding questions of constitutional power except where the acquiescence of the people and the States can be considered as well settled." That had not happened. Various Congresses had voted for and against the Bank. The states had in turn expressed their opposing views in "legislative, judicial, and executive opinions against the bank [that] have been probably to those in its favor as 4 to 1." But even if the Court had in *M'Culloch* "covered the whole ground of this act," that did not matter:

The Congress, the Executive, and the Court must each for itself be guided by its own opinion of the Constitution. Each public officer who takes an oath to support the Constitution swears that he will support it as he understands it, and not as it is understood by others. It is as much the duty of the House of Representatives, of the Senate, and of the President to decide upon the constitutionality of any bill or resolution which may be presented to them for passage or approval as it is of the supreme judges when it may be brought to them for judicial decision. The opinion of the judges has no more authority over Congress than the opinion of Congress has over the judges, and on that point the President is independent of both. The authority of the Supreme Court must not, therefore, be permitted to control the Congress or the Executive when acting in their legislative capacities, but to have only such influence as the force of their reasoning may deserve.

Jackson went on at some length, arguing in particular that a bank in the form proposed was neither "necessary" nor "proper" as those terms should be understood: "There is nothing in its legitimate functions which makes it necessary or proper. Whatever interest or influence, whether public or private, has given birth to this act, it can not be found either in the wishes or necessities of the executive department, by which present action is deemed premature, and the powers conferred upon its agent not only unnecessary, but dangerous to the Government and the country." He emphasized the implications of both a bank and *M'Culloch* for the sovereignty of the states. "Upon the formation of the Constitution," he stressed, "the States guarded their taxing power with particular jealousy. They surrendered it only as regards imports and exports." Jackson conceded that "the States can not rightfully tax the operations of the General Government." But that was not this case. The Bank was a private entity. And *M'Culloch*'s holding on the subject of taxation effected a "subversion of one of the strongest barriers which secured [the states] against federal encroachments."

These were important observations. But the heart of Jackson's veto was clearly his attempt to minimize the role and influence of the Court, and his position represented a stark challenge to its authority. It was also arguably out of character for Jackson himself, as in 1822 he had declared that "all the rights secured to the citizens under the constitution is worth nothing, and a mere buble, except guaranteed them by an independent and virtuous Judiciary." Jackson may well have believed this. But in 1832 he viewed *M'Culloch* not as a case in which the Court did its "imperious duty," but rather one within which it was simply imperious, the enemy of the people and of state rights. Of course, the Bank veto was a political message, not a legal one. And in his closing words in that document, Jackson made it quite clear that the veto and the justifications for it were directed toward the people and not a court of law: "I have now done my duty to my country. If sustained by my fellow citizens, I shall be grateful and happy; if not, I shall find in the motives which impel me ample grounds for contentment and peace."

The people delivered their verdict in two parts. They spoke initially through Congress, which refused to overturn the veto in spite of the best efforts of people like Webster and Clay. That led to the second phase of their response, in which they overwhelmingly approved Jackson's request for a second term. Jackson viewed this victory as a referendum on the Bank and believed that he now had the authorization to proceed as he wished. "Whatever may be the opinion of others," he declared, "the President considers his reelection as a decision of the people against the bank." That may or may not have been the case as an actual matter. There were other issues in the election, and Jackson himself enjoyed a degree of individual popularity that counted for a great deal in how matters played out. But the Bank and the veto were clearly important considerations and factored greatly in both campaign rhetoric and public commentary.

More to the point, what truly mattered was what Jackson believed. The veto had dealt the Bank a strong blow, albeit not necessarily a fatal one. That came when Jackson set in motion the process that led to the withdrawal of all government funds on deposit with the Bank. The House of Representatives held hearings on these matters in February 1833 examining both the question of the security of the government funds and whether the government should sell its stock. It rendered its verdict on March 2 when it voted overwhelmingly, 109 to 46, that Jackson was wrong. The government funds were safe, the House declared, and the government should keep its stock.

Once again Jackson did not care. As he made clear in a paper, *Re-*

moval of the Public Deposits, that he read to his cabinet, the Bank had "dangerous tendencies" and was both "inexpedient and unconstitutional." He had submitted these questions to the people. "Can it now be said that the question of a recharter of the bank was not decided at the election which ensued?" The deposits would be removed.

Unfortunately, the Bank's charter stipulated that only the secretary of the Treasury had the authority to do this. And the incumbent, Louis McLane, refused. McLane was accordingly made secretary of State and a new Treasury secretary, William J. Duane, was installed in June. Duane was a prominent Philadelphia lawyer and the son of the same William Duane who as editor of the *Aurora* had waged a bitter campaign against the Bank. But in September, when told to initiate the process of withdrawal, Duane also refused. He made it clear that this did not reflect newfound support for the Bank. Like his father, he had always opposed the Bank and remained of that mind. But Duane knew that the House had found that the government funds were secure, and he believed that withdrawing them from the Bank would cause significant problems, "shak[ing] public confidence and promot[ing] doubt and mischief in the operations of society."

The solution was obvious. Duane, too, had to go, with Roger Brooke Taney as the logical choice to succeed him. Taney was a key figure in both the Bank War and the history of the Court. The son of Maryland planters, he was educated at Dickinson College in Pennsylvania and then entered the practice of law, fashioning a career within which legal and political advancement were intertwined. Taney supported Jackson in 1824 and in 1828 he was instrumental in securing Maryland for the now victorious candidate. That loyalty paid off in 1831 when Jackson offered Taney the position of attorney general in his reconfigured cabinet. And as one of Jackson's confidants, he became a primary voice for a limited conception of federal authority.

Duane refused to sign the removal order, so Jackson fired him, sending him a letter on September 23 declaring that "your further services as Secretary of the Treasury are no longer required." Jackson then gave Taney a recess appointment, a device that allows presidents to fill vacancies on a temporary basis when Congress is not in session. Taney appointed Kendall as the special agent to oversee the withdrawal, which was accomplished in two ways. As of October 1, all future federal deposits were placed in seven state banks, which became known as the Pet Banks. The daily operating expenses of the government were in turn to be paid by drawing on the funds held by the Bank until none remained.

The removal of the deposits was widely decried and provoked extensive debate in Congress. One result was the refusal of the Senate to confirm Taney in his post. The Senate also passed two resolutions highly critical of Jackson and Taney. The first, which was approved on February 5, 1834, characterized the reasons offered for removal as "unsatisfactory and insufficient." The second was more telling, for on March 28, 1834, the Senate formally censured Jackson for his actions. This provoked a stunned president to lodge a protest against an action he characterized as inconsistent with "the spirit of the Constitution and with the plainest dictates of humanity and justice." And when Jackson remained unrepentant and defiant in the wake of the censure, this posture both cemented his reputation with the people and, in the minds of many, enhanced the power of the presidency by making it clear that that individual could and would operate independently of Congress when he deemed it essential to do so.

The removal of the federal deposits from the Bank marked the beginning of a certain end for that institution. Various petitions and memorials were submitted to Congress and the administration asking that the charter be renewed, but nothing came of them. Biddle in turn responded by contracting the money supply, in theory as a way by which to begin winding up the affairs of the Bank but most likely as his declaration of war against the administration. This had a negative impact on the economy. When a group of individuals complained to Jackson in 1834 that they had become insolvent, his response made it clear where the blame should be laid. "What do you come to me for, then? Go to Nicholas Biddle. We have no money here, gentlemen. Biddle has all the money. He has millions of specie in his vaults at this moment, lying idle, and yet you come to me to save you from breaking."

Jackson's strategy worked. Public opinion now turned completely against the Bank, finding expression in four resolutions passed by the House of Representatives in April 1834. The House declared that it would not recharter the Bank, that the public funds should not be restored, that the state banks were a safe and appropriate repository for federal funds, and that a committee should be formed to investigate the Bank and determine the causes of the economic panic of 1833–1834. Jackson noted in a letter to his son that these votes "put to death, that mamouth of corruption and power, the Bank of the United States." Biddle did not give up, and there were further skirmishes. But in 1835 the Bank began the slow and deliberate process of winding up its affairs. And on March 4, 1836, the charter of the Second Bank expired.

CHAPTER 10

M'Culloch Triumphant

"The death of the Bank was a significant victory for Jackson. He had, after all, vanquished an institution that he hated. Whether this was a true victory for the nation was a different matter entirely. The Second Bank was not perfect. But it had put the troubles it had experienced under William Jones behind it and had become a vital part of the economic and governance systems. And the absence of a central banking and economic authority would prove increasingly troubling as the years passed.

The Bank's demise left only *M'Culloch*, and Jackson and his allies set their sights on removing that judicial stain from the books. John Marshall passed away on July 6, 1835, and Jackson's choice for his successor, Roger Taney, was now chief justice of the United States. Jackson had also been able to make a number of other appointments to the Court, and he and his allies sensed the opportunity to change course.

Senator Thomas Hart Benton of Missouri laid the foundations for what the Jacksonians hoped would become a full-blown assault on *M'Culloch* in 1837 during debate on a motion to expunge the censure of Jackson that had been passed in the wake of his Bank veto. Benton believed that Jackson had provided the necessary foundations for overturning *M'Culloch*. He argued that Jackson "has demonstrated, by the fact itself, that a national bank is not 'necessary' to the fiscal operations of the Federal Government, and in that demonstration he has upset the argument of Hamilton, and the decision of the Supreme Court of the United States, and all that has ever been said in favor of the constitutionality of a national bank." Benton then stressed that Jackson "has prepared the way for the reversal of that decision; and it is a question for lawyers to answer, whether the case is not ripe for the application of that writ of most remedial nature, as Lord Coke calls it, and which was invented lest in any case there should be an oppressive defect of justice — the venerable writ of *audita querela defedentis* — to ascertain the truth of a fact happening since the judgment, and upon the due finding of which the judgment will be vacated."

Benton's theory was that a key element in *M'Culloch* was the Court's determination that the Bank was necessary, and that an application for the writ was called for, as it was a traditional means of reopening a judgment when the necessary factual predicates for it were eliminated by new developments. Benton was of course wrong regarding one key aspect of this, as Marshall had clearly held that the Court was deferring to a conclusion reached by Congress, a legislative finding that the Bank was both necessary and proper. The preconditions for the writ were accordingly absent, even assuming that other jurisdictional problems could be solved. Nevertheless, Benton had made his point. The times had changed, and with them the Court. That posed the very real possibility that *M'Culloch* could be cast aside, if and when a proper case to achieve that end could be fashioned.

But the hopes of *M'Culloch*'s opponents died with President William Henry Harrison, who took office on March 4, 1841, only to pass away on April 4, 1842, the victim of a cold he contracted during his inauguration that developed into pneumonia. He was succeeded by his vice president, John Tyler, who was dubbed by some as "His Accidency." With this, the movement to seek the reversal of *M'Culloch* itself suffered a fatal blow.

When Harrison took office, the Whigs had captured Congress. They clearly favored the creation of a new Bank, and Harrison indicated that he would not oppose them. It was hard to say who was happier: the Bank's supporters, or the individuals who sought *M'Culloch*'s demise. For if a new bank was established, it would certainly be challenged in court. And that was a matter for joy or concern, depending on which side of the bank divide one was on. As Representative Henry A. Wise of Virginia (a bank supporter) noted regarding the Court as it was then constituted: "God forbid that he should say anything disparagingly of that sacred tribunal; but he would ask, if the distinguished gentleman, who removed the public deposits from the Bank of the United States was not at the head of it, and if a majority of its members, was not of that school of politicians, who believed a Bank of the United States to be unconstitutional?"

But Harrison was dead, succeeded by John Tyler, a Virginian who adhered to most of the principles that members of that state's elite traditionally espoused. Tyler believed that the Constitution must be construed narrowly and that state rights must be protected. In 1818 he took these convictions with him when he served as a member of the Spencer Committee's examination of the conduct of the Second Bank. He came to that task with a preconceived negative bias. The Bank's supporters, he noted at the time, had promoted the Bank "under the idea that boundless wealth would result from the adoption." But "the dream, however, is over — instead of riches, penury walks the streets of our towns, and bankruptcy knocks at every man's door." During the floor debates that followed the completion of the committee's report, Tyler was one of the Bank's most relentless critics.

Tyler clung to these views as president. Two measures that in effect created a new bank reached Tyler's desk in August and September 1841. He vetoed both of them. In his first veto message he took a Jacksonian stance and characterized the constitutional questions as "unsettled." He then reminded one and all that he had "uniformly proclaimed to be against the exercise of any such power by this Government." That had been his position throughout his public life, "never concealed." He did not believe that "a bank of discount in the ordinary acceptance of that term was a necessary means or one demanded by propriety in executing those powers" that the government did possess. In his second veto message Tyler stated that he acted with "extreme regret" and "great pain." Whatever it might be called, the entity presented to him "can not be regarded as other than a bank of the United States, with powers seemingly more limited than have heretofore been granted to such an institution." It was his obligation to act on "a settled conviction, founded . . . on a just view of the Constitution."

The vetoes cost Tyler dearly. When the second message was read to what Benton described as a "Senate chamber, and its galleries . . . crowded to its utmost capacity . . . hisses broke forth, followed by applauses." Tyler's cabinet resigned, with the exception of his secretary of state, Daniel Webster, who while wanting a bank was nevertheless appalled by the tactics employed in fashioning the measures that had been presented to Tyler. Tyler was then in effect expelled from the Whig Party and became a president without a political home.

Tyler's two vetoes effectively ended one portion of the political debate. There would be no new bank and no opportunity for its opponents to press their case against *M'Culloch* before the Court. And although the arguments about implied powers continued, they were largely settled by a series of decisions collectively known as the Legal Tender Cases.

Article I, Section eight, Clause 5 of the Constitution gives Congress the power "to coin Money." A literal interpretation of that grant meant that Congress had the authority to do just that: achieve a uniform national circulating medium by coining money, that is, using specie. The Legal Tender Act of 1862 was passed to assist the government in meeting the expenses incurred during the Civil War. It authorized the issue of "United States notes," otherwise known as greenbacks, that were not backed by specie. By the end of the war about $450 million in greenbacks were in circulation. But they depreciated in value and became a source of controversy, especially when they were offered as payment for debts contracted under the assumption that they would be repaid in specie, which had a substantially greater value.

Three cases testing the constitutionality of the Legal Tender Act eventually made their way to the Supreme Court. In the first of these, *Hepburn v. Griswold* (1870), the Court held that the system was unconstitutional. But in a second set of cases that were considered together, *Knox v. Lee* and *Parker v. Davis*, the Court reversed itself: greenbacks were constitutional, after all. Critics of *Knox* saw it as a political decision, a change prompted by the fact that the Court had two new members — one of whom, Justice William Strong, wrote the decision — rather than an appropriate reassessment of what the Constitution required. Whatever the truth of that matter might be, the majority opinion made it quite clear that *M'Culloch* was the guiding spirit for what followed.

Justice Strong began his opinion with the observation that if the Court were to hold the act unconstitutional, "the government is without those means of self-preservation which, all must admit, may, in certain circumstances, become indispensable, even if they were not when the acts of Congress now called in question were enacted." That understanding of the issue echoed a key theme from the founding era, the need for the national government to be armed with those powers necessary to its preservation. In that respect it was important to recall, as Marshall had declared in *M'Culloch*, that the Constitution could not by its very nature specify every power required. More to the point: "It is impossible to know what those non-enumerated powers are, and what is their nature and extent, without considering the purposes they were intended to subserve. Those purposes, it must be noted, reach beyond the mere execution of all powers definitively intrusted to Congress and mentioned in detail. They embrace the execution of all other powers vested by the Constitution in the government of the United States, or in any department or officer thereof. It certainly was intended to confer upon the government the power of self-preservation."

The Legal Tender Act had been passed in a time of great national peril and provided the means required for the nation to survive. The act pursued, as Marshall had explained, a legitimate end, and the means selected were "appropriate and adapted to that end." That arguably sustained the use of greenbacks only in such circumstances. But in the final Legal Tender Case, *Julliard v. Greenman* (1884), the Court closed that potentially damaging loophole by holding that when such currency could be issued was "a political question, to be determined by Congress when the question of exigency arises, and not a judicial question, to be afterwards passed upon by the courts." The political question doctrine is a central part of modern constitutional law, a principle that treats certain types of issues as nonjusticiable, that is, as not fit for consideration by a court. By ruling that the Legal Tender Act presented a political question, the Court in *Julliard* left the matter in the hands of Congress.

Once again, *M'Culloch* provided the analytic framework. The Court stated at the outset that "no question of the scope and extent of the implied powers of Congress under the Constitution can satisfactorily be discussed without repeating much of the reasoning of Chief Justice Marshall in the great judgment of *M'Culloch v. Maryland.*" It then did precisely that, at length, and reached the conclusion that as a matter of law greenbacks were "an appropriate means, conducive and plainly adapted to the execution of the undoubted powers of Congress." As such they were both necessary and proper. The Court then grounded its holding that the timing question was not for the Court in Marshall's admonition that a federal court should not, in the consideration of an otherwise permissible action, "inquire into the degree of necessity," for that "would be to pass the line which circumscribes the judicial department, and to tread on legislative ground."

These decisions established firmly that *M'Culloch* was both an integral part of the Court's legacy and that implied powers were recognized. Jackson's efforts to repudiate or minimize *M'Culloch*, and those of his allies and successors, had failed. And while the current Court has recently proved to be a champion of state sovereignty, the "New Federalism" regime it has embraced has not carried with it a repudiation of *M'Culloch* or the main principles for which it stands.

In *United States v. Lopez* (1995) and *United States v. Morrison* (2000), for example, the Court placed restrictions on congressional authority to legislate pursuant to the commerce clause, holding that the activity regulated must be economic in nature. *Lopez* and *Morrison* were both 5-to-4 decisions within which the same majority — Chief Justice Rehnquist and Justices Sandra Day O'Connor, Antonin Scalia, Anthony M. Kennedy, and Clarence Thomas — expressed concern about federal measures that compromised or violated the sovereignty of the states. In certain important respects their sentiments echoed those voiced by Thomas Jefferson and Spencer Roane, who believed that the Tenth Amendment had enshrined a regime within which the states possessed certain attributes that placed much of what they did beyond federal control, especially that of the Supreme Court.

Critics of *Lopez* and *Morrison* — and of another line of cases within which the Court gave new force to the Eleventh Amendment and the doctrine of state sovereign immunity — have argued that if taken to their logical conclusions the decisions the Court announced presaged a return to the approach embraced in the Articles of Confederacy, under which federal authority was severely limited. The directions in which the Court will ultimately go in this regard remain unclear. This is especially so in a time of transition, when the death of Chief Justice Rehnquist and retirement of Justice O'Connor may — or may not — result in a reconfigured Court pursuing new directions. But it is quite obvious that the doctrines articulated in *M'Culloch* continue to play an important part in these matters. Indeed, *M'Culloch* and its legacy were at the heart of one of the Court's most recent decisions, *Gonzales v. Raich* (2005).

Gonzales involved the application of the Comprehensive Drug Abuse and Prevention Act of 1970 to the use of marijuana by various individuals as treatment for their chronic, debilitating illnesses. California had passed a Compassionate Use Act that authorized "limited marijuana use for medicinal purposes." Two women, Angel Raich and Diane Monson, had the drug prescribed by their physicians after conventional treatments failed to provide relief from the problems imposed by their conditions. In the case of Angel Raich, as the Court noted, her "physician believes that forgoing cannabis treatment would certainly cause Raich excruciating pain and could very well prove fatal." The U.S. Court of Appeals for the Ninth Circuit, relying on *Lopez* and *Morrison*, held that "this separate class of purely local activities was beyond the reach of federal power."

Gonzales was on the surface a hard case, as it presented the arguably wrenching situation of two critically ill women whose sole hope for a life within which they had any hope of functioning effectively seemed to be their physician-prescribed marijuana. But it was actually from a constitutional perspective quite an easy decision. For the manner in which the Court should resolve the question was obvious, assuming that the doctrines articulated by *M'Culloch* and the cases that followed those rules remained in force.

The Court made it clear that this was indeed the situation on June 6, 2005, when it held that the federal measure in general and the particular restriction at issue in this case were valid. Justice John Paul Stevens stated on behalf of the majority, "Our case law firmly established Congress' power to regulate purely local activities that are part of an economic 'class of activities' that have a substantial effect of interstate commerce." Even though the conduct in question, the use of marijuana, was illegal, it was still an economic activity that Congress could regulate if it wished to, as it obviously did. Relief from federal prosecution could not be found in the courts. It lay, rather, with "the democratic process, in which the voices of voters allied with these respondents may one day be heard in the halls of Congress."

In his concurring opinion Justice Scalia made it quite clear that *M'Culloch* in large measure dictated this result. He criticized the dissenting justices for "misundertand[ing] the nature of the Necessary and Proper Clause, which empowers Congress to enact laws in effectuation of its enumerated powers that are not within its authority to enact in isolation," citing *M'Culloch*. And he emphasized that there were restraints on what Congress could do, again turning to Marshall in the Bank case, stating that "the means must be 'appropriate' and 'plainly adapted' to that end" and "not be otherwise 'prohibited' and must be 'consistent with the letter and spirit of the constitution.'" Even Justice Thomas, whose narrow view of the commerce power led him to dissent, began his analysis with an appeal to *M'Culloch*, conceding that it provided the applicable test.

Gonzales was widely criticized by those who believed that the Court had turned its back on two women whose only hope for a quality life lay in their use of marijuana. But it was not a decision in the vein of the aphorism that "hard cases make bad law." Rather, it was an occasion for the Court to remind us that Congress does indeed possess both express and implied powers and that, within the constraints imposed by *M'Culloch*, it is for Congress to decide that a given measure is both necessary and proper.

M'Culloch v. Maryland secured the future of the nation, providing the basis for a doctrine of federal power that fulfilled the promise of the Constitution. That document was born of the impulse to clothe a radically new form of government with the authority necessary to protect itself from threats both external and internal. The government formed by the Articles of Confederation failed because it was unable to marshal the support and cooperation of thirteen relentlessly independent states. It was a nation in name only. And while the Anti-Federalists disagreed with many details of what emerged from the Constitutional Convention, even they largely understood that the obvious and appropriate cure was to draft and ratify a new governing document that gave the national government the authority it needed to curb the states and pursue its destiny.

The Constitution was a necessary first step, the brilliant and innovative product of the collective efforts of some of the most distinguished statesmen ever to have lived. But that document simply began a process by which what James Madison styled as the Compound Republic of America met the Constitution's express goal of securing a "more perfect Union." The new national government needed both the authority to act and protection from the sometimes parochial impulses of the states. *M'Culloch* was ultimately simply one piece of that process. But it was an essential one, the fulcrum on which the future success of the nation turned.

Epilogue

In 1833, William M. Gouge of Philadelphia wrote a book entitled *The Curse of Paper-Money and Banking; or A Short History of Banking in the United States of America*. Gouge was, as his title implied, a hard money man, an individual who believed in specie and decried banknotes at every turn. He was also a harsh critic of the Bank whose assessment of matters in the wake of *M'Culloch* was simple and succinct. "The Bank was saved," he declared, "and the people were ruined."

Gouge's judgment was wrong in the short term, as the absence of the Bank was keenly felt by a nation whose economic affairs remained relatively haphazard for decades. It was also wrong over the long term, as *M'Culloch* now provides the foundations for much of what the federal government finds itself compelled to do as an increasingly complex world poses problems for the nation that the founding generation could never have imagined. Ironically, one of the key but also largely forgotten figures from *M'Culloch* should also have, consistent with Gouge's vision, been ruined. But James William M'Culloh actually emerged from these events an initially chastened but ultimately triumphant individual.

M'Culloh lost his position as cashier on May 18, 1819. His dismissal was initially greeted with surprise and consternation. On May 22, the *Niles Weekly Register* noted that "Mr. John White has been appointed cashier of the branch of the bank of the U.S. at Baltimore, vice Mr. J. W. M'Culloh, removed. The *manner* of this thing appears to be as strange as the appointment is unpopular. But — 'it is none of our business,' as the managers in it will say. The sensation caused by the removal was astonishing — and the effect of the conduct which it is supposed to indicate, is fearfully anticipated by mercantile men in Baltimore, among whom, as in other cities, the chain of connection is so intimate that what operates upon a part is felt by the whole." But as the story of what had happened in the Baltimore branch emerged, public perceptions changed. As one resident of Baltimore, Anna Boyd, observed in a letter to her brother on August 6, 1819, "I think John, one of the most provoking parts of the business is, that these destroyers of widows, and orphans, affect to consider themselves as persecuted men. M'Culloh for example struts about in all the pride and gaiety belonging to an honest heart, and unspotted name boasting as it were; that he is stript of his feathers, that they have determined to bring him down and have succeeded."

M'Culloh's response was to project himself as a victim, rather than the victimizer, and that posture served him well. In June 1819 Hezekiah Niles, for example, complained of the "incessant endeavors of too many persons in Philadelphia to injure Baltimore," an attitude that "shews a want of liberality, or a malignant *envy*, which we feel it our duty to reprehend in severest terms." M'Culloh, Buchanan, and Williams in turn adopted an attacking strategy as a key part of their defense when they were formally indicted for their role in these matters, the end result of an investigation that had been launched by Maryland's attorney general, Luther Martin.

Martin's stroke kept him from completing the task, which fell to others in a trial that was held in Belle Air, Maryland, in March and April 1821. The proceedings had been moved from Baltimore to Belle Air when the defendants — well aware of the damage that their actions had caused — maintained that they could not get a fair trial in Baltimore. They were accused of formulating a conspiracy to defraud the Bank of more than $1.5 million. In the words of the indictment, the three "being evil disposed and dishonest persons, and wickedly devising, contriving and intending, falsely, unlawfully, fraudulently, craftily and unjustly, and by indirect means to cheat and impoverish the said President, Directors and Company of the Bank of the United States . . . [and] did wickedly, falsely, fraudulently and unlawfully, conspire, combine, confederate and agree together, by wrongful and indirect means to cheat, defraud and impoverish [the same]."

The indictments were dismissed by the trial court. Two members of the three-judge panel, C. W. Hanson and William H. Ward, accepted the defense that Maryland had not made such conduct a statutory offense and that it was also unknown to the common law, that is, that this particular crime had not been accepted by the courts. M'Culloh's attorneys also argued, in a neat twist, that even if conspiracy might be a crime, it could not have been illegal as a matter of Maryland law to defraud the Second Bank, which had been placed outside the reach of state authority as a result of the Court's holding in *M'Culloch*.

An appeal was taken, and the trial court verdict was reversed unanimously by the Maryland Court of Appeals in December 1821. The court refused to accept that a conspiracy of this sort was not an offense at common law. The end sought was improper, and the common law recognized that a conspiracy to achieve such a result was a criminal offense. *M'Culloch* in turn was no bar, as this application of Maryland law by Maryland courts in no way involved the Bank itself. It was, rather, a prosecution of private citizens for their criminal conduct.

The court remanded the case for a trial on the facts, which finally took place in March 1823. And this time M'Culloh and Buchanan were acquitted and the indictment against Williams dismissed, results that almost certainly reflected a verdict against the Bank itself rather than a judgment that the three had not actually engaged in massive fraud.

M'Culloh and Buchanan's strategy was simple. Their attorney "admitted that the conduct of the Traversers was indiscreet." But that was not their fault, as "they relied too strongly upon the hopes and calculations in which the whole community indulged; but the failure of their stock speculations was rather to be pitied as a misfortune, than condemned as a crime." Indeed, he maintained, "Those who were now the most eager in prosecuting his clients, were, in 1817, the first to praise the course of conduct for which they were indicted; and those who now believed them guilty of a conspiracy to defraud, were then their most strenuous supporters."

M'Culloh and Buchanan were also the victims of chance. "Adverse circumstances had depressed stock, when, if it had risen, the defendants would have been looked upon as nobles, as the architects of their fortunes, by the very men who now prosecuted them, and lauded to the skies as possessing spirits fraught with enterprize." The Bank, moreover, should at least share the blame, if not be seen as the real culprit. "Did the Bank afterwards pursue the proper course to heal the wounds. Its strange administration was an *incubus* upon it, and was another cause of depreciations of its Stock, so that, in fact, the Bank itself occasioned the losses upon which the present indictment was founded."

James M'Culloh's fortunes then took a strange but perhaps predictable turn. Initially and rightfully condemned, and rendered bankrupt, he soon became a figure of respect and a man of prosperity. In 1825 he was elected to the Maryland House of Delegates as a representative for Baltimore County. And on December 26, 1826, the members of the House elected him Speaker of that body. M'Culloh also began to practice law and again entered the world of business. By the end of the decade he was recognized as one of the most important political figures in the area. He supported Adams in the 1828 election, was a key member of the group of Maryland Whigs who opposed Jackson, and championed many of the causes that the Whigs embraced, including internal improvement.

In the 1830s, M'Culloh became an influential lobbyist on behalf of both the city and county of Baltimore. He was known to have considerable influence in the legislature and, for example, worked actively on behalf of the Chesapeake and Ohio Canal Company in its pursuit of government support for both the canal and a general program of internal improvement. M'Culloh also pursued an active life of community service. In 1837 the legislature designated him as a trustee of the Union Academy in Baltimore. The governor and council in turn allowed him to play a role in the affairs of the institution to which Luther Martin had wished to send him, appointing M'Culloh to serve a term as a director of the Maryland Penitentiary. And M'Culloh was instrumental in securing for the First Unitarian Church of Baltimore a building that remains today, described by its congregation as "a Greek temple, a monument, a building for the ages."

M'Culloh's saga came full circle in 1842 when President John Tyler nominated him for the position of First Comptroller in the Department of the Treasury. That position no longer exists, but it was at the time an important one. As one official publication stated in 1880: "The laws of Congress have made the First Comptroller, in some measure, the law officer, or, as he may be in one sense regarded, the judicial officer, not merely of the Department of the Treasury, but for all the other executive departments, and to a certain extent as to the legislative and judicial branches of the Government, on questions affecting the receipt and expenditure of public money."

Tyler had been a member of the Spencer Committee and was clearly aware of M'Culloh's activities as cashier. He nevertheless submitted his name for this important position, the name of an individual who had engaged in substantial frauds during his prior public service. The irony of this was apparently not lost on the Senate, which approved the nomination on April 1, 1842, with twenty-nine senators voting for him and eight against. The Senate no longer met in secret for its regular business but still considered matters of this sort in executive session. There is accordingly no formal record of the discussion, but the fact that M'Culloh's nomination drew a fair amount of opposition suggests that some members of the Senate remembered his actions at the Bank. His confirmation in turn showed that both Tyler and a substantial majority of the Senate believed that M'Culloh had reformed, for the position became available for him only because the Senate had earlier rejected Tyler's first choice, James N. Barker.

Barker had actually served as First Comptroller from February 1838 through April 1841, when he resigned. It was during that period that the "defalcations" of Samuel Swartwout came to light, and it seems that Barker's role in those matters had come back to haunt him.

Samuel Swartwout was born in 1783 and over the course of his life was involved in a number of key events in the nation's history. The episode that made him a part of this story began when Andrew Jackson — for Swartwout was yet another Jackson man—appointed him to one of the most important posts in the nation, that of customs collector in New York City. Swartwout treated that position in much the same way that M'Culloh seems to have viewed his role as cashier, as an opportunity for personal gain. When he left office in 1838, it was alleged that he had retained in a personal account $1,225,705.69, not quite in the league of James M'Culloh and his partners but a respectable sum nevertheless.

The resulting scandal became known as the Swartwout Defalcations. And as First Comptroller, James Barker played a central role in these events. Barker was directed by the secretary of the Treasury, Levi Woodbury, to investigate the matter and did so. Working with the solicitor of the Treasury Department, Henry Gilpin, Barker did his best to determine the actual amount of the losses and filed a report that included a number of recommendations for corrective action, including the suggestion that embezzlement "should be made a criminal offense" and that severe punishments should be attached to such conduct. Barker's role was ultimately largely confined to writing that report and providing testimony to the special committee that was impaneled by the House of Representatives to investigate the matter. His association with the matter nevertheless apparently came to haunt him.

Tyler submitted Barker's name on December 30, 1841, and the nomination provoked extended debate. It came to a vote on February 11, 1842, and a motion was made to postpone further consideration until February 18. It failed, 18 in favor and 23 against. The Senate then considered the nomination itself, and Barker was rejected, gaining the support of seventeen senators and the opposition of the same twenty-three who had refused to delay the matter.

Once again, there are no records of the discussions. But Barker had two important supporters, both future presidents: James Buchanan of Pennsylvania, and Franklin Pierce of New Hampshire. They offered motions that arguably indicate what happened. Buchanan moved "that the nomination of James N. Barker as Comptroller of the Treasury has not been rejected by the Senate on account of any belief that his official conduct in the case of the Swartwout defalcation was negligent or improper." Pierce, in turn, moved "that the injunction of secrecy be removed from the vote of the Senate on the rejection of the nomination of James N. Barker," an action that presumably allowed the Buchanan motion to become public.

In doing so the two created the very colorable suspicion that it was indeed the Swartwout matter that denied Barker the office and left it open for M'Culloh. Indeed, Buchanan castigated Swartwout during a different debate, observing that "whenever a collector of customs turned politician, it became his interest to accommodate merchants so as to secure their support, and then farewell to honesty." Once again, the irony is profound, as the fates of two individuals, Samuel Swartwout and James M'Culloh, became intertwined, individuals who each committed massive acts of fraud against the nation.

M'Culloh served as First Comptroller until May 31, 1849, when he left the government and again entered private life. He died on June 17, 1861, passing away at the age of seventy-two, presumably in the warm glow of a life initially misdirected but ultimately well spent.

Thus, much like Richard Milhous Nixon, James William M'Culloh — who was indeed a crook — lived out his life a remade individual: a successful politician, lawyer, businessman, and government official, one who initially earned the nation's condemnation but eventually secured its approval. His story was in some ways a typical one for the times, as the urge to prosper led many individuals to do whatever they could to succeed. But it is also both unique and intriguing, given M'Culloh's role in the events that would shape one of the most important decisions ever rendered by the Supreme Court of the United States.

April 30, 1789	George Washington takes his oath of office as the first president of the United States in New York City, which served as the capital at that time.
September 11, 1789	Alexander Hamilton is nominated by President Washington and confirmed by the Senate as the first secretary of the Treasury.
December 1790	Hamilton completes his *Second Report of the Further Provision Necessary for Establishing Public Credit* (the *Report on a National Bank*) and sends it to Congress.
January 20, 1791	The Senate approves the bill for the creation of the First Bank of the United States.
February 1–8, 1791	Debate on the Bank bill in the House of Representatives, with approval coming on February 8.
February 12–15, 1791	Attorney General Edmund Randolph and Secretary of State Thomas Jefferson provide Washington with written opinions arguing that the Bank bill is unconstitutional.
February 23, 1791	Hamilton submits an extensive written defense of the Bank and its constitutionality to Washington.
February 25, 1791	Washington signs the legislation creating the First Bank of the United States.
December 12, 1791	The First Bank begins formal operations at its initial headquarters in Carpenter's Hall in Philadelphia.
June–July 1798	The Alien and Sedition Acts are passed by Congress.
Fall 1798	Madison and Jefferson draft the Virginia and Kentucky Resolutions, protesting the Alien and Sedition Acts.
January 7, 1800	Madison completes his *Report of 1800*, defending the Virginia Resolutions.
November 1800	In the presidential election, Adams finishes behind Jefferson in the electoral vote count, but Jefferson is tied with his vice presidential candidate Aaron

	Burr. The election goes to the House of Representatives, which will eventually select Jefferson on the thirty-sixth ballot.
February 4, 1801	John Marshall takes the judicial oath and becomes chief justice of the United States.
March 26, 1808	The stockholders of the Bank of the United States submit their first memorial to the House of Representatives, requesting that the Bank's charter be renewed. The matter is referred to Jefferson's secretary of the Treasury, Albert Gallatin.
March 2, 1809	Gallatin issues his report on the Bank, recommending renewal of the charter, albeit with changes.
February 19, 1810	After considering the memorials and Gallatin's report, a House committee files a report recommending that the Bank's charter be renewed. A bill to that effect is introduced on April 7.
January 24, 1811	The bill to extend the charter of the Bank is defeated in the House of Representatives by one vote, 65 to 64.
February 20, 1811	The bill to extend the Bank's charter is defeated in the Senate when the vote on the bill ends in a tie, which is broken by the "no" vote of the Senate's presiding officer, Vice President George Clinton.
March 3, 1811	The charter of the First Bank expires.
June 18, 1812	President James Madison signs the declaration of war against England, initiating the War of 1812.
April 6, 1813	The movement to create what will become the Second Bank of the United States begins with a meeting held at the home of John Jacob Astor, where he and a number of other financiers discuss the need for such an institution.
January 20, 1815	A bill proposing that a Second Bank of the United States be created is passed by the Senate and sent to Madison for his consideration.
January 30, 1815	Madison vetoes the bank bill, conceding constitutionality and citing practical concerns as the basis for his action.

April 3, 1816	A new bill creating the Second Bank of the United States passes in the Senate and is sent to President Madison for his approval.
April 10, 1816	Madison signs the bank bill.
January 7, 1817	The Second Bank of the United States formally opens for business at its headquarters in Philadelphia and eventually establishes a branch in Baltimore.
February 1818	The Maryland legislature passes the measure imposing a tax on any bank not incorporated by the state.
May 1818	James William M'Culloh, cashier of the Baltimore branch of the Second Bank, issues a series of banknotes on untaxed paper.
May 18, 1818	John James, collector of the State of Maryland for the Western Shore, files an action of debt against the Bank, claiming that it owes the taxes imposed by the Maryland statute.
May 1818	A Baltimore County court holds that the Bank does owe the tax.
June 1818	The Maryland Court of Appeals, the state's highest court, issues a brief opinion and order holding that the Maryland act is constitutional and that the Bank owes the tax.
Summer 1818	The Second Bank starts the contraction that helps precipitate the Panic of 1819.
September 18, 1818	The U.S. Supreme Court issues a writ of error, accepting what is now styled as *M'Culloch v. Maryland* for review during its February 1819 Term.
November 30, 1818	The House of Representatives appoints a special committee to investigate the Bank, which will be chaired by Representative John C. Spencer of New York.
January 16, 1819	The Spencer Committee files its report with the House, indicating that the Bank had committed a number of errors and that acts of fraud and abuse by Bank officials had taken place.
January 1819	William Jones resigns his position as president of the Second Bank.

February 1819	Extended debate on the Bank in the House of Representatives, which rejects attempts to revoke the Bank's charter.
February 22, 1819	Oral argument begins in *M'Culloch v. Maryland*.
March 3, 1819	Final day of oral argument in *M'Culloch*.
March 6, 1819	Chief Justice John Marshall announces the unanimous decision of the Court, holding that the Bank is constitutional and that Maryland may not tax it.
March 6, 1819	Langdon Cheves takes office as president of the Second Bank, replacing William Jones.
March 30, 1819	The *Richmond Enquirer* publishes the first of two essays by William Brockenbrough, writing as Amphictyon, attacking *M'Culloch* and the Court.
April 24, 1819	The first of two essays written by John Marshall as A Friend to the Union, defending the Court and the decision, is published by the *Philadelphia Union*.
May 7, 1819	Amos Kendall, editor of the *Argus of Western America*, publishes the first of eleven essays attacking *M'Culloch*. The essays lay the foundations for his opposition to the Bank and subsequent actions as a trusted adviser of President Andrew Jackson.
May 18, 1819	James M'Culloh is discharged from his position as cashier of the Baltimore branch of the Bank.
June 11, 1819	The first of four essays by Virginia judge Spencer Roane, writing as Hampden, appears in the *Richmond Enquirer*, attacking Marshall, the Court, and *M'Culloch*.
June 30, 1819	John Marshall responds to Roane as A Friend of the Constitution in the first of nine essays that will appear in the *Alexandria Gazette*.
July 1819	James M'Culloh, James Buchanan, and George Williams are indicted for their actions regarding the Second Bank, charged by the State of Maryland with conspiracy to commit fraud and embezzlement.
September 15, 1819	Ohio state auditor Ralph Osborn enters the Chillicothe, Ohio, branch of the Second Bank and

	confiscates Bank funds as payment for the tax levied on the Bank by the state.
March–April 1821	The first trial of M'Culloh and his colleagues in what will become known as the Conspiracy Cases ends with a verdict holding that a conspiracy to defraud is not a crime in Maryland.
December 1821	The Maryland Court of Appeals reverses the lower court holding and remands the matter for a trial on the merits of the accusations.
January 1823	Nicholas Biddle becomes the third and last president of the Second Bank of the United States, replacing Langdon Cheves.
March 1823	The second trial in the Conspiracy Cases ends with a verdict that M'Culloh and Buchanan are not guilty. The charges against Williams are then dismissed.
March 19, 1824	The Court decides *Osborn v. Ohio*, in which it reaffirms *M'Culloch* in a case arising from the attempt by the State of Ohio to collect the tax it had tried to impose on the branches of the Second Bank.
Fall 1825	James M'Culloh is elected to the Maryland House of Delegates as a representative for Baltimore County.
December 26, 1826	James M'Culloh is elected Speaker of the Maryland House of Delegates by his colleagues.
December 8, 1829	President Andrew Jackson delivers his first annual message, within which he signals his intent to seek the end of the Second Bank.
December 6, 1831	Jackson delivers his third annual message, in which he makes it clear that he will make the Bank an issue in the forthcoming presidential election.
July 3, 1832	The House of Representatives approves the measure that would extend the charter of the Second Bank and sends it to Jackson for his approval.
July 10, 1832	Jackson vetoes the bill extending the Second Bank's charter, arguing in the veto message that *M'Culloch* should not be seen as binding.

November 6, 1832	Jackson is elected to serve a second term as president in an election he subsequently characterizes as a referendum against the Bank.
September 18, 1833	Jackson reads his paper "Removal of the Public Deposits" to his cabinet, confirming his intention to remove federal funds on deposit with the Bank.
July 6, 1835	Chief Justice Marshall dies.
March 4, 1836	The charter of the Second Bank of the United States expires.
March 15, 1836	The Senate confirms the nomination of Roger B. Taney, who succeeds Marshall as chief justice of the United States when he takes the judicial oath on March 28, 1836.
August 16, 1841	President John Tyler, who became president of the United States after William Henry Harrison died one month into his term, vetoes the Fiscal Bank Bill, which would have authorized what would in effect have become a new Bank of the United States.
September 9, 1841	Tyler vetoes a second attempt to create new bank, refusing to approve the Fiscal Corporation Bill.
April 1, 1842	James W. M'Culloh is confirmed by the Senate as First Comptroller of the Treasury, having been nominated for that position by Tyler.
May 31, 1849	M'Culloh leaves his position as First Comptroller of the Treasury.
June 17, 1861	M'Culloh dies.
March 3, 1884	The Court decides the third and final Legal Tender Case, *Julliard v. Greenman*. Taken together, the three decisions make it clear that *M'Culloch* provides the operative rule regarding implied powers and that Jackson's efforts to deny the force of that holding were for naught.
April 26, 1995	The Court decides *United States v. Lopez*, in which it holds for the first time since the 1930s that Congress did not have the authority to enact a measure passed pursuant to its authority under the commerce clause.

May 15, 2000   The Court decides *United States v. Morrison*, confirming its holding in *Lopez* and making it clear that the commerce power extends only to economic activities.

June 6, 2005   The Court decides *Gonzales v. Raich*, a case in which it holds that Congress has the authority to prohibit the medical use of marijuana and reaffirms, yet again, the force and effect of *M'Culloch* as a linchpin in the doctrines of implied powers and deferential judicial review.

BIBLIOGRAPHICAL ESSAY

Note from the series editors: The following bibliographical essay contains the primary and secondary sources the author consulted for this volume. We have asked all authors in the series to omit formal citations in order to make our volumes more readable, inexpensive, and appealing for students and general readers.

Given its importance, the surprising thing about *M'Culloch v. Maryland* is that so much and yet at the same time so little has been written about the decision. *M'Culloch* is routinely mentioned and discussed in virtually every study of the Constitution and the Supreme Court, but until this point only two book-length studies of the decision have been published.

The best is clearly Gerald Gunther's *John Marshall's Defense of* McCulloch v. Maryland (Stanford, Calif.: Stanford University Press, 1969). Gunther's introduction is excellent, an essay that sets up the main purpose of the book, which is to provide the text of the opinion and of the anonymous essays attacking and defending it by William Brockenbrough, Spencer Roane, and Marshall himself. Gunther was the first to realize that Marshall had written two sets of essays. The first appeared, albeit with serious printing mistakes, in the *Philadelphia Union* and was widely known. It was through Gunther that we learned that Marshall wrote nine additional essays that appeared in the *Alexandria Gazette*.

The second book is Bonnie Pettifor and Charles E. Petit, McCulloch v. Maryland: *When Federal and State Powers Conflict* (Berkeley Heights, N.J.: Enslow, 2004), part of the Landmark Supreme Court Cases Series, which is directed at a K–12 audience. It offers an interesting account that is nevertheless exactly what it purports to be, a discussion of the case structured and written for what the publishers characterize as "children and young adults."

A book that grew out of *M'Culloch* but is not about the case itself is Robert Goodloe Harper, ed., *An Exhibit of the Losses Sustained at the Office of Discount and Deposit Baltimore, Under the Administration of James A Buchanan, President, and James W. M'Culloh, Cashier, to which is appended A Report of the Conspiracy Cases, Tried at Hartford County Court in Maryland* (Baltimore: Thomas Murphy, 1823). Harper was a prominent Federalist who collected and published the materials that were compiled as part of the postdecision trial of James M'Culloh and his partners. Generally cited as *A Report of the Conspiracy Cases,* Harper's volume provides a comprehensive history of the prosecution of the three conspirators and their eventual acquittal, including the indictments, evidence presented, arguments of opposing counsel, and opinions of both the trial judges and the Maryland Court of Appeals. It is relatively rare and not especially well organized, which makes working with it a chore. It is nevertheless an important resource for anyone wishing to get a feel for the full story of *M'Culloch*.

Articles within which *M'Culloch* is mentioned or discussed are countless, but, once again, very few are devoted solely or largely to that case. One of the most important is yet again by Gerald Gunther: "John Marshall, 'A Friend of the Constitution': In Defense and Elaboration of *McCulloch v. Maryland*," 21 *Stanford Law Review* 449 (1969). Other articles that deal largely if not exclusively with the decision that are worth reading include J. Randy Beck, "The Heart of Federalism: Pretext Review of Means-End Relationships," 36 *University of California Davis Law Review* 407 (2003); David S. Bogen, "The Scandal of Smith and Buchanan: The Skeletons in the *McCulloch v. Maryland* Closet," 9 *Maryland Law Forum* 125 (1985); A. I. L. Campbell, " 'It Is a Constitution We Are Expounding': Chief Justice Marshall and the 'Necessary and Proper' Clause," 12 *Journal of Legal History* 190 (1991); Martin S. Flaherty, "John Marshall, *McCulloch v. Maryland*, and 'We the People': Revisions in Need of Revising?" 43 *William and Mary Law Review* 1339 (2002); Joseph M. Lynch, "*McCulloch v. Maryland:* A Matter of Money Supply," 18 *Seton Hall Law Review* 223 (1988); R. Kent Newmyer, "John Marshall, *McCulloch v. Maryland*, and the Southern States' Rights Tradition," 33 *John Marshall Law Review* 875 (2000); Harold J. Plous, "*McCulloch v. Maryland*, Right Principle, Wrong Case," 9 *Stanford Law Review* 710 (1957); and Sylvia Snowiss, "Text and Principle in John Marshall's Constitutional Law: The Cases of *Marbury* and *McCulloch*," 33 *John Marshall Law Review* 973 (2000).

The judgment that *M'Culloch* is the "most influential" opinion the Court ever issued is set forth in Montgomery N. Kosma, "Measuring the Influence of Supreme Court Justices," 27 *Journal of Legal Studies* 333 (1998). The approach taken was objective and rigorous. A numerical "historical value index" was calculated for the decisions of the Court, and *M'Culloch* ranked first. There are nevertheless individuals who disagree, arguing both that the decision is overrated and that it was simply wrong, embracing an incorrect view of the Constitution and in particular the powers of the federal government. The former position is set forth in Michael J. Klarman, "How Great Were the 'Great' Marshall Court Decisions?" 87 *Virginia Law Review* 1111 (2001). The latter is found in John Yoo, "*McCulloch v. Maryland*," in William N. Eskridge Jr. and Sanford Levinson, eds., *Constitutional Stupidities, Constitutional Tragedies* (New York: New York University Press, 1998).

The body of literature that focuses on *M'Culloch* is, then, quite small. There is nevertheless a wealth of information available about the Bank of the United States, the Constitution, the Supreme Court, and the various individuals who played a prominent role in the events described in this book.

The best place to start is of course Chief Justice John Marshall's opinion for the Court, which may be found at 17 U.S. (4 Wheat.) 316 (1819), a notation that means that the decision appears in volume 17 of the United States Reports (the official reports of the decisions of the Supreme Court), at page 316, and was decided in 1819. Virtually all courts and scholars cite *M'Culloch* in this manner, with one important exception: the Supreme Court itself, which continues to cite its early decisions in its official reports by the private reporter designation. Thus in any opinion issued by the Court, *M'Culloch* appears as 4 Wheat. 316 (1819), in the same manner that other early decisions of the Court are cited.

One invaluable way to learn about the decision and its importance is to read the newspapers of the day, newspapers that were intensely partisan and that, by dint of both their nature and sheer number, provided a wide spectrum of views about the important events of the day. In most instances using them requires patience, as the norm was to print a small amount of news and a substantial amount of advertising. But that was not always the case, and one of the things that made Hezekiah Niles's *Niles Weekly Register* unique and valuable is that it was devoted entirely to the news. Other important newspapers of the times, at least for the purposes of this book, include the *Daily National Intelligencer*, published in Washington, D.C., generally a voice for the government and a nationalist perspective; the *Richmond Enquirer*, the primary organ for the views of the state rights groups and individuals, and in particular those of the large and influential cadre of Virginians who espoused the state rights position; and William Duane's Philadelphia-based *Aurora General Advertiser* and the *Weekly Aurora*. The *Argus of Western America*, based in Frankfort, Kentucky, and owned and edited by Amos Kendall, is also an important source of information, albeit one that is not as widely available. Most university libraries and a good number of others will have copies of some or all of these and other important early newspapers on microfilm in their periodical collections. The Library of Congress has a major collection of newspapers in both print and microfilm, the latter of which can be obtained via interlibrary loan.

The literature devoted to the First and Second Banks is extensive. In 1908 the Library of Congress compiled *A List of Works Relating to the First and Second Banks of the United States* (Washington, D.C.: Government Printing Office, 1908). Although dated, this remains an excellent resource, providing a comprehensive lists of general works, official reports, the debates in Congress, and congressional documents. A second body of important original source material is found in the four volumes of the series American State Papers devoted to the subject of finance. Originally published by Gales and Seaton of Washington, D.C., in 1834, they are now available in reprint editions published by William S. Hein and Co. of Buffalo, New York, and, as indicated later, on the Internet through the Library of Congress. The information about the Bank in these volumes is detailed and interesting, but it is also widely distributed through them, and finding it requires patience on the part of the reader.

Two early compilations are especially useful in dealing with the Bank and contain a great deal of the original source material. The first is M. St. Claire Clarke and D. A. Hall, eds., *Legislative and Documentary History of the Bank of the United States, Including the Original Bank of North America* (Washington, D.C.: Gales and Seaton, 1832). The record as printed here is incomplete, with many key debates and documents not included. It is nevertheless a valuable compilation and has the added virtue of being available in a reprint edition (New York: Augustus M. Kelley, 1967). The second of these compilations is extremely scarce. It is R. K. Moulton, *Legislative and Documentary History of the Banks of the United States, from the Time of Establishing the Bank of North America, 1781, to October 1834* (New York: G and C Carvill and Co., 1834).

Much of the material in these compilations comes from Congress, either as debates on the floor in each house or in the form of committee reports. But, as indicated, these histories are incomplete, and those wishing to fill in the gaps should consult various publications. For the First Bank the primary source is *The Debates and Proceedings of the Congress of the United States*, more commonly known as the *Annals of Congress*, published by Gales and Seaton. The *Annals* were followed by the *Register of Debates*, which ran from 1824 to 1837 (also published by Gales and Seaton), which was in turn followed by *The Congressional Globe* (published by Blair and Rives), which ran from 1833 through 1873.

All these materials — the American State Papers and the four congressional reporters — may be accessed on the Internet through the Library of Congress Web site in the invaluable collection *A Century of Lawmaking for a New Nation: U.S. Congressional Documents and Debates, 1774–1875*, at http://memory.loc.gov/ammem/amlaw/lawhome.html.

There are also a number of contemporary accounts of the Bank and the controversies it generated, many of which have been reprinted. Two of special interest are William Loughton Smith, *The Politicks and Views of a Certain Party, Displayed* (1792), and John Taylor, *An Enquiry into the Principles and Tendencies of Certain Public Measures* (Philadelphia: Thomas Dobson, 1794). Smith takes a Federalist view in these matters, attacking those who opposed the Bank. Taylor in turn sketches out the Jeffersonian take on these matters, within which the Bank is both itself suspect and its authorization an intrusion on state rights. Other valuable contemporary works include Matthew Carey, *Essays on Banking* (Philadelphia: Carey, 1816), which includes his important essay "Desultory Reflections upon the Ruinous Consequences of a Non-renewal of the Charter of the Bank of the United States" (1810); William J. Duane, *Narrative and Correspondence Concerning the Removal of the Deposits* (Philadelphia, 1838); Albert Gallatin, *Considerations on the Currency and Bank-*

ing System of the United States (Philadelphia: Carey and Lea, 1831); T. F. Gordon, *The War on the Bank of the United States* (Philadelphia: Key and Biddle, 1834); and William M. Gouge, *The Curse of Paper-Money and Banking* (London: Mills, Jowett, and Mills, 1833).

The First and Second Banks have in turn been the subject of numerous detailed studies. The classic work on banking in the United States, within which the First and Second Banks figure prominently, is Bray Hammond, *Banks and Politics in America from the Revolution to the Civil War* (Princeton, N.J.: Princeton University Press, 1957). There are, in turn, three older studies of the First and Second Banks that remain invaluable. Two of these may be found in a volume compiled by the National Monetary Commission, *The First and Second Banks of the United States* (Washington, D.C.: Government Printing Office, 1910). They are John Thom Holdsworth, *The First Bank of the United States*, and Davis R. Dewey, *The Second United States Bank*. The third is Ralph C. H. Catterall, *The Second Bank of the United States* (Chicago: University of Chicago Press, 1902).

A number of more recent studies provide valuable insights. These include Howard Bodenhorn, *State Banking in Early America: A New Economic History* (New York: Oxford University Press, 2003); Marion A. Brown, *The Second Bank of the United States and Ohio (1803–1860)* (Lewiston, N.Y.: Edwin Mellen Press, 1998); David Jack Cowen, *The Origins and Economic Impact of the First Bank of the United States* (New York: Garland, 2000); Edward S. Kaplan, *The Bank of the United States and the American Economy* (Westport, Conn.: Greenwood Press, 1999); Walter Buckingham Smith, *Economic Aspects of the Second Bank of the United States* (Cambridge, Mass.: Harvard University Press, 1953); James O. Wettereau, *Statistical Records of the First Bank of the United States* (New York: Garland, 1985); and Roy Douglas Womack, *An Analysis of the Credit Controls of the Second Bank of the United States* (New York: Arno Press, 1978).

Andrew Jackson's war on the Bank is also the subject of a number of books, among which are Robert V. Remini, *Andrew Jackson and the Bank War* (New York: Norton, 1967); James Roger Sharp, *The Jacksonians versus the Banks: Politics in the States after the Panic of 1837* (New York: Columbia University Press, 1970); George Rogers Taylor, ed., *Jackson versus Biddle: The Struggle over the Second Bank of the United States* (Boston: Heath, 1949); and Jean Alexander Wilburn, *Biddle's Bank: The Crucial Years* (New York: Columbia University Press, 1967).

The economic background of the period is also extremely important. Among the many works available are Bruce H. Mann, *Republic of Debtors: Bankruptcy in the Age of American Independence* (Cambridge, Mass.: Harvard University Press, 2002); Margaret G. Myers, *A Financial History of the United States* (New York: Columbia University Press, 1970); Curtis P. Nettels, *The Emergence of a National Economy 1775–1815* (New York: Holt, Rinehart and

Winston, 1962); Murray N. Rothbard, *The Panic of 1819: Reactions and Policies* (New York: Columbia University Press, 1962); Charles Sellers, *The Market Revolution: Jacksonian America, 1815–1846* (New York: Oxford University Press, 1991); and George Rogers Taylor, *The Transportation Revolution 1815–1860* (New York: Holt, Rinehart and Winston, 1951).

Finally, there is a rich and extensive literature about the Bank in scholarly journals, in particular those devoted to history and economics. Some of the most noteworthy articles are Ernest L. Bogart, "Taxation of the Second Bank of the United States by Ohio," 17 *American Historical Review* 312 (1912); Kenneth L. Brown, "Stephen Girard, Promoter of the Second Bank of the United States," 2 *Journal of Economic History* 125 (1942); Ralph C. H. Catterall, "The Issues of the Second Bank of the United States," 5 *Journal of Political Economy* 421 (1897); Arthur Fraas, "The Second Bank of the United States: An Instrument for an Interregional Monetary Union," 34 *Journal of Economic History* 447 (1974); Benjamin B. Klubes, "The First Federal Congress and the First National Bank: A Case Study in Constitutional Interpretation," 10 *Journal of the Early Republic* 19 (1990); H. Wayne Morgan, "The Origins and Establishment of the First Bank of the United States," 30 *Business History Review* 472 (1956); Peter Temin, "The Economic Consequences of the Bank War," 76 *Journal of Political Economy* 257 (1968); Sandra F. VanBurkleo, " 'The Paws of Banks': The Origins and Significance of Kentucky's Decision to Tax Federal Bankers, 1818–1820," 9 *Journal of the Early Republic* 457 (1989); Raymond Walters Jr., "The Origins of the Second Bank of the United States," 53 *Journal of Political Economy* 115 (1945); and James O. Wettereau, "The Branches of the First Bank of the United States," 2 *Journal of Economic History* 66 (1942).

For articles focusing on Jackson and the Bank, see R. Seymour Long, "Andrew Jackson and the National Bank," 12 *English Historical Review* 85 (1897); Jacob P. Meerman, "The Climax of the Bank War: Biddle's Contraction, 1833–34," 71 *Journal of Political Economy* 378 (1963); Harry N. Scheiber, "The Pet Banks in Jacksonian Politics and Finance, 1833–1841," 23 *Journal of Economic History* 196 (1963); and Charles G. Sellers Jr., "Banking and Politics in Jackson's Tennessee, 1817–1827," 41 *Mississippi Valley Historical Review* 61 (1954).

One particular aspect of the history of the First Bank merits special attention: whether its approval can be tied to the debate about the location of the new nation's permanent capital. For a discussion of those matters, see the book Kenneth R. Bowling, *The Creation of Washington, D.C.: The Idea and Location of the American Capital* (Fairfax, Va.: George Mason University Press, 1991), and the following articles: Jacob E. Cooke, "The Compromise of 1790," 27 *William and Mary Quarterly* 523 (3rd series, 1970); Kenneth R. Bowling, "Dinner at Jefferson's: A Note on Jacob E. Cooke's 'The Compromise of 1790,' " 28 *William and Mary Quarterly* 629 (3rd series, 1971); Kenneth R. Bowling, "The Bank Bill, the Capital City and President Washington," 1 *Capitol Studies* 59 (1972); Norman K. Risjord, "The Compromise of 1790: New Evidence on the Dinner Table Bargain," 33 *William and Mary Quarterly* 309 (3rd series, 1976).

The debate about and history of the Bank are of course also very much a debate about the drafting, ratification, and implementation of the Constitution of the United States. An excellent annotated version, *Constitution of the United States: Analysis and Interpretation* (Washington, D.C.: Government Printing Office, 2006), is prepared by the Congressional Research Service. It prints each section of the text, followed immediately by a lengthy and detailed commentary that analyzes each provision and provides a chronological account of how it has been interpreted and applied by the Supreme Court. Unfortunately, this source tends to be dated. For example, the 1992 edition was published in 1996, and the new edition was promised for 2004 but did not appear until 2006. Thus, although it provides a detailed and important historical treatment, it becomes less valuable if one is interested in current doctrines.

A truly excellent and comprehensive annotation is Philip B. Kurland and Ralph Lerner, eds., *The Founders' Constitution*, 5 vols. (Chicago: University of Chicago Press, 1987). This set provides the text of each section of the Constitution and of the first twelve amendments, followed by extracts taken from contemporary records. These include pre–Constitutional Convention background material, extracts from the convention and state debates, contemporary commentaries, and decisions of the Supreme Court and lower courts interpreting and applying the text. It is avowedly a collection dedicated to what the founding generation understood and intended. As such, it offers an excellent and comprehensive summary of how matters were viewed up to and including the 1820s and 1830s. This collection has also been reprinted and is now available in a reasonably priced version published by the Liberty Fund, Inc., of Indianapolis, Indiana. A valuable supplement to this work, which takes each substantive word or phrase in the text and then offers perspectives on what it might have meant to the founding generation by providing quotations from relevant materials, is Thurston Greene, ed., *The Language of the Constitution* (New York: Greenwood Press, 1991).

The principal contemporary commentary on the Constitution was of course that provided by John Jay, James Madison, and Alexander Hamilton writing as Publius and collectively known as *The Federalist Papers*. These essays were originally published between October 27, 1787, and April 2, 1788, in various newspapers in New York City. Seventy-six papers appeared in this manner. These were eventually compiled and published in two volumes in March and May 1788, which also added eight more essays, bringing the total to eighty-four. The *Papers* have been reprinted frequently. Most students will find the Signet Classics Edition, compiled by Clinton Rossiter and Charles R. Kesler, to be the most affordable version. Scholars in turn have generally preferred Jacob E. Cooke, ed., *The Federalist* (Middletown, Conn.: Wesleyan University Press, 1961). Individuals working with the *Papers* will also want to consult Thomas S. Engeman, Edward J. Erler, and Thomas B. Hofeller, *The Federalist Concordance* (Chicago: University of Chicago Press, 1980), which will allow them to track key words and phrases in the text.

One of the places to read *The Federalist Papers* is in six books, *Commentaries on the Constitution, Public and Private*, which are volumes 13 through 18 of an ongoing project, John P. Kaminski, Gaspare J. Saladino, Richard Leffler, and Charles H. Schoenleber, eds., *The Documentary History of the Ratification of the Constitution*, 17 vols. to date (Madison: Wisconsin Historical Society Press, 1976–). The individual papers are printed in the order in which they appeared, along with any and all other commentaries for the same day. As such, this version places the papers in context, allowing one to assess what Publius had to say within the ebb and flow of what else was being written and/or published at the time, especially in response to what Publius had to say about these matters.

When complete, the *Documentary History* will include all the pertinent documents, debates, and commentaries, both public and private. It will accordingly provide a single, consistent resource for reading and understanding the debates of the Constitutional Convention, the debates in each of the thirteen states, and all the major and most of the minor contemporary commentaries. As such, it will include the materials found in a number of important earlier sources, including: Max Farrand, *The Records of the Federal Convention of 1787*, 4 vols. (New Haven, Conn.: Yale University Press, 1937); Jonathan Elliot, ed., *The Debates in the Several State Conventions on the Adoption of the Federal Constitution*, 5 vols. (Philadelphia: J. B. Lippincott, 1836); and Herbert J. Storing, *The Complete Anti-Federalist*, 7 vols. (Chicago: University of Chicago Press, 1981).

There are any number of other compilations of original source material about the drafting and ratification of the Constitution. One set that provides a comprehensive and affordable group of materials is Bernard Bailyn, ed., *The Debate on the Constitution*, vol. 1, *September 1787 to February 1788*, and vol. 2, *January to August 1788* (New York: Library of America, 1993). These are part of the Library of America series, which, as will be noted later, also includes valuable concise editions of the writings of most of the major members of the founding generation.

Those interested in a general history of the Court's treatment of the text should begin with the various volumes of the *Oliver Wendell Holmes Devise History of the Supreme Court of the United States*. This is in important respects the "official" history of the Court and came about as a result of a decision by Justice Holmes to leave his estate to the United States. The funds lay unused for a number of years, and it was eventually decided that they should provide the financial foundations for a history of the Court. The pertinent volumes, listed by the period covered rather than date of publication (all by Macmillan Publishing Company of New York), are Julius Goebel Jr., *Antecedents and Beginnings to 1801* (vol. 1, 1971); George Haskins and Herbert Johnson, *Foundations of Power: John Marshall, 1801–15* (vol. 2, 1981); G. Edward White, *The Marshall Court and Cultural Change, 1815–35* (vols. 3–4, 1991); and Carl B. Swisher, *The Taney Period, 1836–64* (vol. 5, 1974). The main source for primary materials on the early years of the Court is, in turn, the ongoing project by Maeva Marcus et al., eds., *The Documentary History of the Supreme Court of the United States, 1789–1800*, 8 vols. to date (New York: Columbia University Press, 1985–). There is also a journal dedicated to the Court and its history, initially published as the *Yearbook* of the Supreme Court Historical Society and, since 1990, as the *Journal of Supreme Court History.*

One of the best one-volume discussions of the Court, selected constitutional doctrines, and major Court decisions is Kermit L. Hall, James W. Ely, and Joel B. Grossman, eds., *The Oxford Companion to the Supreme Court of the United States*, 2nd ed. (New York: Oxford University Press, 2005). Most of the individual justices have in turn been the subject of biographies, and numerous books and articles are available on their lives, opinions, and judicial philosophies. Perhaps the best starting point for finding this sort of material is Leon Friedman and Fred Israel, eds., *The Justices of the United States Supreme Court, 1789–1995: Their Lives and Major Opinions*, rev. ed. (New York: Chelsea House, 1995). In addition, the University of South Carolina Press is in the process of publishing a series, Chief Justiceships of the United States Supreme Court, with the pertinent volume for our purposes being Herbert A. Johnson, *The Chief Justiceship of John Marshall, 1801–1835* (1997).

The Court was not the only institution that interpreted the Constitution during the debates about the Bank. For a discussion of how Congress approached these matters, see three volumes by David P. Currie: *The Constitution in Congress: The Federalist Period, 1789–1801* (Chicago: University of Chicago Press, 1997); *The Constitution in Congress: The Jeffersonians, 1801–1829* (Chicago: University of Chicago Press, 2001); and *The Constitution in Congress: Democrats and Whigs, 1829–1861* (Chicago: University of Chicago Press, 2005). The approach taken by the various administrations may be examined in a series of books by Leonard D. White: *The Federalists: A Study in Administrative History* (New York: Macmillan, 1948); *The Jeffersonians: A Study in Administrative History 1801–1829* (New York: Macmillan, 1951); and *The Jacksonians: A Study in Administrative History 1829–1861* (New York:

Macmillan, 1954). The views of the various attorneys general in many matters may be found in H. Jefferson Powell, ed., *The Constitution and the Attorneys General* (Durham, N.C.: Carolina Academic Press, 1999).

There are a number of valuable books for those interested in the background of the Constitution and the various currents that factored into its intellectual development. Perhaps the best, which discusses both pre- and post-ratification events and issues, is Jack N. Rakove, *Original Meanings: Politics and Ideas in the Making of the Constitution* (New York: Knopf, 1996). Another important study is Forrest McDonald, *Novus Ordo Seclorum: The Intellectual Origins of the Constitution* (Lawrence: University Press of Kansas, 1985). Two classic studies of the issues and era are, in turn, Bernard Bailyn, *The Ideological Origins of the American Revolution*, enlarged edition (Cambridge, Mass.: Belknap Press, 1992), and Gordon S. Wood, *The Creation of the American Republic, 1776–1787* (Chapel Hill: University of North Carolina Press, 1998). A recent study that is quite valuable is Calvin H. Johnson, *Righteous Anger at the Wicked States: The Meaning of the Founders' Constitution* (New York: Cambridge University Press, 2005).

For post-ratification events and themes, see, among many others, Roger H. Brown, *Redeeming the Republic: Federalists, Taxation, and the Origins of the Constitution* (Baltimore: Johns Hopkins University Press, 1993); Samuel H. Beer, *To Make a Nation: The Rediscovery of American Federalism* (Cambridge, Mass.: Belknap Press, 1993); Stanley Elkins and Eric McKittrick, *The Age of Federalism: The Early American Republic, 1788–1800* (New York: Oxford University Press, 1993); Joseph M. Lynch, *Negotiating the Constitution: The Earliest Debates over Original Intent* (Ithaca, N.Y.: Cornell University Press, 1999); Drew R. McCoy, *The Elusive Republic: Political Economy in Jeffersonian America* (New York: Norton, 1980); Forrest McDonald, *States' Rights and the Union: Imperium in Imperio 1776–1876* (Lawrence: University Press of Kansas, 2000); and James Roger Sharp, *American Politics in the Early Republic: The New Nation in Crisis* (New Haven, Conn.: Yale University Press, 1993).

The distinctive take on matters constitutional embraced by southerners, especially the Virginians, may be reviewed in James H. Broussard, *The Southern Federalists 1800–1816* (Baton Rouge: Louisiana State University Press, 1978); Timothy S. Huebner, *The Southern Judicial Tradition: State Judges and Sectional Distinctiveness, 1790–1890* (Athens: University of Georgia Press, 1999); F. Thornton Miller, *Juries and Judges versus the Law: Virginia's Provincial Legal Perspective, 1783–1828* (Charlottesville: University Press of Virginia, 1994); and A. G. Roeber, *Faithful Magistrates and Republican Lawyers: Creators of Virginia Legal Culture, 1680–1810* (Chapel Hill: University of North Carolina Press, 1981). Indeed, one interesting aspect of the debates surrounding the Bank is the extent to which many of the arguments reappeared in the debates about secession and, eventually, the Civil War. Individuals interested in these issues may accordingly find the works of the two principal apologists for the Confederacy of interest: Jefferson Davis, *The Rise and Fall of the Confederate Government*, 2 vols. (New York: D. Appleton, 1881; reprint, New York: Da Capo Press, 1990), and Alexander H. Stephens, *A Constitutional View of the Late War between the States*, 2 vols. (Philadelphia: National Publishing Co., 1868–1870; reprint, Harrisonburg, Va.: Sprinkle Publications, 1994). For commentary on these matters, see Brian A. Dirck, *Lincoln and Davis: Imagining America, 1809–1865* (Lawrence: University Press of Kansas, 2001), and an important discussion of the issue of slavery and the Constitution, Mark E. Brandon, *Free in the World: American Slavery and Constitutional Failure* (Princeton, N.J.: Princeton University Press, 1998).

Perhaps the most important figure for these purposes (the judgment is subjective and personal) is James Madison, who has been justly described as the Father of the Constitution. Madison's papers are being compiled and published in four series, each covering a major section of his life. For his early years, from birth to 1801, see William T. Hutchinson and William M. E. Rachal, eds., *The Papers of James Madison*, 17 vols. (Chicago: University of Chicago Press, and Charlottesville: University Press of Virginia, 1962–1991). The middle years (1801–1817) are covered by Robert J. Brugger, ed., *The Papers of James Madison: Secretary of State Series*, 7 vols. to date (Charlottesville: University Press of Virginia, 1986–); and Robert A. Rutland et al., eds., *The Papers of James Madison: Presidential Series*, 5 vols. to date (1984–). These will be followed by a Retirement Series, which is yet to begin. For those wishing to consult a compilation spanning Madison's entire life, there are a number of collections, the best of which is Gaillard Hunt, ed., *The Writings of James Madison*, 9 vols. (New York: Putnam's, 1900–1910). There are also two valuable single-volume compilations: Marvin Meyers, ed., *The Mind of the Founder: Sources of the Political Thought of James Madison* (Indianapolis, Ind.: Bobbs-Merrill, 1973); and Jack N. Rakove, *James Madison: Writings* (New York: Library of America, 1999).

A number of biographies are available. One of the best is also the most compact, the readable and valuable Jack N. Rakove, *James Madison and the Creation of the American Republic*, 2nd ed. (New York: Longman, 2002). An important work that concentrates on Madison as president is Robert Allen Rutland, *The Presidency of James Madison* (Lawrence: University Press of Kansas, 1990). This book is part of the Press's American Presidency Series, which provides a one-volume treatment for the administration of each of the nation's presidents. As will become evident, the series is an invaluable resource for those interested in the Constitution, the Court, and the Bank because so many of the key figures in these matters would later become president.

A number of important books deal with various aspects of Madison's life and accomplishments, among the best and most interesting of which are

Lance Banning, *The Sacred Fire of Liberty: James Madison and the Founding of the Federal Republic* (Ithaca, N.Y.: Cornell University Press, 1995); Richard K. Matthews, *If Men Were Angels: James Madison and the Heartless Empire of Reason* (Lawrence: University Press of Kansas, 1995); Drew R. McCoy, *The Last of the Fathers: James Madison and the Republican Legacy* (New York: Cambridge University Press, 1989); and Gary Rosen, *American Compact: James Madison and the Problem of Founding* (Lawrence: University Press of Kansas, 1999).

John Marshall's papers are being compiled and published as *The Papers of John Marshall*, 11 vols. to date (Chapel Hill: University of North Carolina Press, 1974–), originally with Herbert A. Johnson as editor and now under the direction of Charles F. Hobson. There are also valuable insights to be gleaned from Marshall's biography of George Washington. This was initially published as *The Life of George Washington*, 5 vols. (Philadelphia: C. P. Wayne, 1805–1807), but Marshall was unhappy with this edition and prepared a second, revised and corrected version, *The Life of George Washington*, 2nd ed. (Philadelphia, J. Crissy, 1833). This preferred version may be found in a reprint edition, published in 1926 by the Citizen's Guild of Washington's Boyhood Home, in Fredericksburg, Virginia.

There are a number of biographies, the first of which was provided by Marshall himself: John Stokes Adams, ed., *An Autobiographical Sketch by John Marshall* (Ann Arbor: University of Michigan Press, 1937). The first major discussion of Marshall's life and work, and in some respects still the most important, was Albert J. Beveridge, *The Life of John Marshall*, 4 vols. (Boston: Houghton Mifflin, 1919). The most recent and arguably the best biographies are R. Kent Newmyer, *John Marshall and the Heroic Age of the Supreme Court* (Baton Rouge: Louisiana State University Press, 2001); and Charles F. Hobson, *The Great Chief Justice: John Marshall and the Rule of Law* (Lawrence: University Press of Kansas, 1996). Important books on Marshall and his thought include Robert K. Faulkner, *The Jurisprudence of John Marshall* (Princeton, N.J.: Princeton University Press, 1968); Samuel J. Konefsky, *John Marshall and Alexander Hamilton: Architects of the American Constitution* (New York: Macmillan, 1964); R. Kent Newmyer, *The Supreme Court under Marshall and Taney* (New York: Crowell, 1968); James F. Simon, *What Kind of Nation: Thomas Jefferson, John Marshall, and the Epic Struggle to Create a United States* (New York: Simon and Schuster, 2002); and William F. Swindler, *The Constitution and Chief Justice Marshall* (New York: Dodd, Mead, 1978).

A third key figure is the Father of the Bank, Alexander Hamilton. Hamilton is the only one of the major members of the founding generation whose papers have been published in full: Harold C. Syrett and Jacob E. Cooke, eds., *The Papers of Alexander Hamilton*, 26 vols. plus index (New York: Columbia University Press, 1961–1987). Hamilton's important papers on financial matters may be found in Samuel McKee, ed., *Papers on Public Credit, Commerce and Finance by Alexander Hamilton* (New York: Columbia University Press, 1961). There also is a valuable one-volume survey of his work in Joanne B. Freeman, *Alexander Hamilton: Writings* (New York: Library of America, 2001).

For many years the standard Hamilton biography was a two-volume effort by Broadus Mitchell, *Alexander Hamilton: Youth to Maturity* (New York: Macmillan, 1957), and *Alexander Hamilton: The National Adventure 1788–1804* (New York: Macmillan, 1962). The most recent and what will likely become the definitive story of Hamilton's life and work is Ron Chernow, *Alexander Hamilton* (New York: Penguin, 2004). A number of books examine various aspects of Hamilton's life and thoughts, including Harvey Flaumenhaft, *The Effective Republic: Administration and Constitution in the Thought of Alexander Hamilton* (Durham, N.C.: Duke University Press, 1992); and Robert E. Wright, *Hamilton Unbound: Finance and the Creation of the American Republic* (Westport, Conn.: Greenwood Press, 2002).

Thomas Jefferson was also a key figure, an individual whose strong state rights orientation and bitter opposition to Hamilton and his programs had important repercussions for the Bank. The modern edition of his papers is Julian P. Boyd et al., eds., *The Papers of Thomas Jefferson*, 32 vols. to date (Princeton, N.J.: Princeton University Press, 1950–). These volumes will eventually take one through the end of Jefferson's two terms as president. The years after that will be covered by J. Jefferson Looney, ed., *The Papers of Thomas Jefferson: Retirement Series*, 1 vol. to date (Princeton, N.J.: Princeton University Press, 2004–). There is also a valuable one-volume compilation, Tom Wicker and Merrill D. Peterson, eds., *Public and Private Papers by Thomas Jefferson* (New York: Vintage Books/Library of America, 1990).

There are any number of biographies of Jefferson. For many years the key work was Dumas Malone, *Jefferson and His Time*, 6 vols. (Boston: Little, Brown, 1948–1981; reprint, Charlottesville: University Press of Virginia, 2005). Malone's work was comprehensive but tended not to be critical. For valuable perspectives on Jefferson's time as president, see Forrest McDonald, *The Presidency of Thomas Jefferson* (Lawrence: University Press of Kansas, 1976). Jefferson was not involved in the drafting or ratification of the Constitution but was nevertheless an influential figure in its interpretation and implementation. The most important study of that aspect of his life is David N. Mayer, *The Constitutional Thought of Thomas Jefferson* (Charlottesville: University Press of Virginia, 1994). Additional interesting works include Lance Banning, *The Jeffersonian Persuasion: Evolution of a Party Ideology* (Ithaca, N.Y.: Cornell University Press, 1978); Richard E. Ellis, *The Jeffersonian Crisis: Courts and Politics in the Young Republic* (New York: Oxford University Press, 1971); and Richard K. Matthews, *The Radical Politics of Thomas Jefferson: A Revisionist View* (Lawrence: University Press of Kansas, 1984).

The final major figure in the story of the Bank was its most dedicated foe,

Andrew Jackson. Jackson's papers, now under the editorship of Daniel Feller, are being published by the University of Tennessee Press (1980 to date, 6 volumes to date). The standard major biography is by Robert V. Remini: *Andrew Jackson and the Course of American Empire, 1767–1821* (New York: Harper and Row, 1977); *Andrew Jackson and the Course of American Freedom 1822–1832* (New York: Harper and Row, 1981); and *Andrew Jackson and the Course of American Democracy, 1832–1845* (New York: Harper and Row, 1984). Jackson's presidency is chronicled in Donald B. Cole, *The Presidency of Andrew Jackson* (Lawrence: University Press of Kansas, 1993). Some very interesting work on Jackson and the Constitution is in turn being done by Gerard N. Magliocca. Three articles are now in print: "Veto! The Jacksonian Revolution in Constitutional Law," 78 *Nebraska Law Review* 205 (1999); "Preemptive Opinions: The Secret History of *Worcester v. Georgia* and *Dred Scott*," 63 *University of Pittsburgh Law Review* 487 (2002); and "The Cherokee Removal and the Fourteenth Amendment," 53 *Duke Law Journal* 875 (2003). These will eventually be combined and supplemented in a book, *One Turn of the Wheel: Andrew Jackson and the Modern Constitution*, to be published by the University Press of Kansas.

There are any number of other key figures in the story of the Bank and *M'Culloch*. One was Joseph Story, Marshall's great friend and ally on the Court. An early account of his life is found in a work by his son, William W. Story, ed., *Life and Letters of Joseph Story*, 2 vols. (Boston: C. C. Little and J. Brown, 1851; reprints, Freeport, N.Y.: Books for Libraries Press, 1971, and Union, N.J.: Lawbook Exchange, 2000). There is also William W. Story, ed., *The Miscellaneous Writings of Joseph Story* (Boston: C. C. Little and J. Brown, 1852; reprint, Union, N.J.: Lawbook Exchange, 2000). The best biography is R. Kent Newmyer, *Supreme Court Justice Joseph Story: Statesman of the Old Republic* (Chapel Hill: University of North Carolina Press, 1985).

George Washington played a key role in these matters, and one should look at two works in particular, Forrest McDonald, *The Presidency of George Washington* (Lawrence: University Press of Kansas, 1974); and Glenn A. Phelps, *George Washington and American Constitutionalism* (Lawrence: University Press of Kansas, 1994). For a selection of his writings, see John H. Rhodehamel, *George Washington: Writings* (New York: Library of America, 1997).

Another important figure is John Taylor, characterized by some as the Philosopher of the Jeffersonian Republicans. He was a prolific albeit irritatingly opaque author, and many of his works are available in modern reprints. Those that bear on the Bank or the issues raised by the Bank include *An Inquiry into the Principles and Policy of the Government of the United States* (Fredericksburg, Va.: Green and Cady, 1814; reprint, Union, N.J.: Lawbook Exchange, 2000); *Construction Construed and Constitutions Vindicated* (Richmond, Va.: Shepherd and Pollard, 1820; reprint, Union, N.J.: Lawbook Exchange,

1998); *Tyranny Unmasked* (Washington, D.C.: Davis and Force, 1822; reprint, Indianapolis, Ind.: Liberty Fund, 1992); and *New Views of the Constitution of the United States* (Washington, D.C.: Way and Gideon, 1823; reprint, Union, N.J.: Lawbook Exchange, 2002). For discussions of Taylor and his life, see Robert E. Shalhope, *John Taylor of Carolene: Pastoral Republican* (Columbia: University of South Carolina Press, 1980); and Eugene T. Mudge, *The Social Philosophy of John Taylor of Carolene: A Study in Jeffersonian Democracy* (New York: Columbia University Press, 1939).

Roger Brooke Taney played a key role in these matters, both as the individual Jackson chose as executioner for the Bank and as Marshall's successor as chief justice of the United States. Many important observations about the era and the Court in particular may be found in Samuel Tyler, ed., *Memoir of Roger Brooke Taney* (Baltimore: J. Murphy, 1872; reprint, New York: Da Capo Press, 1970). The standard biographies are Carl Brent Swisher, *Roger B. Taney* (Hamden, Conn.: Archon Books, 1961); and Lewis Walker, *Without Fear or Favor: A Biography of Chief Justice Roger Brooke Taney* (Boston: Houghton Mifflin, 1955). Taney's account of the Bank War may be found in Carl Brent Swisher, "Roger B. Taney's 'Bank War Manuscript,'" 53 *Maryland Historical Magazine* 103–152, 215–237 (1958).

Daniel Webster, John C. Calhoun, and Henry Clay were also important figures for the Bank and the nation. Webster's papers are a rich source of material, as are Clay's. Studies of the three of special interest include Maurice G. Baxter, *Daniel Webster and the Supreme Court* (Amherst: University of Massachusetts Press, 1966); Maurice G. Baxter, *One and Inseparable: Daniel Webster and the Union* (Cambridge, Mass.: Belknap Press, 1984); Maurice G. Baxter, *Henry Clay and the American System* (Lexington: University Press of Kentucky, 1995); Maurice G. Baxter, *Henry Clay the Lawyer* (Lexington: University Press of Kentucky, 2000); John Niven, *John C. Calhoun and the Price of Union: A Biography* (Baton Rouge: Louisiana State University Press, 1988); Merrill D. Peterson, *The Great Triumvirate: Webster, Clay, and Calhoun* (New York: Oxford University Press, 1987); and Robert V. Remini, *Daniel Webster: The Man and His Time* (New York: Norton, 1997).

One should also look closely at the lives and views of the presidents who preceded and followed Jackson. For discussions of the nation's first father-son presidential combination, see Ralph Adams Brown, *The Presidency of John Adams* (Lawrence: University Press of Kansas, 1975); and Mary W. M. Hargreaves, *The Presidency of John Quincy Adams* (Lawrence: University Press of Kansas, 1985). In addition, see Noble E. Cunningham Jr., *The Presidency of James Monroe* (Lawrence: University Press of Kansas, 1995); Major L. Wilson, *The Presidency of Martin Van Buren* (Lawrence: University Press of Kansas, 1984); Norma Lois Peterson, *The Presidencies of William Henry Harrison and John Tyler* (Lawrence: University Press of Kansas, 1989); and Paul H.

Bergeron, *The Presidency of James K. Polk* (Lawrence: University Press of Kansas, 1987).

Finally, one of the realities of *M'Culloch* is that very little has been written about the individual who gave the case his misspelled name, James William M'Culloh. Some details about his life are available in Bayly Ellen Marks, *Hilton Heritage* (Catonsville, Md.: Catonsville Community College Printing Services, 1973). His role as a lobbyist and influential politician is discussed in Whitman H. Ridgway, *Community Leadership in Maryland, 1790–1840* (Chapel Hill: University of North Carolina Press, 1979).

INDEX